UNDOING THE KNOTS

FIVE GENERATIONS OF AMERICAN CATHOLIC ANTI-BLACKNESS

MAUREEN H. O'CONNELL

BEACON PRESS, BOSTON

BEACON PRESS
Boston, Massachusetts
www.beacon.org

Beacon Press books
are published under the auspices of
the Unitarian Universalist Association of Congregations.

24 23 22 21   8 7 6 5 4 3 2 1

This book is printed on acid-free paper that meets the uncoated paper
ANSI/NISO specifications for permanence as revised in 1992.

Text design and composition by Kim Arney

Library of Congress Cataloging-in-Publication Data
Name: O'Connell, Maureen H., author.
Title: Undoing the knots : five generations of American Catholic
anti-Blackness / Maureen H. O'Connell.
Description: Boston, Massachusetts : Beacon Press, [2021] | Includes
bibliographical references and index. | Summary: "The author goes on a
pilgrimage of her family's history in Catholic parishes throughout one
of the largest dioceses in the country to excavate the legacy of
American Catholic anti-Blackness she has inherited and discover
spiritual resources for resisting it"— Provided by publisher.
Identifiers: LCCN 2021032642 (print) | LCCN 2021032643 (ebook) |
ISBN 9780807016657 (hardcover) | ISBN 9780807016756 (ebook)
Subjects: LCSH: African American Catholics—Pennsylvania—
Philadelphia—Biography. | Catholic Church—Pennsylvania—Philadelphia—
History. | Race relations—Religious aspects—Catholic Church.
Classification: LCC BX1407.B63 O26 2021 (print) |
LCC BX1407.B63 (ebook) | DDC 282/.7481089—dc23
LC record available at https://lccn.loc.gov/2021032642
LC ebook record available at https://lccn.loc.gov/2021032643

For my family, here and gone ahead;
and for my teachers, especially the unexpected ones

CONTENTS

MATTERING

St. Vincent de Paul

THE INHABITANTS OF PHILADELPHIA, the City of Brotherly Love and Sisterly Affection, have wrestled with the moral and civic quandary of who matters when it comes to loving each other ever since King Charles II paid a debt to the Penn family with a forty-thousand-square-mile land grant in North America in 1681. William Penn tolerated both Catholics and slavery in his Holy Experiment, and eventually five generations of my Catholic family became a part of that unholy mixture.

Philadelphia became the Birthplace of Freedom and the Cradle of Liberty when the Founding Fathers signed the Declaration of Independence—the only Catholic to do so also being a slave owner—and drafted the Constitution in Independence Hall. But only white landowning men enjoyed those liberties and freedoms. The nine hundred enslaved Black people in Philadelphia at the time were not deemed worthy of being loved with that kind of justice.[1]

Later, when European immigrants poured into the Workshop of the World, native Black artisans and machinists struggled to get a toehold in the factories that dominated the cityscape. During the Golden Age of American Catholicism in the early twentieth century, Philadelphia became the City of Neighborhoods, and with the help of priests and the endorsement of the archbishop, it maintained racialized neighborhood boundaries. It morphed into "Up South" with the arrival of Southern Blacks, refugees of economic, if not actual, lynching. By the 1950s, white

Catholics were already building a sprawling "just out of Philadelphia" (JOP) Catholic infrastructure in the city's suburbs. Home loans for Black Philadelphians who wished to move JOP were not forthcoming.

By the time I was born in 1973, ten years after the March on Washington for jobs and equality and on the cusp of the city's throw-down bicentennial celebration, post-industrial Philadelphia was already devolving into "Filthadelphia." In the 1990s we became "Killadelphia," with one of the highest gun-murder rates in the country, the majority of the dead being Black men.

Today, Philadelphia is two decades into its "The Place that Loves You Back" phase, a moniker intended to lure tourists and bolster our "eds and meds" economy. But Black service workers in hotels and restaurants, as well as Black homeowners in some of the gentrifying neighborhoods where my people used to live, aren't exactly feeling the love. Nor was the corporate leadership of Starbucks in April 2018 when a white barista called the police on two Black business partners in a Center City store, prompting the closure of 8,000 stores nationwide for a day of anti-bias training with 175,000 employees.[2] Philadelphia's "love" made national headlines when on June 1, 2020, the chief of police gave the green light to use tear gas on peaceful activists trapped on an embankment of Interstate 676 while protesting the murder of George Floyd.[3]

THIS IS MY CITY. And it is the context in which, in the spring of 2017, some members of my parish in the Germantown section of Philadelphia, home to the world's first anti-slavery movement in 1688, wanted to hang a Black Lives Matter banner out in front of the church. We were latecomers to the movement for Black lives. Other more progressive denominations in our Philadelphia neighborhood had already proclaimed this slogan for months, so our silence was conspicuous. Yet we were also light-years ahead of most other Catholic parishes when it came to taking public stands for marginalized groups. It was not unusual for the litany of announcements about justice-related activities to delay the recessional hymn by fifteen minutes on Sundays.

"A Black Lives Matter banner is a no-brainer for St. Vincent's," I thought, when another parishioner named Chris told me about the plan. By that spring we were four years into a merger with two predominantly Black parishes in Germantown. The violence assailing Black people in

Philadelphia was not "out there" somewhere in the nation's poorest big city. It was right here under the peeling frescoes of St. Vincent de Paul and St. Louise de Marillac on the church's domed ceiling. It was gripping the people who filled the aisle with hugs during the exuberant sign of peace, showing each other how much they mattered.

Chris is one of the most fascinating Catholics I have ever met. It's not just his dreadlocks or the tambourine he shakes in time with the choir. Or how when I sit directly behind him at Mass I can feel the reverberations of his audible expressions—"Amen!" or "That's right!" or "My Lord"—in the kneeler where I prop my feet. What captivates me is his devotion to our traditions despite the US Catholic Church's disdain for Black Catholics like him. He does not hold back in professing the pain of being excluded by our Church, and he insists on the radical promise of inclusion at the core of the Gospel's message. The paradox of his anguished hope gives him a charismatic holiness. People seek out his hugs at the sign of peace. They clap in time with his tambourine. They listen to what he has to say about what it means to be a Catholic in the midst of anti-Black racism.

As for me, I had searched in vain for that kind of propheticism from Catholic leaders after the deaths of one unarmed Black person after another. Not long after joining St. Vincent's, I found myself intoning Chris with my simple prayer of gratitude for having landed in a parish with the courage to stand up for Black lives: "Thank you, *Jesus*."

"The time is ripe for the banner," I said impatiently to Chris. "If not now, when?"

Chris shared the concerns about the banner that he'd raised with our pastor and the lay leaders in the parish. My certainty gave way to the all too familiar sinking feeling I get whenever I am about to be confronted by my whiteness. For example, Chris asked, did the Peace and Justice Committee realize that the banner could evoke pushback from white parishioners? Some were already nostalgic for the whiter days and ways of "the Old St. Vincent's" before the merger. And what about possible "Blue Lives Matter" pushback from the police? Would the neighbors in the parish's predominantly Black neighborhood end up dealing with potential fallout?

Chris also wondered if the committee assumed the message was intended only for an external audience. Did we as a faith community have an accurate sense of whether or not our Black parishioners felt as though they mattered in St. Vincent's? What did it even mean for Catholics to claim that Black Lives Matter anyway?

None of his questions had ever crossed my mind. I was embarrassed by my ignorance, my shortsightedness. My white-sightedness. I felt like an amateur.

This, despite the fact that I am a white Catholic worshipping among Catholics who look like the Afrocentric Jesus on the cross we process by each Sunday. I'm someone who served on the parish's Reconciliation and Unity Ministry initiated in the wake of the crisis in Ferguson, Missouri. For the last six semesters, I've taught an undergraduate course on theology and racism at a Catholic university where nearly 20 percent of the student body is Black. I'm even an active member of an interfaith organizing coalition that puts resisting racism at the heart of our work.

My oversight took my breath away.

The implications of hanging the banner were not the only dimension I'd missed. To acknowledge Chris's concerns, the Peace and Justice Committee proposed conducting a referendum at each of the three liturgies the following Sunday. The pews would be stocked with small pencils and ballots usually reserved for parish council elections, and parishioners could decide whether or not we'd hang the banner.

Chris dropped his forehead into his left palm. His fingers disappeared into the roots of his dreadlocks to massage the top of his head, perhaps preemptively tending to wounds sustained by other well-intentioned white Catholics.

"Well," I said hesitatingly, as I pondered the alternatives, "that seems like a reasonable solution."

"I understand that the committee wants to *do* something," he replied. "But think about it: Did we have to vote on whether to support the sanctuary movement for undocumented immigrants? Did we vote on whether to publicly welcome LGBT brothers and sisters?"

"No, we didn't," I admitted.

"So the only time we take a vote is when it has to do with Black people," he said.

My whiteness was exposed. Again.

How could the painful symbolism of putting the banner to a vote have been lost on me? We were not even a month past Donald Trump's inauguration, which itself must have felt like a referendum on Black lives. Not to mention the fact that white women like me, and white Catholics as a whole, had a hand in putting Trump in office. Fifty-five percent of white Americans now believed *we* were victims of discrimination.[4] The view from Chris's standpoint was bleak. And if white folks at St. Vincent's didn't get it, with our commitments to social justice and our rare proximity to Black Catholics, then what hope was there for white Catholics in far more conservative and segregated parishes—parishes where the phrase Black Lives Matter was practically heretical?

I was suddenly struck by how good-intentioned and do-gooding white Catholics like me are ill-equipped for the discipleship required if Black lives are really going to matter. As a Catholic theologian steeped in social ethics, engaged in critical race theory, trained in the fundamentals of anti-racism, and actively teaching and lecturing about whiteness, I was probably one of Chris's best hopes. And while I may have failed to see how our approach to the whole banner initiative excluded and put at risk the Black people we'd intended to support, I could not miss the pain on Chris's face.

As his pain registered, I could feel my defenses go up, protecting me from dangerous talk about racism. Why was it always the same people in the parish who felt responsible for figuring out how to fix this racism problem? Why does it always seem as though white people can't do anything right when it comes to tackling racism? What did Black Catholics want from us, anyway? Maybe it is better, easier, safer to do nothing given how our misguided actions reinforce the very racism we are trying to undo.

Racism ties me into knots when it shows up, especially in the moments—like those with Chris—when I am trying as a white Catholic woman to resist it. It makes me feel ignorant about things I would otherwise know if my life had not been sheltered from harsh truths of social inequality. I agonize over my missteps and miscommunications. I am ashamed at not copping to my racial biases, especially when they are painfully evident, and feel guilty over wrongdoing that predates me. I get angry at the people responsible for my Catholic education who left me unprepared to deal with something so inherent in the American way of life. I freeze at the thought of all I do not know or could never fully understand when it comes to the complexity of this problem. I start wondering if everything I'm doing to be a good white person—if all my reading, teaching, lecturing, researching, writing about racism—will ever be valued by my white brothers and sisters or be enough for my Black ones. I get upset at the white people who I assume don't care about Black people and I begrudge Black people for not acknowledging all I'm trying to do.

I panic about making bad situations worse, about getting embroiled in conflict, about being outed as a racist.

It seems that whenever I try to undo the knots of racism I only end up getting more tangled in them.

The controversy over the banner was unfolding at St. Vincent's just as Chris and I had a chance to hear a keynote address—a sermon really—from Rev. Traci Blackmon, a pastor of a congregation in Ferguson, at a four-day gathering of faith-based community organizers from around the country.

"What happened to Michael Brown started before he was born," she said, as she laid bare the deep roots of racism in American culture.

"That's right!" Chris hollered back at her, shaking his tambourine. As I clapped in agreement, I wondered if what was tying me into knots had started before I was born too.

"Reconciliation requires confession, and confession must begin with the Church," Blackmon insisted, turning our focus from the sin of American racism to the sins of racism in American Christianity.[5]

I decided that if Black lives were going to matter in St. Vincent's or anywhere else, if they were going to matter to *me*, then undoing these knots would have to matter too. To do that, I would need to concentrate on the relationship between the two things that bound Chris and me together long before we were born: Catholicism and racism.

ASIDE FROM OUR CATHOLICISM and even our Philadelphian natures, many of my people—my American ancestors across five generations—share something else in common. We all have been entangled with the *color line* in the City of Brotherly Love. W. E. B. Du Bois infamously used that term, first coined by Frederick Douglass, in 1900 after spending a year studying the Black community in Philadelphia. "The problem of the twentieth century," Du Bois prophesized, "is the problem of colour line."[6] The earliest of my relatives to arrive in Philadelphia had already been here for eighty years at that point, steering clear of the abolitionist fray down along the northern side of the Mason–Dixon Line in Chester County. Today, my niece and nephews—the first generation of the twenty-first century and all born during the nation's first Black presidency—are coming of age with a "Hate Has No Home Here" sign on their front lawn in a school district that is 60 percent whiter than its adjacent counterpart in

Philadelphia and receives $30,000 more in funding per pupil.[7] The color line is indeed America's most persistent problem.

Like Penn with his holy hypothesis, my devoutly Catholic parents raised me and my siblings with our own moral and civic guiding principle: of those to whom much is given, much is expected. For most of my life—all but a little more than a decade of it spent in mostly Catholic communities in the City of Brotherly Love and Sisterly Affection—I thought that to be holy I needed to be good and give back. As much as I credit our family mantra for setting me on my current professional path as a Catholic theologian with a curiosity about faith and social justice, it actually set me up for failure when it comes to faith and *racial* justice. Being good and giving back is no match for racialized social inequality, especially in a place like Philadelphia where the experiences of enslaved people and free Black people presented a contradiction to the moral and civic vision of Penn's Holy Experiment, the Founding Fathers' Declaration of Independence, and the Framers' Constitution.

As of early March of 2020, the City of Brotherly Love is the poorest of America's big cities, with 24.5 percent or one in four residents living below the poverty line and 14 percent living in deep poverty or with incomes of less than $12,300 a year.[8] Poverty in Philadelphia discriminates. According to an August 2020 report from the Economy League of Greater Philadelphia, "Black households make up 55.6 percent of all households earning less than $10,000 a year," an increase of 4 percent between 2017 and 2018, and are "1.5 times more likely to be making less than $40,000" than their white counterparts who "show the greatest representation in the highest income brackets with a 76.8 percent representation in households earning $200,000 or more."[9] All of this in a city where the median household income is $44,000.[10] Poverty in Philadelphia is also geographic. While at least 20 percent of residents in most zip codes are poor, the impoverished are concentrated in census tracts in North and West Philadelphia, many with poverty rates exceeding 45 percent.[11] Despite a high "citywide diversity index" in light of an influx of immigrants since 2000, Philadelphia was the fourth most segregated city in the country in 2015 and second only to Chicago among the nation's big cities, in light of its low "neighborhood diversity index." Only 38.6 percent of Philadelphians have neighbors who "belong to a different racial group."[12]

Racial segregation defines more than our wealth gap and neighborhoods. Philadelphia's students are educated in separate and unequal schools. Another 2020 report from the Economy League of Greater Philadelphia literally mapped the performance of Philadelphia public and charter schools onto the employment levels, wealth, and racial makeup of the neighborhoods in which they are located. They found evidence of "deep structural racism" in the "disproportionate share" of high performing "model" and "reinforce" schools in "majority Non-Hispanic-White" neighborhoods, which also boast the "highest proportion of full-time workers and the highest median household incomes." The highest proportion of "watch" and "intervene" schools were in majority Black neighborhoods, already disadvantaged by "the lowest proportion of full-time workers" and "second lowest aggregated median household income."[13]

Philadelphia's economic resurgence may be driven by "eds and meds," but according to reporter Mark Dent of the online news source, BillyPenn, "Philly-area universities have enrolled a lower percentage of black students in the last 20 years"; and a study referenced by the *Philadelphia Inquirer* found that Black residents who live in predominantly Black neighborhoods are twenty-eight times more likely to have less access to health care.[14] Philadelphia's Department of Public Health notes that clusters of predominantly Black census tracts have higher infant mortality rates, teen birth rates, and cancer rates and lower life expectancies than citywide averages.[15] In light of these preexisting structural conditions, as of August 2020 Black Philadelphians had the highest rates of COVID-19 infections, hospitalizations, and deaths.[16] According to Pew, "Black and Hispanic residents of Philadelphia were two and three times more likely than White residents, respectively, to lose jobs and income, and to know someone who died from the coronavirus."[17] And then there are the racial implications of the estimated 36,000 Black men missing from Philadelphia's economy due to incarceration or death by homicide.[18]

Since Pew reports that Philadelphia's poverty rate has grown 10 percent between 1970 and 2016, about as long as I have been at this "doing good and giving back" thing, I have to wonder: What if it turns out that these moral impulses—so central to my identity as a Philadelphia Catholic—have kept racial inequality squarely in place for as many generations as my people have been here?[19] What if being good and giving back is the worst possible way to love my brothers and sisters of color since it only grows my inheritance while ensuring their disinheritance?

My white Philadelphia Catholic family is tied up in knots that keep us mired in the dehumanizing muck of racism. Some of our knots are just the price of doing business in a racialized society when ours has been touted as the most valued skin type. We move through the world with a sense of entitlement that comes at the expense of our empathy for others. We have distanced ourselves from people of color to protect our wages, property values, test scores, and inheritances. In preserving upward mobility, we breed exhausting anxiety that is suspicious of vulnerability and obsesses over perfection instead. We have bought into the fragile myths of how we got here and promote false rationales as to why others haven't been able to achieve the same things.

My people feel the knots of racism in our bodies, although we probably can't diagnose them and certainly won't talk about them. Our stomachs churn with guilt and our faces flush hot with shame when we find ourselves in over our heads in situations of racial disparity. Our hearts race with fear and our throats tighten with defensiveness when we try to explain what we never intended or meant. Our eyes roll with exasperation when the "race card" gets played. We square our shoulders with denial or grit our teeth with the prospect of being lumped in with the *real* racists. Some of us have tried to loosen these bodily knots through alcohol, long hours at the office, charitable giving, political activism, novenas, or working to be perceived on the right side of racial conflicts.

But like suturing wounds that haven't been properly cleaned, things only fester. In fact, Black philosopher George Yancy likens whites' experience with racism to that of being "sutured"—sewn shut, tightly bound, sealed in and sealed off.[20] My Philadelphia Catholic family is stitched together with knots of ignorance, false innocence, isolation, guilt, shame, and fear.

My experience growing up, worshipping, teaching theology, and organizing in Catholic Philadelphia suggests to me that white Catholics cannot make meaningful contributions to movements for racial justice if we are tangled up in these knots, especially the distinctively Catholic ones. For example, if we don't know the history of slavery and its impact in our families, our parishes, and our archdiocese, then we are bound to repeat otherwise avoidable mistakes with each new generation, further tethering us to a legacy that would appall us. If we prefer charitable giving in response to need rather than asking why there is a need in the first place, then we won't fix social problems. If we wrongly equate justice with deferring to authority figures who either see moral relativism as the biggest threat and cut through it with binary thinking or view public safety as the greatest good and protect it through appeals to law and order, then we will struggle to build safe communities. If we prefer a sacramental life that hinges on seeking absolution for individual sinfulness, then we will leave sinful Catholic cultures and institutions beyond reproach. If we resent accusations that we may not be as innocent, as good, as moral as we've been led to believe, then we will never learn and grow. If we continue the generations-old practice of sacrificing our spiritual and cultural traditions to the idol of whiteness, then we will have a hard time seeing ourselves in the multicultural future of the American Catholic Church. We have yet to realize, to paraphrase Du Bois, that the problem of American Catholicism, specifically of white American Catholics, is the problem of the color line.

The catch-22 in all of this, as people of color like Chris have helped me to see it, is that the urgent responsibility for racial justice—for building individuals and communities that flourish by erasing the color line—rests on the shoulders of the people that racism has rendered most unprepared to accept that responsibility. Black Catholic theologian Bryan Massingale insists that white comfort always has and will continue to set the limits of racial justice movements in this country.[21] If I learned anything from the Black Lives Matter banner initiative in my parish, it's that even when responding to the call of racial justice, white Catholics aren't always aware of and committed to what this justice requires of us. How can we possibly think, for example, that history won't repeat itself if we remain ignorant of it? Or that communities of color in Philadelphia can trust whites in the risky struggle for racial justice if we're too afraid to do this uncomfortable work in our own families and parish communities? How can we have compassion for others' pain if we continually dodge our own with self-righteous denial of any racial wrongdoing on our part? How can we envision a radically different future if we've allowed the status quo to distort our moral imagination for generations? How can we move forward if we are afraid of making mistakes? The work of racial justice is certainly the work of white Catholics, but not when we are tied in knots.

JAMES BALDWIN'S ADVICE to white people suggests to me how I might undo my knots: "Go back where you started, as far back as you can, examine all of it, travel your road again and tell the truth about it."[22] That is what I aim to do in this book—to go back as far as I can in my family's history in Catholic Philadelphia, examine all of it, and travel those roads again, like a pilgrim, telling the truth about it.

You could say that what follows is a kind of reckoning. I am reckoning with memories of racism held collectively by people who identify as Catholic and as white in Philadelphia, a city where Catholics map each other by parish on a landscape of white supremacy codified by the Founding Fathers in our own Independence Hall. I've been trying to do this kind of reckoning with white people, most of them Catholics, with varying levels of success. I've reckoned with college students through reflective writing and interactive classroom activities, with suburbanites in parish hall lectures and breakout conversations, and with communities of nuns and priests at reflection gatherings. Rarely do we take the uncomfortable but essential turn toward the specific contours of our own entanglements with the color line, our own participation in a culture of anti-Blackness, our own sacrificial offerings to the idol of white supremacy. It's easier to deconstruct theory or debate hypotheticals than to accept our part in the reality of others' suffering or to probe our own wounds.

But I suspect that when it comes to racism, Baldwin wants whites to wrestle with those dimensions of our own personal histories, the shadow sides of our family-creation stories. So in this book I will reckon with memories specific to the people in *my* family as far back as I can go. While I've heard all sorts of tall tales about some of these ancestral characters, this is my first trek down *this* road—the well-trodden but less celebrated memory lane of American Catholic racism, American Catholic white dominance, American Catholic white supremacy. In trying to learn from the truths encountered on this journey, it is my hope to share two pieces of wisdom with possible import for other white Americans whose family histories mirror my own and who may feel a bit like me—proud and yet ashamed, grieving for others but not yet ourselves, fearful and yet resolved.

First, the lived experience of my family members reveals that whiteness is part of the tradition of American Catholicism. It has kept white Catholics tied up in knots since our people's earliest encounters with Catholicism in this country. Going back to my great-great-great grandparents, my family's ways of being Catholic in a variety of spaces in and around Philadelphia—in parish churches and schools, on the block or at work, around the family dinner table or in the pew—suggest that whiteness itself is part of the Catholic tradition in the US. It is a body of knowledge and a bodily process of handing down that knowledge from generation to generation.

Across the generations, ideas about what it means to be white resonate with ideas about what it means to be Catholic: people are naturally or innately superior or inferior, being good requires deferring to authority, security comes with upholding law and order, charity absolves responsibility for inequality, unborn life must be protected even at the cost of many other lives. These were formal ideas promulgated by the Pope and by conferences of bishops. They were also ideas that came more informally from the pulpit and in the parish bulletin, or over the public address system and in the curriculum in the parochial school.

What's more, these ideas about being Catholic and being white are passed down from one generation to the next through a set of embodied practices we recognize as the rituals of American Catholicism: reserving communion for Catholics in good moral standing; inviting white children to the front of the First Communion line; learning to acquiesce to the authority of those addressed as Father or Sister or Officer and likewise to their perspectives on complex situations; prioritizing the sexual purity of a fair-skinned Virgin Mary and protecting those who look like her from hypersexualized people with darker skin; doing acts of charity to ease the guilt of social inequality; confessing individual sins of racial bias but not those of moral cooperation in structural racism; insisting that the right to life of the unborn is the human right that most counts in the voting booth; claiming it is more accurate to say "all lives matter" than to believe those whose experience proves otherwise. Catholicism provides what Joe Feagin calls the "hidden curriculum of beliefs, images, emotions and narratives" of the white racial frame by which we understand ourselves and the workings of the world. He suggests that performances of whiteness serve as the "muscles and tendons that make up the bones of structural racism," imagery that resonates deeply with the corporal nature of Catholicism.[23]

The second piece of wisdom I hope to share is about how traditions are constantly evolving. By learning more about the white supremacy I've inherited from my Catholic tradition, I can disrupt its ongoing *inertial force* beyond the boundaries of my faith tradition. I can be more prepared to work with others in adapting my rich Catholic tradition to take up the work of anti-racism. Becoming an anti-racist entails surveying how my family became and remains white over five generations in Catholic Philadelphia. I can take an inventory of ideas and practices of whiteness that have been handed down to me, examining who handed them on and why. I can notice the culturally distinct pieces of the Catholic tradition that were dropped along my ancestors' journeys to becoming Americans, to becoming white by being anti-Black. Some of this inheritance I will want to leave by the wayside, such as tacit beliefs about our superiority, images of white-only saints, downplaying unearned advantages. Some heirlooms, however, I will want to reclaim in order to better travel the road ahead: forgotten cultural feast days on the liturgical calendar, stories of small feats of resistance, moments of transgressing the color line. Either way, I want to get a better handle on who I am as a white American Catholic today by reckoning with how my ancestors became Catholic and white in Philadelphia. With these reckonings of the Catholic tradition in hand—in heart, really—I then want to travel my road again.

One of my doctoral professors, James Keenan, SJ continues to teach me that mercy is "the willingness to enter into the chaos of another."[24] He goes so far as to say that mercy defines Catholicism. Journeying the color line in my Catholic family, I contend that *racial* mercy ought to define Catholicism for white American Catholics. This is particularly true given our aversion to the chaos of racism in our own lives, in the lives of people of color, in our neighborhoods and parishes, and in our faith tradition itself. If we understand justice as Dr. Martin Luther King Jr. did—"Justice is love correcting that which revolts against love"—then racial mercy holds up before us those revolting, disgusting, disheartening tendencies cultivated in us over generations of getting tangled up in the color line.[25] Racial mercy then gives us the courage to probe those tendencies, cleanse their festering wounds, and heal what they have infected. If justice is what love looks like in public, as Cornel West passionately intones, then racial mercy is the precondition for public expressions of love that resist racism. Racial mercy is what love looks like in the midst of our personal and public relationships, all of which have been distorted by our proximity to and participation in a culture of white supremacy in American Catholicism. Racial mercy is the antidote to the spiritual bypassing that white Catholics have learned when traveling the road to Jericho, when traveling the color line in America.

MY CATHOLIC ANCESTORS in seventeenth- and eighteenth-century Ireland—the people who eventually became American Catholics and white in Philadelphia—likely practiced the penitential ritual of *rounding*.[26] After confessing their sins, they would have exiled themselves to a nearby space in the natural landscape they believed was imbued with the holy. It may have been a rock outcropping that had long caught the eye. Maybe it was a spring or natural well, or a spot where Irish saints were reputed to have rested while on a pilgrimage. Whatever made the space liminal, my Irish Catholic ancestors would have walked in a clockwise direction around and around a particular point at its center, offering prayers of contrition with each step. Their confessor would have determined the number of prayers and rounds to be made. Depending on the circumstances, shoes may not have been an option. My Irish ancestors would have counted each "round" by placing a small stone or a pebble on a growing mound at the circle's center, symbolizing their refusal to carry the weight of sin a step further. Still others may have left buttons as a symbol of unfastening or loosening themselves from sin's suffocating grip. Some would have left threads or pieces of fabric on the branches of nearby shrubs and trees, casting intercessory prayers for forgiveness to the damp winds, signaling to future penitents the spot's power for detachment from sinful conditions.

There must have been something cathartic about that ritual, wandering out in the elements, moving their bodies, leaving something behind. Rounding wasn't about worrying the knots of life, or reactively tugging at their loose ends in an effort to be set free. Rather, with each short lap, my ancestors would have experienced, in the rhythm of their walking and their prayerful whispering, a loosening of the tightness in the chest, a softening of the heart, an expansion of the soul. Step by step, round by round, surrounded by reminders that they were not alone in their desire to be set free from whatever bound them, the knots of the sinful self would gradually become undone. Room for something new to take root would have opened up. Upon completing their rounding, my ancestors would put their shoes on and walk the well-worn track back to their lives with a resolve to begin again. This rounding ritual was so transformational that my ancestors would have called it a *tura*, meaning pilgrimage.

My journey along the color line in Catholic Philadelphia is a *tura*—a penitential pilgrimage filled with rounds. Like my Old World ancestors, I seek a cathartic penance that might promise unburdening, loosening, and detachment. I desire to experience forgiveness by moving through and around liminal holy spaces or spots in the City of Philadelphia that link past and present. I seek penance for the sins of white supremacy while I circle the stories and memories of these places, a loosening from the grip of anti-Blackness inherent in my family's experience of Catholicism in America. I want to be able to return to my life with a renewed sense of hope that my yearnings for racial justice will interrupt the legacy of white supremacy in American Catholicism. I want to leave something behind to signal to other penitents that this kind of change is indeed possible. That is my hope for this book—that it serves as a *tura* of racial mercy.

Each of the following chapters will consider—critically and compassionately—how different members of my family across five generations in and around Catholic Philadelphia have been entangled in the color line, as well as efforts they and others like them made to undo the knots of racism. In some cases, I commune with these folks because of their need for racial mercy given their particular entanglements with the color line in Philadelphia. If white supremacy is indeed socially reproduced, then it's likely I've inherited many of the knots that bound them. Others I visit because they were agents of racial mercy—whether in seeking it for themselves or in offering it to others. If white supremacy endures because of a collective failure to resist it, then these are memories I want to uncover. To do all of this, it is my intention to walk a bit in my ancestors' shoes. I want to appreciate the choices they faced in terms of developing their individual and collective identities and discover the ways in which their Catholic identity and their whiteness were so deeply intertwined. I want to probe the wounds that whiteness inflicted upon them and attend to the damage and hurt that reverberates down the generations and beyond the branches of my family into the wider Body of Christ.

Some of these folks I know by their stoic gazes in the midst of the extensive framed photo array on a mantel in my parents' home. A profile photograph of a stern woman, streams of white ruffles cascading from her throat, and the amiable and yet unsmiling portrait of her saloon-owning husband, in his twenties and already the father of two, striking a pose that conveys a blissful ignorance of Prohibition and the Great Depression looming on the horizon. I recognize these people by their grins amidst a shot of the neighborhood group down the shore, tucked under the arms of dates who would never become spouses or shoulder to shoulder with broad-chested pals who would not make it back from Europe. A 1930s bride stepping out of a black Ford, veil billowing behind her in a September breeze as she reaches back to free a hem; wedding party portraits with morning coats and cascading bouquets, cheeks tinted by the latest photographic technology. Little girls veiled in First Communion white, clasping prayer books with shy, only-daughter smiles. They're growing families, herded together in the front yard of the newly purchased suburban twin home or posing for a quick intergenerational picture at the end of a Sunday visit with the grandparents.

Going back even further, I have come to know many of these people as apparitions in the documentary history of the country and the Archdiocese of Philadelphia. Government censuses dating back to the 1820s capture all of the essentials of their citizenship in a thin black script worthy of becoming an official font given its consistency across the decades. They appear in similar sacramental censuses conducted by dutiful priests in rectories across the metro area, time-stamping baptisms, marriages, and burials. These family members also make themselves known to me through their signatures—on World War I draft cards indicating prohibitive medical conditions, passport applications to take the oldest boy back to Sligo to meet the family, or the death certificates of mothers or younger brothers—many with uncanny similarities in penmanship to descendants they never knew.

I want to round the sacred spaces where my family simultaneously learned how to be Catholic and become anti-Black, learned to see Blackness and Black people as liabilities, threats, unholy others to be kept at a distance, contained, managed, thus continually demarcating the color line in Philadelphia. In each of the book's eight chapters, we will examine the different options facing my family in terms of their entanglements and the impact of the choices they made on themselves and on African Americans. We begin with my first memory of the knots of racism, rounding the MOVE standoff in West Philadelphia in 1985 and the Catholic dimensions of that tragedy, which I carried through most of my adolescence and young adulthood. Chapters two and three take us back to the origins of my family in the Philadelphia area and consider the dynamics of the forced choice they faced in the antebellum period when settling in a county sandwiched between Philadelphia, with a large free Black population, and the northern borders of Delaware and Maryland, where slavery was legal. Did they support abolition or simply put their heads down and assimilate into the anti-Black American and Catholic culture? Chapter four explores the experiences of the first generation to come of age as American Catholics in the late nineteenth century. We'll round their parish neighborhood in South Philadelphia to discover how they contributed to the manufacturing of race during the Reconstruction period in what was called the Workshop of the World. Chapter five explores the golden age of American Catholicism in the 1920s when my family, now in a more affluent parish in central North Philadelphia, experienced the tension between remaining within tightly drawn parish boundaries or boldly stepping out into the American culture beyond them. Here we will round the sesquicentennial celebration in Philadelphia in 1926, where Catholic participation revealed the social forces of the color line in my family's yearnings to finally—and unequivocally—belong in the American project.

Through a pair of chapters, I then explore the way Catholics held that line in terms of housing integration, setting in motion the conditions for our current wealth gap and hyper-segregated neighborhoods and parishes. Chapter six rounds the Gesu Parish in the 1930s, where my father's maternal grandparents were involved in initiatives spearheaded by the Jesuits to protect a "grand old neighborhood" from an "invasion of the colored" from the South. From there we move in chapter seven to St. Francis of Assisi Parish in suburban Philadelphia, where in the years immediately following World War II, my maternal grandfather built two hundred homes in a subdivision where he only sold to white families. Our pilgrimage concludes in chapter eight with a rounding of the Catholic university context in which I now find myself, to examine the ways in which everything from endowments and mission statements have long been entangled with the color line.

"RECONCILIATION BEGINS WITH CONFESSION, and Confession must begin in the Church," Rev. Blackmon told Chris and me at that gathering of community organizers back in 2017.[27] The sins of racism in American Catholicism, in Philadelphia Catholicism, in my own Philadelphia Catholic family, need to be confessed. We need racial mercy to begin that confessional process, to begin the work of reconciliation. We need racial mercy to untie our knots so that, in the spirit of James Baldwin, we can become better, more truthful storytellers about ourselves and our tradition. In other words, we need racial mercy to be witnesses to the truth. *Witness* is a word with layers of theological significance. A witness does not simply offer some kind of factual testimony about an event that she has observed from the margins. Rather, a witness shares knowledge she has accumulated from encountering an event or significant moment in a fully embodied way. This isn't just any kind of knowledge either, but rather, it often contains countercultural ideas and radical perspectives with the potential to transform those who share it and those who take it in. Witnesses often impart a dangerous wisdom, which is why the word *martyr* comes from the Greek word *martys*, meaning "witness."

White American Catholics have been witnesses to the inequalities and violence of racism, especially at the hands of and in the name of white American Catholicism, but we have yet to give witness. I don't think we can undo the knots of racism until we risk doing so. To speak truthfully about what we have seen, heard, or experienced in the past allows us to live differently in the present, and in living differently in the present we make a different future possible. Given the costs already accrued and a future clearly at stake, this is a risk I am compelled to take. It's time to undo the knots.

My pilgrimage starts with the first knot of white supremacy I recall being tied up in: May 13, 1985—the day of the MOVE raid in West Philadelphia.

CHAPTER ONE

WITNESSING

St. James

"ATTENTION, MOVE! This is America!"

My father should have been a historian. He's got *Philadelphia Inquirer* newspapers from many of the major events of his lifetime: the first man on the moon, the Phillies winning the World Series in 1980, the Clinton impeachment. Dad made reel-to-reel audiotapes of John F. Kennedy's funeral and photographed the train carrying Robert F. Kennedy's casket on its way from DC to Boston in June of 1968. Historical sites, mostly colonial, were often family vacation destinations—Williamsburg in Virginia, Mystic Seaport in Connecticut, Old Sturbridge Village in Massachusetts—if not ancillary side trips before the main attraction. Never mind what today we'd call pop-up excursions on random Saturdays to more local history-laden sites like Pennsbury Manor, William Penn's homestead on the Delaware River, or the Gettysburg battlefields, where we'd ponder how hot it must have been doing all that fighting in wool uniforms. Dad was all about experiential history.

So it was not out of character for him to rouse my younger sister and me out of our beds on a mid-May Monday evening in 1985 and drive our wood-paneled Dodge Aspen station wagon to the local elementary school, not even a half-mile from our development of colonial-style homes (ours a Williamsburg blue, of course). Dad helped Corinne and me climb up on a picnic table at the crest of a small rise at the back of the school. Then we tracked the direction of his pointed finger to take in the orange sky just to the south and west. She and I didn't know, as we stood there in our pajamas gazing at the eerie glow, that earlier that morning the Philadelphia Police Department had fired ten thousand rounds of ammunition in the space of ninety minutes on a house filled with twelve people, six of them children, in a middle-class Black neighborhood in West Philadelphia. This was an attempt to evict the residents and arrest several—without any prior efforts in meaningful conflict resolution by city officials or agencies. We didn't know that in the late afternoon, untrained members of the bomb unit of the Philadelphia Police Department dropped, from a helicopter, a knapsack containing C-4 that exploded on the roof of the home and started the blaze. We didn't know that firefighters were initially ordered stand down, so that "fire could be used as a tactical weapon," or that the fire became an inferno that consumed almost an entire square block of traditional Philadelphia row homes.[1] But Dad knew something significant was happening, and like any aspiring historian, he thought Corinne and I—aged ten and twelve at the time—should be witnesses to Philadelphia history.

We were witnesses, in the most passive sense of that word. We were mere observers, or so we thought, of the violent culmination of a decade-long standoff between a back-to-nature Black liberationist group, MOVE (meaning The Movement), and the Philadelphia Police Department. The city awoke the next morning to the news of eleven dead (six adults and five children); sixty-one houses in the Cobbs Creek neighborhood of West Philadelphia burned to the ground, and 250 residents left homeless.[2]

Dad, Corinne, and I watched from a safe distance, quite possibly on the cartographer's line separating suburban Montgomery and urban Philadelphia counties. Chronologically speaking, we took it in from the vantage point of two generations of government-sponsored white flight. Those were the days of social welfare that ensured the economic mobility of the white people who watched the event unfold on live TV in their greenlined neighborhoods. Meanwhile, those watching from redlined communities knew that but for the grace of God theirs could have been the neighborhood ablaze. We watched as innocent bystanders, presumed nonparticipants in the horror we gazed upon. I remember feeling scared and confused. While we were close enough to see the orange sky above it, 6221 Osage Avenue might as well as have been on Mars for the connection that folks like us in Elkins Park felt to the standoff that had been mounting since 1978. That was MOVE's first violent incident with the police in West Philadelphia, which left one officer dead and nine MOVE members convicted with life sentences. And like most witnesses, we also

failed to realize how our positionality—how we came to be on our picnic table perch on the city line, our ages and genders, and especially our
race—filtered everything we were taking in, conditioning any testimony
we would offer in the days to come.

But the opportunity for testimony never arose. As one commentator
noted on the twentieth anniversary of the bombing, "When it came to
outrage, Philadelphia shrugged."[3] We simply didn't talk about MOVE.
Anywhere. Not at home, not at school or Mass in St. James Parish. Not
even in the racially integrated track club we belonged to, the only place beyond our housing development where I interacted with Black kids—both
of those spaces being anomalies for suburban Philly in the mid-1980s.
It was as if the MOVE bombing hadn't happened, at least not for those
of us living in Philadelphia's predominantly white suburbs. Certainly the
aftermath of the bombing, the five weeks of televised public hearings of a
special investigation commission, and the trial of the lone adult to survive,
Ramona Africa, dominated the news cycle for months. And there were
intermittent reminders in the ensuing years: the houses the City of Philadelphia had been required to build in the wake of a class action lawsuit
filed by those who had lost their homes turned out to be constructed by a
corrupt developer. They had to be condemned not long after the original
Osage Avenue residents had reluctantly relocated.[4] But we never really
talked about what we had witnessed. Not as a family, not with our Black
neighbors, not in our parish.

It is possible that follow-up conversations with my parents didn't reg-
ister in quite the same depths of my twelve-year-old brain as that orange sky had. But it is more likely that the predominantly Catholic adults
around me were simply practicing what they had learned from their Catholic parents when it came to witnessing the horrors of racism: say some
prayers for those poor people, and don't ask questions for which there
are no easy—or exonerating—answers. And this was a response my family learned from faith leaders in Philadelphia's Catholic community, who
have yet to bring our tradition of social justice or rituals of reconciliation and healing to bear on that event. The US bishops' first teaching
on racism—*Brothers and Sisters to Us* promulgated in 1979, a year after
MOVE's standoff with police in the Powelton Village neighborhood and
less than a decade before the MOVE bombing—was not much help since
it couched racism in interpersonal rather than structural ways or as institutional abuses of power.[5]

In May 2021, another dimension of the MOVE tragedy came to light: city officials had mishandled the remains of two of the children killed in the fire. It was only then that I learned from a Black Catholic blog that a Catholic priest, Monsignor Charles Devlin, was part of faith-based attempts to negotiate a peaceful resolution to the conflict between MOVE and police in 1978, which set the stage for the final standoff in 1985.[6] Devlin was director of the cardinal's Commission on Human Relations and expressed concerns for human rights violations in the city's starvation blockade to evict the group from their dwelling.[7] His stance met with resistance from some Philadelphia Catholics and placed him in opposition to one the most prominent among them, Frank Rizzo, a former police commissioner and Philadelphia's mayor at the time. In the end, after engagements with city officials and MOVE members in the final hours before the confrontation, Devlin also seemed to accept the violence as inevitable.[8] Aside from offering the funeral Mass for the officer killed in 1978, James Ramp, he stepped away from MOVE as remaining members regrouped in Cobbs Creek where the deadly confrontation happened in 1985.

That silence about the MOVE bombing in 1985 wasn't simply because I was too young to understand. It followed me through sixteen years of Catholic education in the Philadelphia Archdiocese—from elementary school, which my parents and their siblings had also attended, and which, when I attended, had just a few remaining Sisters of St. Joseph on staff; through high school with the Sisters of Mercy, with all of our charity runs into the city with cans and coats and frozen turkeys and wrapped Christmas toys; and then through my college years with the Jesuits in a West Philadelphia neighborhood not too far from Osage Avenue, where learning how to become "men and women for and with others" was the hallmark of my education. MOVE simply never came up.

The silence followed me to my doctoral program in theological ethics at Boston College. The lone Black professor in the department assisted me in reorienting my dissertation away from my initial curiosity about women and work toward a reconstruction of compassion that would help Christians after 9/11 better face and respond to the unjust suffering of everyone, from the Jews of Auschwitz to those displaced by Hurricane Katrina. And yet the suffering I had actually been pulled out of bed to witness in May of 1985 still remained safely out of mind. Nor did it surface in the ensuing decade, while I wrote a book on how murals in Philadelphia were effective in responding to entrenched problems like racism. In all of my research for that book, the interviews and wanderings through Philadelphia neighborhoods—pilgrimages that led to the family origin questions at the heart of *this* book—never once did I wonder why none of Philadelphia's 3,500 community murals have broached the MOVE event.

Even in the past ten years, as I've turned my vocational attention as a teacher and scholar to understanding racism and collaborating with others to undo it in the context of Catholic higher education, my memories of MOVE have remained interred in my psyche, with no calls of conscience to exhume them. Nor have I even thought to incorporate it into a course on theology and racism I now teach in one of Philadelphia's Catholic universities that was founded by the Christian Brothers. In fact, I've only anecdotally recalled that night on the picnic bench with my dad and my sister as evidentiary proof of my father's quirkiness, failing to notice that the bigger picture itself points to the ongoing legacy of white supremacy in the various communities of silence to which I have belonged and in which I am beloved.

Not even the thirtieth anniversary of the tragedy—which coincided with African Americans in Baltimore publicly protesting for justice for Freddie Grey—sparked theological reflection on *why* May 13, 1985, had happened and how thirty years of white silence around that tragedy continues to function as its own kind of testimony. No wonder I was initially apprehensive as the chair of the department of religion and theology when a junior colleague informed me he had invited Ramona Africa, the only adult survivor of the MOVE bombing, to his course on Black religion in America that April. As a new arrival to the city, clearly he was impervious to our unspoken vow of silence around MOVE in Catholic Philadelphia. Ms. Africa, still in her MOVE-inspired dreadlocks, wore jeans and a pale yellow sweatshirt with a picture of a bouquet of flowers stitched on the front. I shook her hand, thanked her for making the time to be with us, grasped at straws for questions I might ask her. As dutiful Catholics, we had learned our lessons well—the vast majority of our students hailed from the Philadelphia area and had never heard of her, MOVE, or the fire on Osage Avenue. The chasm between her experience growing up in Catholic Philadelphia and that of the students, as well as my own, remained unbridged. This time, *my* shame was the reason for the silence.

On May 13, 1985, an announcement delivered by bullhorn by the chief of police broke the Monday morning quiet on Osage Avenue. He gave MOVE members one last chance to evacuate: "Attention, MOVE!

This is America!" In the end, we white folks were probably the only ones who didn't realize just how accurate that declaration turned out to be. With 10,000 rounds of police ammunition spent, a bomb dropped, 61 homes burned to the ground, 253 people displaced, and 11 Black people dead, 5 of them children, May 13 was indeed America. It was the America of thirty generations of white violence against people of color in the name of maintaining law and order, in the name of assimilation to the dominant white culture, in the name of what historian Carol Anderson calls "white rage" at the prospect of Black assertiveness or advancement.[9] Not to mention that this declaration was also made in Philadelphia, the city where the Founding Fathers declared that "we hold these truths to be self-evident"—but only for property-owning white men—and where "we the people" formally legalized slavery and appeased Southern concerns about governmental underrepresentation by counting five enslaved Africans as three constituents while denying them the rights of citizenship, all "in order to build a more perfect union." MOVE members more than likely knew better than anybody else what the chief of police was actually declaring before unleashing fire and fury on them and an entire Black neighborhood: "Attention, America! *This* is America!"

White America is now confronted by videos of police-initiated shootings, domestic terrorism perpetrated by young white men against people of color and their allies, and chants about lives that matter from people who feel as though they do not. We are reluctantly waking up to the tragedy of this ugly contradiction: that from our country's origins in the seventeenth century through our politics in the twenty-first, white supremacy *is* America. To put it another way, America created and now is trapped by what Eddie Glaude calls a "value gap" between whites and people of color that pervades our national ethos, shapes our individual and collective self-understandings, dictates our social imaginations, and directs our interactions within and across the racial groups the value gap created in the first place.[10]

But white Catholics like myself, and like so many of my family members and colleagues and students, remain among the most reluctant to wake up from what Ta-Nehisi Coates disturbingly describes as "the Dream" of America—the "Memorial Day cookouts, block associations, drives" and "treehouses and the Cub Scouts" that we fold over our heads like a blanket to escape our harshest and, for Black people, most dangerous contradictions.[11] We prefer to sleep on in silence than to believe the cacophony of truth. If Rebecca Solnit is even partially correct in claiming that "trauma is inherited silence, a silence it takes generations to learn to hear," then clearly it is high time for a declaration via bullhorn: "Attention, white Catholics! This white supremacy is American Catholicism!"[12]

THE CATHOLIC WALLS OF RACISM

In the weeks following the MOVE catastrophe, while I was having nightmares about house fires, my sister Corinne refused to sleep with her bedroom windows open. Since MOVE members had barricaded the front door of their house on Osage Avenue in preparation for the eventual standoff with police, TV footage often featured members rappelling from second-floor windows. Corinne's bedroom sat directly over our own front door, with two windows opening onto what she considered an easy-access porch roof, so she felt she needed to do her part to keep our family safe. This required a real commitment as warm May nights eventually gave way to muggier June and July. No oscillating fan could deal with the heat in that bedroom (although we had it, central air did not square with my parents' frugality). Nor could any amount of rationalizing ease her torment.

That image of Corinne lying wide-eyed and frozen with fear in her sweaty bed—haunted by unprocessed memories, confused as to what exactly had gone down and why, anxious about what might happen next, and succumbing to a futilely defensive stance that cut her off from fresh air—strikes me as a poignant metaphor for growing up a white Catholic after generations of America's racism.

Somewhere in my ongoing journey toward anti-racism, I was exposed to an analogy (whose source I no longer remember) that presents whites' experience of racism as akin to being hermetically sealed by four walls: a wall of separation and isolation as a result of generations of segregation in housing; a wall of amnesia about history; a wall of illusions about our own innocence and delusions about the magnitude of racial disparities; and a wall of power and privileges awarded us by our pigmentation. My white Catholic family has been living behind those walls in the City of Philadelphia since my first ancestor, Andrew Little, arrived here sometime in the early 1820s at the age of nineteen. As I reflect on my history, I realize I stand in his legacy in more ways than one.

Putting up the *wall of separation* through voluntary segregation from people of color was an essential step in the process of becoming American for Catholic Christians from other places, who soon after arriving on these shores faced a litmus test for belonging that involved ensuring that others could not. For many, building this wall was a forced choice exercise that pitted your future well-being and that of your family, for whom you had sacrificed greatly, against the well-being of others with equally sacrificial, albeit differently colored, skin in the game. Either deny the full humanity of Black people or join them in their less than human status. Catholics were not exempted from this process. Indentured Catholic laborers in the colonial era quickly learned not to cast their lot with their African counterparts, despite being equally inferior in the emerging American economy. For Irish Catholics in the antebellum period, like my great-great-grandparents Maurice and Margaret Donovan O'Connell and William and Mary Smith Gallagher, this segregation more than likely came by choosing to join the pro-slavery Democratic party rather than affiliate with the abolitionist Republicans—even though the latter's passion for liberty and equality would have resonated with their pre-famine experience of British-occupied Ireland.

For waves of Catholic arrivals in the early twentieth century, like my great-grandparents Edward and Belinda Dempsey Hargadon, segregation meant isolating yourself in white-only labor unions—whether in urban centers or rural mining towns—or, in Edward's case, operating a whites-only taproom in North Philadelphia in the midst of the first wave of Black migrants from the Jim Crow South just before World War I. During the economic recovery from the Great Depression, when Catholics like my grandparents William and Catherine Hargadon Gallagher and Maurice and Georgia Yeager O'Connell had become the largest denomination in the country, walls of isolation were built in greenlined neighborhoods on the fringes of cities—green with not only lawns and trees, but also, more importantly, with federal subsidies distributed to the most Anglo among us. "Non-whites"—initially Southern and Eastern Europeans and Jews, but eventually just Blacks and Hispanics—were relegated in 1937 to Philadelphia neighborhoods coded by the federal Home Owners' Loan Corporation with blue, yellow, or red lines that reflected the presumed pigmentation of residents, whose lack of whiteness deemed them risky investments for mortgages or loans.[13]

The walls of segregation only became higher in the years following World War II, as federal assistance for GIs disproportionately advantaged white vets when it came to housing and education. White Catholics like my parents, George and Kathleen Gallagher O'Connell, could grow up in all-white neighborhoods, buffered by government policies from ideas about Black people and the economic insecurity that Ibram X. Kendi claims in his book about the historical roots and evolution of ideas that Black inferiority was "stamped" on them "from the beginning."[14] Mom and Dad could attend predominantly white schools—Catholic or public, from kindergarten through college—in suburban districts beyond the reach of mandatory integration. So did their children, and now so do their grandchildren.

With nearly three generations of voluntary isolation from people of color under our belts, today's homogeneity strikes many Catholics as natural, as de facto, as "just the way things are." The economic disparity between our voluntarily walled off white neighborhoods and those like the one that burned to the ground in West Philadelphia thirty years ago is likely to strike us as a demarcation in the metropolitan landscape rather than the result of choices our family members made in search of social mobility and economic security. That we are even less likely to recognize our myopia is evidence of our habituation in our predominantly white racial habitats.[15]

Then there's the *wall of amnesia*. Most of us don't know much about this history. *Amnesia* is the correct word for our relationship to it, since at various points our ancestors *did* know about or experience the injustices of racism given their standing on the lower rungs of the social hierarchy. We've instead operated with a selective memory, choosing the bits that serve both the myth of Anglo-Saxon exceptionalism and the American Catholic corollary of "respectability politics." In both cases, the desire to be accepted into and respected by a racially biased status quo morphs into maintenance of it through our ability to pass assimilation tests or strict adherence to law and order. Rather than turn to face those memories and learn from them, we've chosen to forget, which is another way white Catholics have walled ourselves off. We don't know our racist history as a faith community, and too frequently, the history we do know we don't remember accurately. Or we recall it in ways that fail to re-member the Body of Christ that is broken by the violence of racism.

For example, the name Charles Carroll may ring a bell, since he was the only Roman Catholic to sign the Declaration of Independence. But how many of us know that Carroll was not only among the slave-holding majority of signatories to the Declaration of Independence but also the most expansive, owning between four and five hundred people at the time of the Revolution?[16] Despite owning slaves, Carroll and others signed that sacred American text that claims the rights to life, liberty, and the pursuit of happiness are inalienable for all—except those who did not look like them? Or that the first Catholic Supreme Court Justice, Roger B. Taney, also wrote the majority opinion in the 1857 Dred Scott case that denied enslaved people citizenship and extended slavery into free territories, or that Homer Plessy, the plaintiff in the 1896 *Plessy v. Ferguson* case, which legalized "separate but equal" Jim Crow laws, was a Black Catholic?[17] How many graduates of Catholic colleges and universities are aware of the connections between their alma mater's institutional wealth, held in land and endowments, and what sociologist Joe Feagin calls the "slave-centered economic complex"?[18] How many Catholics peer out from among the blurry faces in photographs of the 4,075 lynchings of Black people between Reconstruction and World War II, or are among the economic beneficiaries of today's "new Jim Crow," as scholar and activist Michelle Alexander calls it, whether as stakeholders or shareholders in the $5.1 billion private prison industry?[19] How many white Catholics have inherited the wealth of homeownership, in no small part thanks to parish-led campaigns to resist racially integrated neighborhoods and parochial schools during the Great Migration in the name of protecting property values, or as a result of suburban federal housing subsidies after World War II that fueled the expansion of archdioceses across the country? And what of the 58 percent of white Catholics who voted for Donald Trump in 2016 and the 50 percent who did so again in 2020, despite his unapologetic race-baiting campaign tactics, mixed public track record on abortion, and policies on the environment, immigration, refugees, capital punishment, and health care that contradicted Catholic social teaching?[20]

Unfortunately, our ignorance does not stop there. The wall of amnesia also keeps us from remembering courageous people and countercultural movements that defied the color line and advanced anti-racism in the US. Iconic white Catholics like Dorothy Day and Thomas Merton broke the silence around racial injustice with spoken, written, and embodied public testimonies, and Philadelphia's own St. Katharine Drexel took her massive personal fortune and worked to bridge the education gap between whites and people of color before the Supreme Court demanded that the states do this in 1954. She also wrote to President Roosevelt in 1934 demanding that he support the Costigan–Wagner anti-lynching bill.[21] The

wall of amnesia ensures that the anti-racist contributions of these prophetic figures remain largely unsung, and their visions of a beloved community, visions that set the moral compass of their lives, slip further out
of our sights.

We've also forgotten the ordinary people among this important community of witnesses—everyday Catholics like those from a national network of Catholic Interracial Councils who marched on Washington or
Selma; or Anna McGarry, who led Catholic integration campaigns like
the one in the Jesuit Gesu Parish community in North Philadelphia; or
my grandfather William Gallagher, who paid into the social security account of Lillian Bagley, the family's Black housekeeper, even though he
wasn't legally required to do so; or Monsignor Charles Devlin, who attempted to negotiate a peaceful resolution with MOVE before the 1978
police raid. It is not that these people were flawless in their responses to
racism, but rather that they refused to indulge the fear that racism instills
in whites to wall ourselves off from neighbors, employees, coworkers, or
strangers in the name of upholding social mores or following unjust laws.

Behind a third *wall of illusion of innocence and delusion of magnitude*,
Catholics like me are paralyzed by our unquestioned confidence in what
we think we know about racism, whether handed down in the tales of discrimination our immigrant ancestors faced or in the consensus we reach in
the echo chamber of our white-only conversations in predominately white
academies and boardrooms, high schools and universities, parish councils and community service teams. Our belief in our own moral goodness
goes unchallenged and in fact is reinforced by our inequality-sustaining
charity that fails to ask why the ceaseless need exists in the first place.
Why the never-ending canned food drives, special collections at Mass,
independent mission schools, service-learning courses, spring break trips
to poor rural or urban communities? As "voluntourists" to others' suffering, we are blinded by our judgments about the people on the receiving
end of our charity. "Good people, bad choices," we tell ourselves reassur-
ingly, to remain at the level of individual analysis that keeps us morally
off the hook. Rarely do we delve into structural analysis, which deflates
our do-good-to-feel-good high by raising questions of our complicity in
systems, institutions, and policies that have advantaged us precisely by
disadvantaging people of color.[22]

Not only do white Catholics short-circuit more deliberative and
relationship-building processes of restorative justice with our fix-it-now

pragmatism, we also end up missing the assets that communities of color bring to the work of racial justice. These cultural traditions, stories of brave ancestors, food and music, and religious rituals simultaneously heal, soften, and strengthen hearts. They are assets that our ancestors also once had before trading them in for the chance to start building all these walls of whiteness.

Ultimately, our reliance on charity speaks to our delusion about the depth of racial inequality and its crippling effects on our economy and the social fabric of our communities. After-school tutoring programs do not solve the racial bias in the distribution of state and federal education dollars that create educational disparities among students of color. Sacramental accompaniment and college degree programs inside our prisons will not ebb the rising tide of the last thirty years of hyper-incarceration that now imprisons Black people at a rate six times higher than it does whites.[23] While building houses with Habitat for Humanity may slow the process of gentrification, it does not address the hurdles in the urban housing market prospective home buyers of color must clear, or the way race colors eviction. Food and clothing drives fail to see the connection between depressed wages in service sector jobs that are disproportionately held by people of color and spending power.

Finally, sealed off behind a *wall of privilege and power*, we often feel burdened by gifts we don't even know we've been given by our dominant culture, defensively asserting that it's not our fault that we have them: unquestioned belonging, amplified voices, presumptions of innocence, a sense of entitlement, offense when those entitlements get challenged, and fragility when we get called out. Acknowledging privilege is an important step in showing up for racial justice work, especially the ultimate privilege of being able to opt into or out of that work. Catholic ethicist Bryan Massingale names this clearly: "White comfort sets the limit on racial justice."[24] It keeps us as the central focus rather than the people most negatively impacted by racial injustice. It leads us to believe that racial justice simply requires interpersonal awareness. It does little to address imbalances of power that racism creates and sustains.

So in order to dismantle these walls of racism, I will be naming the many manifestations of racism I encounter but will remain particularly attentive to racism as an expression of power that dehumanizes and exploits. This seems particularly important for me as a Catholic, since the ultimate power whites have exercised is our ability to name who God is and as such who is most like God or what it means to be made in God's image.[25] This helps me understand racism as a perversion of power, which Joseph Barndt understands as "the ability or the capacity to become all that God intends us to be, individually and collectively."[26] To his mind, racism abuses power in three ways. It promises white people power over others by creating a society that allows whites to control systems, institutions, and cultures. It disempowers people of color by dehumanizing them and cultivating internalized inferiority. And it destroys all people by holding us captives in the internalized self and collective understandings of either superiority or inferiority that ultimately separate us from our true selves and each other.[27] We won't be motivated to tear down racism's walls, or be effective in attempts to do so, if we don't acknowledge racism's pernicious impact on *us*.

THE UPPER ROOM OF WHITENESS

The analogy of being hermetically sealed behind walls of racism is not without theological significance. Just as my sister attempted to wall herself off from the horror of the MOVE bombing in the summer of 1985, white Catholics have shut out the realities of white supremacy and are stewing in some pretty unsavory juices in that tight, airless space. To that end, we're not much different from the disciples in the hours and days after the Crucifixion of Jesus. We have witnessed terrifying events and horrifying exchanges across the generations of our discipleship, and like our predecessors in the Gospel accounts, we have chosen to hide ourselves away in tight spaces—geographical, demographical, psychological, spiritual—in a desperate attempt to shut out the madness, to avoid suspicion, to make things go back to the way they were before, to preserve our moral standing, our legacy, our very selves. I'm compelled by Barndt's suggestion that we'd be more effective approaching racism as a sin of captivity, rather than a sin of omission or commission.[28] In other words, racism is a collective experience of separation marked by "isolation, separation, hostility and mistrust," whether between white and Black people, or even among whites ourselves, that then forces us to think and do and say things we don't necessarily want to think or do or say.[29] White Catholics like me have learned from our parents, from our teachers, from our pastors, from our bishops, that the best response to racism is to retreat from its catastrophes and lock ourselves into an upper room, or what I have come to understand through my own experience as an *upper room of whiteness.*

Like the disciples in Jerusalem in the aftermath of Good Friday, we are hiding behind walls of fear and confusion, guilt and shame, ignorance and denial, grief and exhaustion. Like them, we are trapped in the liminal space of a present where we assume nothing new is possible, since we're neither learning from the past nor imagining a different future. We're stifled by the racial sameness in this room, its lack of different perspectives, memories, strategies of making sense of it all. Having only ever really considered racism from the tight space of the upper room, with its clannish similarities and like-mindedness, we're clueless as to how to contribute to movements of integration and inclusion. We're paralyzed by fear in here too. Just as the disciples worried that what the authorities did to Jesus would be done to them, we wonder if what we have done to African Americans will be done to us. In this upper room of whiteness, we are cut off from the wisdom of the lived experience of people of color when it comes to understanding the dynamics of racism. We are also mired in a mental space where we reject the idea that we, too, are in need of healing, whether through an acquired distaste for becoming vulnerable enough to admit harming and being harmed, or out of fear of what such admissions of weakness might spark. After all, we're empathetic enough to wonder whether we ourselves would be able to refrain from reacting with violence if ever faced with the injustices that have been heaped upon communities of color. From behind that locked door, it is quite difficult to move toward the threshold of something entirely new and different.

Returning to the idea of being held captive, Barndt goes on to say that in being held captive by racism, whites "lose our humanity, our authenticity, and our freedom."[30] Unlike people of color who have these things *taken* from them by a culture of white dominance, for generations we whites have *handed over* our humanity, our authenticity, our freedom in order to gain access to the higher rungs in America's racial pecking order and to maintain our white dominance there. Trading on what W. E. B. Du Bois called our "psychological wages of whiteness," we stubbornly remain content with "eating Jim Crow," as Martin Luther King Jr. once described the economic disadvantages racial inequity creates for white people too, rather than hungering for a far more satisfying racial justice that comes when working across the color line.[31] Even among affluent white Catholics we see growing levels of anxiety and depression; eyes turned away from abuse in our families, workplaces, and faith communities; declining young adult affiliation with the Church; insistence on blaming individuals for their hardships; and reluctance to work across denominational or racial lines in taking on shared threats to our common good. We fervently assert our innocence in an effort to ward off our gnawing doubt of that very innocence. The anxiety, defensiveness, rationalizing, and posturing are exhausting in the end, and so we shut down and retreat, diminishing our humanity as we pull away, as we retreat further into the upper rooms of our whiteness.

Pope Francis seems to acknowledge as much when he describes what happens to Christians who "are enclosed in our groups, our movements, our parishes, in our little worlds." He says, "When a room is closed, it begins to get dank. If a person is closed up in that room, he or she becomes ill! Whenever Christians are enclosed in their groups, parishes, and movements, they take ill."[32]

Looking back, I realize that my family lost out in the aftermath of the MOVE crisis. We were held captive by racism, compelled to do things we didn't want to do, our integrity and freedom and authenticity compromised. Within two years, as Black families began to outpace whites in purchasing the remaining lots in the development where we lived, and with a renewed fear in the white subconscious of the "dangerous Black man," housing prices in our neighborhood began to decline. The familiar choice presented itself yet again—should we stay or should we join other white families with the means to move? Should we stay put in a house we loved—with my father's first fireplace, which we fueled with wood he sawed himself in the wooded acres that surrounded the property where he played as a kid; with its screened-in porch where we ate every family meal in the summer; with its vegetable garden and compost pile? Could we leave a house ensconced in patios, brick walkways, and colonial-inspired gardens that Dad had planted and pruned himself, a tire swing and elaborate bird feeding stations, a playhouse in the backyard and spotlighted whiffle ball diamond out front?

Should we bail on the experiment of racially integrated housing, the possibility of which was so hard-earned in the '60s and was just starting to hit its stride in neighborhoods around the country in the early '80s? Should we rend the social fabric of a racially integrated neighborhood where kids of all stripes—African American, Filipino, Jewish, Argentinian, three different denominations of Protestant—orbited on bikes around an oak tree seedling my father had planted at the center cul-de-sac? Should we protect the wealth tied up in our home, wealth eked out initially from my mom's salary at her job right out of high school with Bell Telephone while my dad completed his law degree before starting at a small law firm? Wealth needed to pay for all of that private Catholic secondary and higher education on the horizon, or to care for aging grandparents, one of whom had breathed her last with us from our back bedroom after a battle with lung cancer only a month before the whole MOVE crisis?

In the end, we left. My parents found another house in an adjacent township whose distance from the city line provided a bit more insurance, despite a bigger mortgage.

Mom and Dad sold the first house they had bought together, their first piece of the American Dream, where my siblings and I created our own childhood memories amidst the kind of integrated diversity that Martin Luther King Jr. dreamed of: kids of all colors and creeds riding bikes, sledding, picking wild raspberries, pitching tents, catching lightning bugs, playing baby in the air and ghost in the graveyard. I don't remember saying goodbye to my friends—to Chris, Justin, Jacob, and Chi Chi or Jennifer and Seth. I wonder if they remember us and if our abrupt leaving still wounds them too.

All of this remembering lately makes me think of the word *reckon*, a great concept for racism given its etymological roots in Anglo-Saxon English (the root of white supremacy). Among its many uses, I find "dealing with contradictions" to be the most compelling definition for *reckoning*. I have been reckoning with my memories of MOVE. I have wrestled or grappled with the contradictions that surface, the incongruence I feel about myself and my family, the unexpected information or insight that comes to mind when I step away from the defensive "okay but what about" mindset and try instead to believe the truth of that event in my life. In my brief experience doing anti-racist teaching, scholarship, and organizing, I have quickly come to realize there is no end to the contradictions that confront me as a white person, particularly a white Catholic woman; no end to deconstructing things I know with truths that are entirely new; no end to wrestling with a host of ideas and emotions that are breaking the bones of my white supremacy.

This idea of reckoning resonates with the rich Christian tradition of conversion: to make a turn or a shift—whether in our desires, our values, or our frameworks of meaning—away from excess toward balance, away from incompleteness toward fullness, away from indifference toward empathy, away from *ego* (self-centered love) toward *philia* (other-centered love). In this way, reckoning morphs into another meaning: to reconcile. Reconciling requires a deliberate process that begins with acknowledgment and ends with redress, all the while seeking mercy. In the case of my reckonings, it is racial mercy.

BEFORE COMMITMENTS TO RACIAL JUSTICE, ENCOUNTERS WITH RACIAL MERCY

My thirty years in post-MOVE Catholic Philadelphia—behind our walls of segregation, amnesia, illusions and delusions, and power and privilege—reveals to me that white Catholics cannot engage in nor make meaningful contributions to movements for racial justice from the upper room of whiteness. Justice requires that we more fully know our histories, that we engage in structural analysis of social problems, that we think with imaginations unfettered by the status quo, that we privilege those closest to the pain with leading the way. My own experience of Catholicism in Philadelphia suggests white Catholics do not possess these critical capabilities right now precisely because of our Catholic whiteness.

For example, Catholics do not know the history of MOVE, nor that of racism itself in the unfolding story of William Penn's "holy experiment," not to mention the unique role the Catholic Archdiocese of Philadelphia played in it all. We've been part of the chorus that pathologized and incarcerated surviving MOVE members but remain silent about the continued flow of wealth out of communities of color and into the hands of a concentrated few, a reality that the Church historically facilitated in Philadelphia and that MOVE shouted against through their megaphones. We remain stubbornly ignorant of our privileges. Our ability to retort righteously and defensively that "all lives matter" when confronted by people of color who insist on *their* human dignity serves as a primary example. We far prefer charitable giving to folks in need or asking them to do the heavy lifting to change the systems that oppress them over standing with them in working together for social change. We sacrificed our spiritual and cultural traditions on the altar of becoming homogenous Americans generations ago, and we have a hard time seeing ourselves in the multicultural future of the American Catholic Church. We resent accusations that we may not be as innocent, as good, as moral as we've been led to believe by a sacramental life that hinges on seeking absolution for individual sinfulness while leaving sinful Catholic cultures and institutions beyond reproach.

The catch-22 in all of this, as people of color have helped me to see it, is the fact that the urgent responsibility for racial justice—for building flourishing individuals and communities primarily by living in good and faithful relationships with multicultural others—rests on the shoulders of the people that racism has rendered most unprepared to accept this responsibility. How can we possibly think, for example, that communities of color in Philadelphia can trust whites enough to work with us toward racial justice if we're too paralyzed by guilt and shame to face dangerous memories like those of MOVE? How can we know the depth of the pain that keeps others from flourishing if we are hemmed in by self-righteous denial at racial wrongdoing in the first place? How can we move together toward a vision of what might be possible when for generations we've largely tethered ourselves to strategies that maintained the status quo by reminding us of who we are not and what should never be? "We may be Catholic, but at least we're not Black," has been the implied moral of the stories of failed integration of housing, parishes, schools, and universities. How can we develop the courage to move forward, knowing we'll make mistakes, if we haven't publicly acknowledged the mistakes of the past or if the stories of those who actually attempted racial justice remain untold?

The work of justice is uniquely ours to do, but not from inside the upper room.

Scripture shows us that the disciples faced a similar Catch-22 situation: the only way to experience relief from the anxieties of the upper room, to taste the joy of the Resurrection, was to reckon, again and again, with the memory of the Crucifixion. The only way out was through. And mercy, which Jesus modeled for them again and again in that upper room, was the path. In that same room Jesus anticipated—with mercy—the epic failures of his friends in his final hours before his brutal execution and loved them anyway so that they might accept his invitation to always begin again. It is with mercy that in that room Jesus took the bread, blessed it, broke it, and shared it—asking the disciples to do this in his memory, so they would remember a love that didn't draw boundaries between people but rather drew people across them. It is with mercy that Jesus passed through the locked door of that room in order to appear in their midst with offerings of peace and with the invitation to probe his wounds so they could move beyond paralyzing guilt and denial toward a reconciliation that would make them whole people again. It is with the breath of mercy that the Spirit rushed through that upper room, pushing and pulling the disciples across its threshold and into the chaos of the world from which they sought refuge but to which they had so much to offer.

If Keenan claims that mercy is the willingness to enter into the chaos of another, to move toward each other rather than retreat, then I contend that *racial* mercy ought to define Catholicism for white American Catholics, given our aversion to the chaos of racism—in our own lives, in the lives of people of color, in our neighborhoods and our faith tradition.[33] By racial mercy I mean a willingness to enter into the chaos of racism. Racial mercy heals white Catholics by helping us face difficult truths about ourselves, freeing us from the anxieties that come with whiteness, and emboldening us to use our privilege and power differently. We need racial mercy to free our American Catholic tradition from a culture of white supremacy, to free ourselves to work together toward imagining the beloved community.

In the end, if Pope Francis is right in claiming that "mercy is God's identity card," then racial mercy is a loving encounter with a God who "mercifies" or chooses us not in spite of our failings but because of what they make us capable of.[34] With racial mercy we can acknowledge our wrongs and shortcomings, our desire to be forgiven, and then commit ourselves to making things whole again. Racial mercy helps us reject the empty promises of whiteness and to long instead to accept our remarkable status as God's beloved. Racial mercy helps us channel forgiveness into the courage to always begin again. As witnesses of the horrors of racial injustice, we need to become witnesses to the blessings of racial mercy before we can become agents of racial justice. Racial mercy offers the key that unlocks the door to the upper room—allowing God to draw near to us in our guilt and shame and confusion and freeing us to cross its threshold as beloved agents for God's justice on the other side. Racial mercy gives us the empathy and courage to get down to the reckoning work of justice.

RECKONING WITH contradictory truths about ourselves is not something white Catholics have been taught to do by our American Catholic tradition. Consider that my own Catholic upbringing and education buffered me from a truth that I had been dragged out of bed to witness nearly forty years ago. I am struck by all it has taken in order for that memory of May 13, 1985, to really lay a claim on me, to demand that I listen to the narratives swirling just below the surface of all of that Catholic silence, to demand that I believe the truths it holds: six years of graduate-level theological training; sixteen years of teaching, reading, and writing; twelve years of anti-racism training and community organizing and strategizing; eight years of worshipping among Black Catholics; eight years of teaching courses on theology and racism in racially mixed undergraduate classrooms; countless lectures and invited talks on racism and racial justice; and even one brief moment of coming face to face with the lone survivor of that horror. And yet I have never really processed my MOVE memories, whether intellectually or spiritually. I am still not sure I believe my MOVE memories.

My dad made me a twelve-year-old witness to the violence of white supremacy. Since then, I have lived in a Catholic silence that normalized that violence and expected little of me by way of reckoning with it. As a result, my extensive Catholic formation renders me largely incapable of effectively joining brothers and sisters of color who have been struggling to make their lives matter long before hashtags—students, colleagues, fellow parishioners, neighbors. I am limited in my ability to respond, to love those neighbors, because I've not been forced to examine the truth about myself, about my family, about my Church, about my tradition where racism is concerned. My well-developed Catholic inclination to retort to suggestions of my complicity in white supremacy with appeals to my moral innocence and goodness—an inclination reinforced by those decades of silence and low expectations—keeps me trapped under the very label I seek to reject: racist. That is my tragic conflict—that I am bound to a racist identity by a tradition to which I have dedicated my vocational life precisely, ironically, because of its liberatory appeal. Despite all of my knowledge and good intentions, I cannot get out of my own white Catholic way.

CHAPTER TWO

ALIGNING

Christ's Church

ACCORDING TO HIS June 1886 obituary in the borough of West Chester's *Daily Local News*, Andrew Little, who from historical records appears to be my first ancestor in North America, arrived at about age nineteen from Ireland sometime in the early 1820s along with roughly six thousand other Irish.[1] He initially found work as a "lime burner," likely in one of the three large quarries in Chester County that harvested the fossilized remains of the sea life that covered the great valley of Montgomery, Chester, and Lancaster counties 375 million years ago. His neighbors used the limestone to build their houses and fertilize their fields.[2]

Before writing this book I knew nothing of Andrew Little. He came to rest atop my family tree thanks to the files at the Chester County Historical Society. I spent a month scouring these alphabetized scrapbooks of inch-wide clippings from the county's various newspapers dating back to the early 1800s. I discovered much with little effort. So much care was taken to record the life events of these people—wedding announcements, illnesses, obituaries, promotions. The census counted their heads and the county surveyed their land. Every detail of their funerals was preserved, down to the arrival time of trains carrying back for interment the bodies of those who had migrated away from West Chester. Their lives mattered.

From these snippets of yellowed newspaper, I patched together Andrew's story. He married a local woman also from Ireland named Catherine, and they raised two girls and five boys. Andrew eventually earned enough to buy a hundred-acre farm on Wilmington Road, two miles southeast of West Chester Borough, the county seat. I picked out his plot, marked by easily discernible script on the lower corner of the 1873 county atlas. In 1866, their youngest, Emily, married John Carroll, a newer Irish immigrant to West Chester. The Carrolls ran the West Chester Hotel, where they raised five children.[3]

One rectangle of hand-set type took my breath away. In 1871, Andrew took out an ad in *The Jeffersonian*, a local paper with a Democratic bent, announcing the sale of some of his "personal property." The ad speaks to his success as a farmer and the scope of work it required in the nineteenth century. Suddenly, the Littles' life in West Chester came into sharper focus: "three good horses, one a first rate driver; thirteen excellent cows . . . all of them first rate butter cows." There was a two-horse wagon, a one-horse car, a threshing machine, a grist mill, and a "Cope's improved mower and reapers in good order." In addition to an array of harnesses and saddles, Andrew looked to liquidate a host of "dairy fixtures"— horse- and hand-powered butter churns, butter scales and weights, and pans and trays. A sleigh and two strings of sleigh bells made me smile.[4] I looked up to see if there was an archivist I could share my find with.

I stood on the brink of discovering something new about my family's arrival to a threshold space at a threshold time. The Littles lived just miles from the official boundary between slave and free states, in a county that was home to a Black population caught between those two worlds, and during the abolition period when the country teetered back and forth between the two. What's more, the Littles were the threshold people in my family—the first to straddle Ireland and America, old and new world Catholicism, the life they left behind and the new one that lay ahead. In that moment of discovery in the archives, I was like them: not quite sure how this story was going to turn out, especially in light of a question that most of us who invoke an Irish immigrant history rarely feel we need to ask. The more time I spent in those clippings, especially the Black history file—easily a half-foot high—the less confident I felt about the answer.

Did my people own slaves?

TENSIONS IN AN EMANCIPATION BORDERLAND

Andrew unknowingly arrived in the southernmost northern state in the Union as national tensions over slavery were mounting. Settling on the outskirts of West Chester Borough put his brood just twenty miles west of Philadelphia, abolition's "keystone city" and home to the largest freed Black population in the US. The Littles were also just twelve miles north of the Mason–Dixon Line, with nearly four million enslaved people residing below it by 1860. Finally, they arrived about ninety miles from Baltimore, the most active slave port of the upper south with more than two hundred registered slave traders at that time.[5] As the Littles put down roots in the "emancipation borderland" of Chester County, they encountered often violently contradictory messages about and actions toward Black people.[6]

Reading local histories, I learned that the Littles lived in a political, economic, and moral battleground and must have experienced the tension between abolition and pro-slavery camps that was tearing the country, the Commonwealth, and Chester County apart.[7] Pennsylvania had a strong tradition of anti-slavery. The Quakers and Mennonites of Germantown Village, just outside of Philadelphia, spearheaded the world's first anti-slavery movement in 1688. In 1780, the Pennsylvania Assembly passed the world's first piece of abolition legislation, the Gradual Abolition Act, which required the manumission (meaning the release from slavery) of all enslaved peoples in the Commonwealth by 1808. Chester County historian William Kashatus notes that in 1780 there were 142 slaveholders and 470 enslaved people living in Chester County; as of 1800 there were 58 enslaved people in the county.

Andrew and Catherine were exposed to prominent abolitionists since many took refuge in Chester County from the violence they experienced in Philadelphia—most notably in 1838 when Pennsylvania Hall, a newly constructed gathering space for abolitionists, was burned to the ground by pro-slavery rioters. The Littles read accounts of wealthy individuals and groups of like-minded citizens in West Chester pooling their money to buy the freedom of Black citizens of the borough who were on the run from former owners in Maryland. For example, Abner Hoopes contributed to funds to pay off slave catchers marauding through the county on the hunt for fugitives. His grandsons, Josiah and Abner Hoopes, founded the nursery in which Andrew and Catherine's future son-in-law, Maurice Connell, would find work upon his arrival in West Chester in 1845. In 1848, Jacob Nathan Sharpless—who later owned the White Hall Hotel, a competitor of the West Chester Hotel operated by their daughter Emily and son-in-law John Carroll—bought the freedom of a "kidnapped negress" hauled back over the line from West Chester by "advanc[ing] the amount claimed by her master."[8]

And yet, I was shocked to discover that despite some who took a prophetic stance against slavery, relatively few people in southeastern Pennsylvania were anti-slavery and even fewer were abolitionists. It may have had something to do with the Commonwealth's history. William Penn tolerated slavery as much as he tolerated religious difference. He permitted the *Isabella* to bring 150 enslaved people into the Port of Philadelphia in 1684 just two years after he founded his Quaker City. The first Fugitive Slave Act, passed in 1790, kept slavery alive by insisting that Black bondage was the national preference even in abolitionist strongholds. The *very* gradual nature of Pennsylvania's 1780 Abolition Act was another likely culprit. It only applied to people born into slavery on or after the date of its passage, so it didn't demand the freedom of all of the estimated 7,000 enslaved Black Pennsylvanians at time of its passage. Moreover, Black people born into slavery after the act was passed were only to be freed upon turning twenty-eight, basically guaranteeing "years of your productive life [spent] working for your mother's owner."[9] Eventually, the Pennsylvania Assembly took a contentious vote to ban slavery outright—but that wasn't until 1847. Andrew Little had lived in West Chester for nearly twenty years at that point.

The Littles were also bombarded with strong appeals for their allegiance to the opposing causes of slavery and abolition. Since the passage of the federal Fugitive Slave Act in 1850, which made the harboring of runaways a felony and legally mandated participation in their immediate return, the Littles lived in a geographical territory that historians describe as "the battle ground struggle between disgruntled southern slave owners and northern abolitionists."[10] Andrew may have recalled talk as early as the 1820s of legislation in Harrisburg to prohibit slave owners in Virginia and Maryland from transporting their human property in chains across the Commonwealth on their westward journeys to the new territories. He and Catherine likely read calls in the local papers to attend anti-slavery lectures and public rallies and even an Anti-Slavery Convention in West Chester to debate establishing a local anti-slavery society. "It is confidently hoped that the [Anti-Slavery] Convention will be large, that every friend of the oppressed, will give his attendance on this occasion," expressed a March 1837 advertisement for the event in a local West Chester paper. The only viable excuse for not attending: being "rendered unable by some providential circumstance."[11]

Then again, they also would have read damning commentary about abolitionists and their activities. *The Jeffersonian*, where Andrew Little placed his ad in 1871, offered the following report of an abolitionist gathering in 1854 under the headline "The Nigga Meetin": "There was quite a large collection of negroes, mulattos, quadroons, and some few white persons, attracted by curiosity. Few, very few, of our own citizens were present at any of their meetings; they do not sympathize with them."[12] I found myself wondering with whom the Littles were sympathetic.

A second factor that surely complicated my family's ideas about Black people was the contradiction they experienced in American understandings of emancipation. Certainly emancipation was a familiar idea to some of the older Catholic families in West Chester, particularly those of Irish descent. The first English ship to sail up the Delaware river in 1682, *The Welcome*, had Irish Quakers on board, and some of these families had Irish indentured servants, known as "redemptioners," on board. A good many of them and the waves of indentured peoples that followed them to Penn's colony were Catholic. These folks shared much in common with enslaved Africans. "An unknown number of Irish were either kidnapped (a word that came into the English language in the 1680s as a result of this program) or lured into transportation on false premises," explains colonial historian Kevin Starr, who likens their experience to "a program of de facto enslavement."[13] Redemptioners also ran away.

And yet, while English and Irish servants could look forward to "redeeming" their freedom through grueling labor in the span of three or four years (should they survive), enslaved Africans could not. The shared impulse to escape oppression became the first wedge that white landowners drove between enslaved Blacks and indentured whites when a 1660 law in Virginia increased the sentence for any white people caught running away with Black people. Even as the Founding Fathers were condemning tyranny with appeals to inalienable rights of liberty and the pursuit of happiness, emancipation was not intended for Black people. I was unsettled by the fact that the Littles likely scanned ads in West Chester papers selling Black people. I never realized my people were so close to slavery.

Third, the Littles would have seen that freedom for Black people was different from freedom for Irish immigrants like themselves. For the

Black people of Chester County—whether freeborn persons, people who had been freed or who had purchased their freedom, or fugitives on the run—this "twilight zone between slavery and freedom," was also a place of "economic dependency."[14] Free Black people "were inheritors of a system that had replaced slavery in Pennsylvania, as in other states, without significantly altering the economic order that slavery had helped to make possible or the social order that had sustained it."[15] There were slave codes, curfews, and even patrols. Families were still separated from each other, and Black workers earned far less than their white counterparts on the farms or in trades. How else, Pennsylvania farmers asked themselves, could they keep pace with their counterparts on the Maryland side of the Mason–Dixon Line, where 87,000 enslaved people labored before the outbreak of the Civil War?[16]

For the more than 5,000 freed Blacks in Chester County in 1850, living in a free state may have made it illegal for them to be enslaved, but it didn't necessarily mean a life of flourishing. It also did not guarantee the liberties that lead to prosperity—rights to wages, education, political participation—that the Littles themselves came to West Chester in search of. Given these similarities for Black people above and below the Mason–Dixon Line, the Littles also learned that Blackness was the determining factor when it came to living free or, in the words of theologian Kelly Brown Douglas, being a commodity.[17] For example, Andrew Little may indeed have hired Black laborers on the farm, but that did not mean he paid them the same as white laborers or that the Littles considered them neighbors. Black people may have been free in West Chester, but they didn't dine or lodge in the West Chester Hotel or any other white-owned establishment.[18] From the perspective of white people, freedom for Black people simply meant the end of bondage and little more.

Finally, there was significant human traffic across that most significant border, the Mason–Dixon Line, and it flowed in both directions. Andrew and Catherine settled just ten miles north of the most historically significant border in US history as the movement of Black people back and forth across it peaked. In fact, the Littles came into their own at the height of activity on the Underground Railroad, between 1839 and 1860. The Southeastern Corridor, which crisscrossed Chester County, was the busiest line in the Commonwealth due to the short distance between northern Maryland or Delaware and Philadelphia and the number of freed Black people and abolitionists serving as conductors or station agents. Black refugees either crossed the Susquehanna River near Havre de Grace and made their way into Lancaster County, or they came up through Wilmington, Delaware, into Chester and Delaware counties in Pennsylvania. Chester County itself was territory between two high-volume stations, one in Wilmington belonging to white Quaker Thomas Garrett and the other belonging to William Still, the Black station agent in Philadelphia. Between the two of them, and the hundreds of station agents and conductors in between, including the 132 people in Chester County known to have participated in the Underground Railroad, it is estimated that between 1,000 and 2,000 people escaped using this branch of the network. From West Chester, refugees either went north toward Norristown in Montgomery County (which will feature in my family's story a century later) or west on to Philadelphia. A Chester County Quaker who kept a diary indicated that ninety refugees passed through his farm alone in just four months in 1842.[19]

Had the Littles harbored anyone on the run for freedom?

I was struck by a March 1860 headline in the *Village Record*, which read: "An Underground Railroad Heading South."[20] It was one of many reports in the 1850s of Black people literally being hauled out of Chester County—regardless of their freedom status—and transported back over the Line by armed white men, some of them police or constables in the employ of slave owners in Maryland and Virginia. Black people were always looking over their shoulders for the slave catchers, also known as "borderers," who had crossed over from Maryland on the hunt for anyone who would meet the minimal requirement for capture: being dark skinned. There were also "negro stealers" trying to get in on the act and make a sizable sum on the black market centered around Baltimore's slave pens and auction houses.[21]

THE LITTLES AND RACIAL PROJECTS

The more I read from the Black history clippings, the more anxious I became about my family's relationship to slavery and enslaved peoples in Chester County. Granted, I took some comfort in the fact that census reports indicated that no enslaved people lived with them. Also, since Andrew Little took out his ad in *The Jeffersonian* in 1871, Black people could not have been part of the property he hoped to liquidate. Nevertheless, it was likely that Black people played some kind of role in Andrew's rise from lime burner to prominent farmer. Encountering the shadow side of West Chester's history, I got the gut feeling that the Littles participated in an intense racial project in West Chester. Sociologists Michael Omi and Howard Winant define *racial projects* as ongoing and collective commitments to interpret, represent, or explain racial identities and organize and distribute resources accordingly. In other words, racial projects maintain "the centrality of race in the organization of political life in the United States."[22] There are three basic steps to racial projects: first, we arbitrarily construct what "races" are and classify people according to them; next, we imbue these racial categories with evolving meanings; and finally, we rely on those racialized meanings to distribute the material benefits of our social systems.[23] I may not have found evidence that my people owned anybody, but I uncovered traces of their participation in a serious racial project in West Chester.

Since the Littles had little previous experience with people who looked different from them, they undoubtedly learned to racialize others or to "make people up" using the arbitrary category of race. Omi and Winant note that there is a "corporeal dimension to the race-concept," and as newcomers the Littles would have immediately tapped into its "ocular" dimensions. They noticed differences in human features—like skin color and hair texture—then quickly tapped into meanings associated with those differences, which had long been encoded to signify conquest, enslavement, and domination.[24] Living in West Chester, for example, they would have soon perceived that one's freedom status in America was color-dependent, since Black people were denied full liberty regardless of whether they were freeborn, manumitted, or runaways. They also saw that whiteness conferred the power to determine those conditions of freedom. To help them make sense of an arrangement that contradicted the very values of their new homeland and assured their allegiance to it, the Littles' new neighbors bombarded them with what Joe Feagin calls "racial frames"—beliefs, emotions, images, stories, and ideologies that "structur[e] the thinking process and shap[e] what people see, or do not see, in important societal settings."[25] My family quickly ingested America's dominant "white racial frame" that "assertively accented a very positive view of white superiority, virtue, and goodness" while framing Black people in particular as less than human on multiple counts.[26]

So how did the Littles "make people" using race? They may not have witnessed enslavement, but as bystanders to a number of high-profile violent abductions of Black people back across the Mason–Dixon Line, the Littles acquiesced to the racial frames that made "slaves out of free people" by "replacing human singularity with fashioned salability."[27] Moreover, since they arrived at a time when the master frame in the United States was being called into question by the very existence of free Black people— as well as the movement for the abolition of a system that kept them in bondage—at the very least they heard public debates about the veracity of claims about Black people that justified their enslavement. They may have even witnessed what happened to people who publicly articulated doubts about the central premise of America's racial project: shaming, vigilante violence, lawsuits. For example, I came across postings for anti-slavery meetings in a variety of public spaces that dismissed fears of "unruly and mobocratic" attendees, suggesting that some in the West Chester popu- lace found abolitionists a threat to the American experiment.[28] The Littles also saw that, in the words of historian Gary Nash, "the more free Black people achieved in building churches, schools, and mutual aid societies, the more white people resented them."[29]

Finally, given when and where they arrived, the Littles had a front-row seat to the racial politics unfolding around them, which revealed that "race is strategic" and does "ideological and political work" when it comes to distributing the very basic social good of freedom.[30] Chester County his- torian William Kashatus notes that because of its proximity to Maryland, Southeastern Pennsylvania was a "legislative battleground over slavery."[31] A Marylander claimed in 1851 that "no state in the Union has violated the solemn compact on the subject of fugitive slaves more violently than Pennsylvania."[32] Some historians suggest that the first bloodshed of the Civil War was actually spilled in Chester County in 1851 over the en- forcement of the Fugitive Slave Act, when four runaways seeking refuge in the home of a freed Black man named William Parker defended them- selves against a band of seven white men, two of them hired constables, attempting to return them to their owner in Maryland.

I found myself wondering how West Chester's racial project formed the Littles. Given their proximity to legally free and yet economically and politically disinherited Black people, my family likely developed practices of denial to manage the anxiety Black people provoked—anxieties about the duplicity of America, about remaining in the favor of those making decisions, about who got access to its opportunities, about the violence that erupted around ideas about or efforts toward Black freedom. The

Littles learned to compartmentalize that anxiety by compartmentalizing the people who generated it, sidelining Black people from white spaces and retreating into white-only spaces.

The Littles also learned that white disputes could be more easily settled if there were Black bodies on the bargaining table. They learned from national examples of political compromises between political and economic elites: the three-fifths compromise in the Constitution that brought the slaveholding states into the Union in 1787 by bolstering their representation in Congress with disenfranchised Black people;[33] the removal of the land-owning prerequisite from the Naturalization Act of 1790 that expanded the vote so long as Black people remained disenfranchised;[34] the Missouri Compromise in 1820 that pushed off secession for a generation by extending slavery into the first state west of the Mississippi;[35] or the Compromise of 1850, which made the admittance of California as a free state, although pro-slavery representatives could be elected, contingent upon the passage of the Fugitive Slave Act of 1850, which was used for fifteen years to "force all white citizens, however they felt, to support slavery" by criminalizing the abetting of fugitives and incentivizing their return.[36] Indeed, the Mason–Dixon Line itself was a compromise from the time it was drawn in 1767, and it dictated the political climate of West Chester. Pennsylvania was ground zero for working out compromises that upheld slavery in the land of the free, especially in the courts tasked with enforcing the Fugitive Slave Acts of 1793 and 1850 in the midst of Quaker abolition.

Finally, the Littles learned that the ultimate fallback position for white people, especially around divisive issues like Black freedom, was to align themselves with those in positions of power. No matter how much slavery contradicted the professed values of their new homeland, the state rarely ruled in favor of Black or white people who supported Black emancipation or suffrage.[37] In his book *How the Irish Became White*, historian Noel Ignatiev points to what the Littles knew when it came to discerning where they stood vis-à-vis slavery and the Black people in West Chester: to be American is to uphold American institutions, not necessarily American values.[38] All of these dynamics worked on their individual and collective self-understandings to such an ongoing extent that race "[became] common sense—a way of comprehending, explaining, and acting in the world."[39] I cannot help but think that these early dynamics set the tune for the familiar white refrain to questions about racial inequity that echoed down the generations: "That's just the way things were." But in truth, racial projects like the one that unfolded in antebellum West Chester ensured that the way things were actually *was* the way things are intended or *supposed* to be. The significance of that realization hadn't even settled into my consciousness before my dive into my people's Catholic parish in West Chester revealed that racial inequality was how whites thought things were *divinely intended* to be.

A CATHOLIC RELIGIO-RACIAL PROJECT IN AN EMANCIPATION BORDERLAND

In 1794, just five years after Pope Pius VI formally established the Catholic Church in the US, eight Catholics in West Chester decided that the time had come to build a Catholic church. By then there were about three hundred Catholics living in Chester County and they had outgrown the house church the Jesuits had initiated in 1730 on Thomas Wilcox's property. These leaders were a diverse group. Among them were a farmer, a paper mill owner, a bricklayer, a tailor, and two potters; two Irish and a German; and two veterans of the War of Independence. A third-generation Pennsylvania Quaker and veteran of the Revolutionary War, John Hannum, supported their cause. He donated a quarter-acre of land for the parish at the end of Gaye Street in the borough. The trustees raised funds to build a one-story brick building with three windows on each side, situated on a small hill—the first church in West Chester Borough. They named it Christ's Church, a quixotically un-Catholic choice that the first long-term pastor, John Prendergast, rectified in 1851 when he changed the name to St. Agnes. Until 1840, only a hundred and fifty parishioners could gather within its walls on the random Sundays when an itinerant priest, often a Jesuit, offered Mass and administered the sacraments. Befitting its self-ascribed status as the "pioneer church of Chester County," Christ's Church stood as the only physical church building within the boundaries of West Chester Borough until 1812.[40]

All of this history seemed innocuous enough until I considered the larger historical context swirling around Christ's Church. As the fifth-oldest parish in what would become the diocese of Philadelphia in 1808, these Catholic trustees founded Christ's Church at a time of both racial *and* racist progress in the country: just thirteen years after the abolition of slavery in Pennsylvania and three years after Congress passed the Naturalization Act that restricted voting to white landowning men. It was established in the same decade that Philadelphia's free Black population reached five thousand, making it the largest urban center of free Blacks in America, but also in the same year that Congress passed its first Fugitive Slave Act that gave slaveholders legal rights to retrieve runaways from any state and fined anyone protecting runaways $500.[41] Finally, Catholics gathered in Christ's Church for the first time a year before the invention of the cotton gin, which expanded the American economy and ensnared everyone on both sides of the Mason–Dixon Line in the horrors of slavery.[42]

Moreover, the trustees founded Christ's Church in auspicious Catholic terrain. West Chester itself was located along well-trod routes between the two epicenters of Catholicism in North America during the colonial period—Baltimore and Philadelphia. Jesuits in particular served Catholics clustered around home churches or small chapels in Maryland, northern Delaware, and southeastern Pennsylvania. These itinerant priests offered Mass in the Chester County homes of the Wilcoxes, Hearns, and Fitzgeralds on their way to or from their first mission center in Pennsylvania at Conewago, which was just above the state line and eighty miles to the west of Chester County, or their northernmost mission center at Old St. Joseph's in Philadelphia.[43]

I was struck by the extensive records about Christ's Church in the Chester County archives, which included a copy of a history written in 1894 to mark its centennial, an artifact that itself was more than 125 years old when I pored over it. Catholics had been in West Chester a long time and took great pride in that fact. I did too—until I realized that Black people were almost entirely absent from this otherwise extensive parish historical record. There was no mention of the political tumult in the emancipation borderland of Chester County or the clandestine activities of the switching station on the busiest line of the Underground Railroad or the pre–Civil War skirmishes involving the enforcement of the Fugitive Slave Act. Why the silence? What were the Catholics hiding when it came to the history of Christ's Church? I reread the opening line of that first parish history with an eye for an unintended truth it reveals: "The story that it tells is in a great measure the history of the rise and progress of Catholicity in this country."[44] Christ's Church is the story of the rise and progress of *white* Catholicity. As such, it was an epicenter of what theologian Jeannine Hill Fletcher calls a "religio-racial project" that added a Christian dimension to the white master frame. In other words,

Christ's Church had helped ensure that America continued to become a white *Christian* nation by "elevating Whiteness and Christianness and devalu[ing] or destroy[ing] others" by equating difference with deficiency.[45] I saw evidence of a religio-racial project at Christ's Church in three places: its connection to Jesuit missions in Maryland, its very self-understanding as a mission church and later as a mission center, and the few interactions between parish leaders and Indigenous and Black people described in the historical record.

The first point came into focus as I sketched the ecclesial husbandry of Christ's Church, which took me further and further south of the Mason–Dixon Line. Christ's Church was established as a *mission church*—an offshoot, tentacle, or satellite—of St. Mary's Chapel, which itself was established in 1790 at Coffee Run just north of Wilmington. Coffee Run was a two-hundred-acre Jesuit farm founded in 1772 that eventually became the first Catholic chapel in Delaware. Coffee Run was also a mission church of one of the earliest Catholic plantations in Maryland, a three-hundred-acre tract called Old Bohemia, which was established in 1704 and served as an epicenter of Jesuit endeavors in the mid-Atlantic colonies.[46] In short, Catholic initiatives in the lineage of Christ's Church were thoroughly Jesuit.

In cobbling together the history of Jesuits in the mid-Atlantic, I was struck by the fact that they called these original outposts in Maryland *plantations.* Certainly at the time this word was used simply to describe tracts of colonized farmable land. But Jesuit farmable lands featured the very thing I have always associated with plantations: slavery. Jesuits were aboard the first ships that landed on Maryland's Eastern Shore in 1634. They brought indentured servants with them from England: two were described as "Molato" and one as "Black" but none were identified as enslaved. By 1717, however, they had embraced slavery according to the earliest documented record, although it is believed they were engaged in slavery before that. Jesuits owned 12,677 acres by 1765 and 192 enslaved people who worked them.[47] It would be difficult to deny that enslaved Black labor on these plantations in Maryland and Delaware enabled the Jesuits to establish a growing network of mission churches throughout southeastern Pennsylvania—ones like my family's own Christ's Church in West Chester.

I doubt that revenues from these Jesuit plantations provided seed money for Christ's Church in West Chester, since under the trusteeship model, its founding members contributed and then bequeathed monies needed to keep the mission church open. What I don't question, however, is that since their expansive growth went hand in hand with their slave owning, the Jesuits pollinated attitudes about and practices toward Black people in their ministerial travels. Christ's Church congregants were informed by Catholic priests buoyed not just by the capital of their slave owning in Maryland but also by the theological craftiness necessary to justify their collusion in it. In fact, they practiced what theologian James Perkinson disturbingly calls "the witchcraft of White supremacy," or a brew of language and practices that cursed Black and brown people with enslavement, exploitation, and violence in the name of white domination.[48]

Moreover, Hill Fletcher helps me see how these itinerant Jesuit priests carried with them to Christ's Church the symbolic capital—the power, privileges, and benefits—that came with their ability to invoke their Catholicity and whiteness to deny the full humanity of Black people.[49] For example, their very ability to invoke the power to name God in their own image and likeness—male, European, Christian, and elite—empowered them to describe those who did not share their traits as un-Godlike and therefore less than human. Sociologist Santiago Slabodsky suggests this sliding scale of humanity cultivated a Christian frame that viewed all non-white people monolithically and as lacking humanity, whether in terms of "religion, history, civilization, development, and ultimately democracy."[50] Religious racialization framed non-whites as "opposing Euro-Christianity and, therefore, of having the wrong-pre-condition."[51] Their opposition was addressed through evangelization and violence, neither of which were mutually exclusive and both of which determined access to material and spiritual goods—hence the need for missionaries.

This leads me to my second piece of evidence regarding Christ's Church as a religio-racial project. In his 1894 hagiographical centenary tribute about the parish, historian William Barrett notes that in its earliest days, West Chester's Catholics "gathered in neighboring houses, at rare intervals, when some sturdy and devoted *missionary* appeared in their midst [emphasis mine]," at which point they "worshipped as devoutly as though kneeling before guided altars of some stately cathedral."[52] I'm struck by that word choice, since the parish itself was considered a *mission* church, first by the Jesuits and later by the diocese of Philadelphia. In fact, as soon as it was assigned a permanent pastor in 1840, Christ's Church evolved from a mission church, or outpost of Catholic outreach in Chester County and neighboring Lancaster County, into a *mission center* or epicenter for missionary activity into less adequately served parts of the county. Over the next several decades, the pastors who attended to Christ's Church offered Mass twice a week in West Chester then took to the road, administering sacraments in a growing network of Mass houses and chapels—"stations" according to Roberts—in the region.[53] The goal was to evolve those mission churches into mission centers themselves, growing the human and physical Catholic infrastructure across the new republic.

A history of Christianity in the "discovery" of the New World illuminates how this missionary designation was not as neutral as it sounds. Theologian Willie James Jennings explains how being part of a mission church created what he calls "tragedy-inflicting conditions for identity formation" for Catholics in West Chester.[54] According to him, missionaries were one of three agents in the New World who recreated the worlds of those who originally inhabited the Americas and later those who settled here. If the merchant claimed natural resources for profit and established relationships of exchange, and the soldier defended the spaces the merchants needed to do their business, then the missionary kept everyone aligned with the goals and modalities of both. They did so by sanctifying the work of the merchant, normalizing the violence of the soldier, and domesticating an otherwise alien people assumed to be deficient or inferior.[55]

I saw evidence of this missionary desire for alignment of economic and ecclesial interests in the interactions that one of the leaders of Christ's Church, Fr. Patrick Kenny, had with Indigenous and Black people. One of the more regular itinerant priests, the Irish-born priest served Christ's Church from 1808 through 1827 and kept a diary of much of his twenty-three years of service to Catholics in southeastern Pennsylvania and northern Delaware from his home base at Coffee Run. He meticulously noted the size of the congregation or the number baptized in the various homes, chapels, and churches he tended to between Wilmington and Philadelphia. An entry from 1811 caught my eye. In it he detailed his encounter with "seven Indian chiefs—of the Machimacinac Tribe" during his brief stint as one of the pastors at Trinity parish, founded in 1784 in Philadelphia. After describing their physiques and dress—"all were straight, able-bodied men, painted with red strakes . . . all had feathers in their long black hair"—he reported how he "shew'd them Trinity Church," which drew a large crowd. Kenny noted that "they behaved in no manner like savages."[56] I can't help but think that Kenny was flummoxed by these Indigenous visitors whose civility did fit not fit the frame imposed on them. Did he show them the church to further bring them into alignment with the dominant Christian culture? His report of the incident suggests that he was more taken with their physical appearance than with what they might have offered in terms of their own spiritual gifts. This was a one-way cultural exchange and they were a spectacle. Kenny's accounts reflect even greater transactional relationships of exchange with Black people in various states of freedom in his comings and goings between Wilmington and Philadelphia. In 1805, he documented paying $1 toward "redeeming the time of a slave," although it's not entirely clear who he paid for the work.[57] In February of 1812 he "engaged a French black woman as a servant" at his home in Coffee Run for "125 c" per week.[58] When passing through Wilmington, he regularly boarded with Mrs. Laurette Noel, a very "worthy woman" who had been formerly enslaved by a prominent Wilmington Catholic. He stored his vestments with her and often said Mass from her home.[59] He was lodging with her in 1828 when her son suddenly died; Kenny offered Andrew's funeral Mass and noted that Mrs. Noel and her two daughters "exhibited as became real Catholics" while "catholics of the whole district, & from members of other persuasions, & from the colour'd population of Wilmington" paid "a full tribute of respect."[60]

I interpret Kenny's failure to mention the violence and economic exclusion surely faced by the various Black people he encountered as evidence of Catholics trying to align themselves with the anti-Blackness inherent in the dominant white frame. This alignment was an urgent task since that same white frame was suspicious of their Catholicism. In 1822 he worried about the futility of a personal donation to help repair Christ's Church since "the people of West Chester cease not to injure the building and insult the Catholics as they pass through the borough . . . This insolence," he surmised, "is a spark from Philadelphia fire and may end in the destruction of the building."[61] If Catholics in West Chester were themselves objects of a Protestant religio-racial project that tried to frame them as insufficiently American, I couldn't help but think that participating in the dominant culture's treatment of Black people was a way that Catholics could better align themselves with that white Protestant master frame.

I also found evidence of white Catholics normalizing the violence Black people faced in the record of Christ's Church itself. Certainly the fact that I only came across two mentions of Black people in the entirety of the parish's historical record—despite the significant Black figures named elsewhere in West Chester's history and the violence against Black people happening all around them—implied that parishioners and pastors viewed this violence as normal and not worth mentioning, much less responding to. But even the two accounts that the parish's first historian, William Barrett, describes in his centennial history are telling as they reflect "the feelings of Catholics toward a race whose bondage almost proved the wedge which was to rend our country in twain."[62] One of Christ's Church's early permanent pastors, Fr. Patrick Sheridan, "received several converts, including a few Negroes into the Church" during his tenure in the early 1840s.[63] That these people, the circumstances that brought them to the church, or even the responses of the congregation go unmentioned suggests their baptisms were hardly an act of integration or even inclusion but rather a perfunctory duty of evangelizing missionaries. It also reflects the missionary posture Sheridan took: European Catholicism was the mode that Black converts needed to adapt; it was they who moved toward the Church and not the other way around.

The other account of Black Catholics in West Chester was equally as telling. At some point in the 1830s, "a black man, ostensibly a Catholic and a member of the congregation of Christ's Church, was to be buried in the graveyard around the church."[64] Apparently this did not sit well with some parishioners, whose "protests reflect[ed] the prevailing socially acceptable attitude of the time."[65] An unnamed priest intervened, however, and "reminded the objectors that the Church includes all races" and the Black Catholic was buried.[66] While this seems a prophetic stance, it still reflects an anti-Black, Catholic-missionary impulse. For example, the historical record is also problematically incomplete—when did this sacrament rite happen, who were the players, and what was the history of the deceased? Moreover, the unnamed priest's actions reflect the charitable impulse of the day—to tend to Black souls but leave unaddressed ideas about Black inferiority and white structures that denied them material goods even within the Church itself, even in death. This stands in stark contrast with the work of other Christians in Chester County, most notably Black people themselves, in the liberation of refugees from the South. In fact, after Quakers, free Black people in Chester County were the largest participants in the Underground Railroad. They ran safe houses out of their homes at great risk. Black residents of West Chester like Abraham

Shadd, John Smith, Thomas Brown, and Benjamin Freedman guided people to and from the sanctuaries provided by white Quaker families in the borough with the names of Darlington, Price, Painter, and Sharpless.[67]

This points to the starkest evidence I found of Catholic missionaries' aims to invest in infrastructure that builds social progress and empowers white people. As Blacks and abolitionists began to build a network of stations across Chester County intended to ferry enslaved Black people to futures of freedom and hopefully prosperity, Catholics, too, were building "stations," a word used by Fr. Kenny's first biographer, John Wilcox, himself a Chester County Catholic.[68] But these weren't safe houses for Black refugees. Rather they were Catholic houses that welcomed priests like him who were working to secure the freedom and prosperity of the institutional Catholic Church in America. Moreover, the advancement of Catholicism and justice for Black people in Pennsylvania appear to be antithetical. In an extensive examination of the Underground Railroad throughout the Commonwealth, one historian concluded that "there are no clear references in any of the sources to Roman Catholic churches or priests being actively involved in the Underground Railroad in Pennsylvania."[69] There is no evidence of public stances about the moral problems of slavery in Christ's Church or later St. Agnes, its new name at the end of the trusteeship period when the diocese assumed control of parish affairs. I found this silence deafening given that Christ's Church was the first congregation in West Chester Borough.[70] More to the point, other churches in Chester County had begun to discuss options for enslaved people—from their emancipation to their recolonization in Africa—so Catholic silence struck me as an anomaly. And I couldn't chalk it up to ignorance. Individual parishioners—my own family members—lived in close proximity to active resistance to slavery, whether out on the Littles' farm, on the streets around the White Hall Hotel, or in public meeting places across the county.

As the trustees who originally founded and funded Christ's Church yielded to diocesan control, they unknowingly helped lay groundwork for the long game in Catholic ecclesial supremacy in the US. Like its twin, white supremacy, Catholic ecclesial supremacy saw Black people as liabilities, if not a direct threat to their efforts. While white Catholics relied on unpaid or underpaid Black laborers to secure their economic footing and grow the Church, a missionary stance did not prioritize protecting those Black people, many of whom were Catholics themselves, from violence.

Nor did white Catholicism support meaningful Black flourishing. All of this Catholic networking through mission churches and mission centers, the scaffolding of what would become one of the nation's largest dioceses, was done in the name of white Catholic security, advancement, well-being, and alignment with white superiority—a way of plowing the benefits earned by disadvantaging some into the further advancement of others. The fruit of this investment was celebrated in a newspaper article about the parish's one-hundredth anniversary in 1893. "St. Agnes has a large congregation of citizens of our borough, useful in almost every walk of life, and filling every requirement of service with fidelity to duty, alertness and faithfulness not excelled anywhere in like avocations," the article boasted. "Many of their homes are equal to the best in the borough, and for good citizenship the fidelity of the people of this congregation has never been called into question."[71] I was unsettled in learning my family members were involved with this. Hill Fletcher insists this kind of growth necessitated "shifting the weight of the world onto their non-White neighbors."[72]

ROUNDING CHRIST'S CHURCH: RACIAL MERCY AND THRESHOLDS

What I've learned from this chapter in my family's history is that to take an initial step in the journey toward racial mercy—the capability to enter into the chaos that racism wreaks—we first need to pay attention to thresholds: the places at the edge, the spaces in between, the moments of ambiguity, the crossroads. In the Celtic spirituality my ancestors would have known, literal and figurative thresholds invite moments of discernment and breakthrough because they are spaces of wonder, moments of great "imaginal" possibility between what is and what might be. But thresholds also challenge us because when we find ourselves in between spaces or times we also discover that we are no longer in control—of the past or of the future. Only when we release control, however, is transformation possible. "We can only become something new when we have released the old faces we have been wearing," contemporary Celtic mystic Christine Valters Paintner explains, "even if it means not knowing quite who we are in the space in between."[73]

Moving through the threshold space of antebellum West Chester and imagining the lives of my first ancestors in America there, I discovered that the oldest face I have worn, the face that prevents me from accurately seeing the past and moving with a different intention into the future, is the face of innocence where slavery is concerned. My whole life I have lived with the moral confidence of most Americans with immigrant histories, particularly Irish ones, because I have had the ultimate "get out of jail free" card in reckoning with racism: "My family didn't own slaves."

Andrew and Catherine's threshold tale, however, pulls that face away. In addition to living in a threshold place—an emancipation borderland—and at a threshold time—on the brink of the Civil War—the Littles also lived in close proximity to Black people enduring a terrifying threshold: between being dead while still alive and living as though already dead. In his historical and comparative study of slavery called *Slavery and Social Death*, historian Orlando Patterson helped me understand how slavery denied Black people life-sustaining inheritances—whether heritage, family memories and ties, wealth or prized possessions, or even bodily integrity—while they lived, creating a kind of living death.[74] Slavery also required ongoing death-dealing violence that was both structural (embedded in laws and deployed by institutions) and interpersonal (doled out at the hands of individual people). Here's the kicker. Theological ethicist Katie Walker Grimes contends that Black people didn't have to be enslaved to experience social death since the characteristics of slavery in North America ensured that they "could be reduced to slavery simply for having a body that came to be categorized as 'black.'"[75] In other words, the Littles didn't need to own Black people to participate in these structural and personal forms of domination in West Chester, because white people, not just white slave owners, ensured this domination extended to *all* Black people.

My family participated in the social death of Black people.

With this realization in mind, I stand on that historical threshold of antebellum West Chester and see a very different picture of Andrew and Catherine Little's experience there. They became American Catholics in the midst of the death-dealing dynamics of slavery, even in West Chester County. They observed violent domination in headline-making incidents of abductions, kidnappings, and skirmishes throughout Chester County in which whites abducted Black people assumed to be fugitives and transported them back across the Mason–Dixon Line into slavery. They also saw elements of what Grimes calls the pleasure embedded in the master-slave relationship, whether in the zeal of search parties of "borders" who roamed the county with impunity, empowered by masters to return their missing property, or in the "merciful" efforts of abolitionists to "buy" the freedom of fugitives running from them.[76] Both activities reinforced the fact that whites did indeed have ultimate power over Black people, since they proved in different ways that freedom was something that could be granted or bought by whites rather than automatically claimed by Blacks by virtue of their humanity.

They also experienced the death-dealing dynamics of slavery in their parish, Christ's Church. Because white Christians considered Black people deficient in the eyes of God, they also considered slavery as an alternative to the death they believed Black people actually deserved. So whites took pleasure in granting disempowered Black people the ability to survive from day to day through their own "largesse and mercy," such as burying them in the parish cemetery without fanfare or historical note.[77] To my mind, this was little more than domination masked as charity. There was a big difference between being a station on the Underground Railroad and a mission church in an emancipation borderland. The Littles' Catholic Church chose a missionary sensibility—a way of allowing supposedly inferior people a chance to assimilate to the dominant culture through sacramental care of their souls, with little regard given to the violent discrimination exacted on their bodies or the way disadvantaging them served to advance white Catholics. Little did I know just how frequently that missionary impulse would repeat itself through Philadelphia Catholic history.

In short, Andrew and Catherine Little didn't need to own slaves to "participate in the powers and pleasures of mastership."[78] They merely had to participate in anti-Blackness that linked Black people with slave status in order to perpetuate the social death of slavery. Doing so also ensured their own social advancement as newly arrived Americans whose descendants would soon be accepted as white. From that perspective, I realized that Andrew's ad in *The Jeffersonian* was damning for a different reason. His success illuminates how invested in and aligned with the social death of slavery he and Catherine were. They were the genesis of my family's participation in an intergenerational process—a project really—to "dispossess Black Americans while securing benefits for Whites."[79]

With that thought in mind, I found myself standing at a new threshold. Preoccupation with whether or not the Littles owned slaves is not only irrelevant but also detrimental because it has allowed me to bypass a harsh truth. Up until learning Andrew and Catherine's story, I had assumed my ancestral tale in America was about how my people "became white" or how we gradually assimilated into the dominant culture in America despite our objectionable immigrant and Catholic identities. I knew that attitudes and behaviors around Black people were part of that assimilation process, but I wrongly assumed that we were innocent of the most egregious of those attitudes and behaviors. After all, slavery was not part of our story. In West Chester I uncovered the origins of a more accurate trajectory: my Catholic family didn't just become white in Catholic Philadelphia, we became anti-Black here. It started with Andrew and Catherine's proximity to the social death of slavery and their responses, or lack thereof, to that epidemic. At best they were voyeurs who experienced some cognitive dissonance at what they witnessed, or bystanders who lacked the courage to interrogate those contradictions publicly or to participate with Christian neighbors in disrupting the status quo. Perhaps they gave charitably to meet individual needs, a stance modeled for them by the missionary sensibilities of their leaders at Christ's Church. But like other white Catholics in West Chester, they did not enter into the chaos unfolding around them.

When I allow that shameful realization to settle in a bit—we didn't become white Catholics in America, we became anti-Black Catholics here—I usually want to shake it off and return to the less damning and more passive "becoming white" self-understanding. But standing in that threshold, I recall Joe Feagin's idea about replicating racial frames: "How we interpret and experience our racialized present depends substantially on our knowledge of and interpretation of our racialized past."[80] So I need to be honest with my history. To use Feagin's words, we cannot successfully reframe new approaches if we don't deframe the old ones or "consciously take apart and critically analyze" those inherited beliefs and stories and images and emotions.[81]

Racial mercy invites lingering in uncomfortable threshold spaces to settle into a more honest reckoning with the past. Acknowledging the anti-Blackness at the very beginning of my family's story can be liberating in its candor and calming in the integrity it offers. I find myself spending less energy dancing around an uncomfortable truth and more energy in purposefully discerning responsibility for it. When I am able to acknowledge the anti-Blackness in my tradition and in my family history, I am also better able to embrace anti-racist strategies that align with efforts to dismantle the structures of inequality rather than simply remaining satisfied being someone who is not racist in the midst of them.

CHAPTER THREE

GRAFTING

St. Agnes

MAURICE CONNELL, my namesake, became a gardener not long after he arrived in West Chester in the late 1840s.[1] He worked for a Quaker-owned nursery during what has been called America's golden age of fruit growing. Hoopes Brothers and Thomas was one of the largest growers in the country in terms of acreage and inventory: 80 varieties of apple trees, 60 kinds of pears, 30 types of peaches, and 108 varieties of roses. Maurice's brother-in-law, William Donovan, got him the job and the two of them worked long days. At one point in 1867, they helped fill an order of 18,000 potted plants for a firm in Baltimore. By the time two of Maurice's four sons followed him there, the nursery boasted 17 greenhouses with 15,000 hothouse plants in their inventory. It was the pride of West Chester.

As he coaxed green things to life in America, I wonder if Maurice ever recognized the irony of his situation. Back in the Irish village of Lisgoold in County Cork, he had been surrounded by greenery stitched together by seams of stone walls. But as the youngest of three sons in a family of five, the chances of any of it ever belonging to him were slim. His father, Patrick, was not a "strong farmer."[2] It had nothing to do with his physical strength. Patrick simply didn't own or lease enough land to pay the landlord the required two-thirds of his harvest and sustain a family on what remained. The strain may have killed Patrick by the time Maurice was five. If that wasn't enough, the "stem family" practice protected the Connells' coveted plot from further subdivision by ensuring that Maurice's oldest brother, Michael, seven years his senior, inherited the lease when Patrick died in 1827.[3] But since leases timed out after thirty-one years, even Michael's future wasn't entirely secure. Maurice's oldest sister, Mary, was destined to marry an oldest son somewhere in Cork. He and his other siblings, Margaret and Nicholas, had to fend for themselves in a patriarchal and authoritarian family structure where family loyalty was expected but not easy.

Standing amidst all that land that would never be his, did Maurice dream of the situation like the one he found in West Chester?

Paging through Hoopes Brothers and Thomas archival material in the Chester County Historical Society—weather logs and payroll ledgers, planting schedules for seedlings, and international catalogues of ornamental and fruit trees—I learned more about Maurice's vocation as a nurseryman. He likely spent several weeks each spring grafting to increase rates of propagation and varietal characteristics of the nursery's collection. The process fascinated me. To graft two distinct plants together, Maurice took the stem or a bud of one plant, called a scion, and sliced it upwards to make a wedge. He then lined the scion up with the stem of another plant, called the rootstock, that he had sliced in a downward wedge. He aligned the cambium, or the generative tissue at their respective centers, then bound the two pieces together, most likely with hot wax, so that the sap between them would flow. He left part of the incision on the scion uncovered. This open wound, called the church window, allowed for some stability as the graft healed and the two plants grew together. The scion determined the variety of fruit and the rootstock the plant's size.[4]

Grafting provides a helpful analogy for making sense of what I learned about Maurice's emigration experiences and the sap of racism oozing through my family tree. After all, he was grafted onto America. The scion of his Irish heritage was joined to the rootstock of American culture, and in turn, the two propagated subsequent generations of Irish Americans like the Connells.

As I dug a bit deeper into the context of Maurice's story, three of his contemporaries, men with whom he had indirect if not direct contact in the environs of Ireland and West Chester, deepen this grafting analogy for me: Daniel O'Connell, "The Liberator" of Ireland; Frederick Douglass, whom some Irish called the "Black O'Connell"; and Bishop Francis Kenrick, the "St. Patrick of Pennsylvania." Through them I can see the sap that flowed between Maurice's Irish and American identities, the ties that bound him to the rootstock of America, and the church window that allowed his fusion to take.

THE SCION: CATHOLIC OPPRESSION IN IRELAND

In some ways, I can understand why Maurice Connell left Ireland. Even with the perspective of two hundred years, I couldn't see much on his horizon. When he was born in 1822, Ireland was one of the poorest countries in Europe with a quarter of its population desperately poor. He was part of the three-quarters of Irish males tethered to land that didn't produce enough food or income. And British colonization ensured that there was no hope of Ireland developing an autonomous industrial economy. The British employed three strategies: deny Irish autonomy, exploit Irish resources, and keep an Irish elite from gaining a political or economic foothold.[5] The success of all three hinged on setting Irish Catholics apart as a separate and uncivilized group not worthy of equal treatment under the law. To my mind, this is the very definition of racism.

I was surprised to learn that in Maurice's own county of Cork, the Protestant Penns had confiscated Catholic land in the 1650s. The Penns' youngest son, William, served as executor of the family's Irish holdings in the late 1660s. He traversed their extensive plantation on horseback and collected rents from tenant farmers. He also converted to the Society of Friends in Cork. While he never mentioned Catholics by name in his diary, William Penn did "pass derogatory remarks about their barbarous, superstitious customs."[6] In 1681, King Charles granted William Penn land in North America to repay a debt the Crown owed his father. Maurice made his way to Penn's Woods, aka Pennsylvania, 140 years later.

A litany of the limits on Catholic freedoms in eighteenth-century Ireland strikes me as being much like those imposed on Indigenous or enslaved peoples across the growing British empire. By the early 1700s, Catholics in Ireland made up three-quarters of the population of the island but owned one in nine acres of its land. English penal laws from 1704 to 1829 decreased Irish Catholic landownership to one in sixteen acres, and Catholics could not buy or lease it for longer than thirty-one years. Catholics could not become lawyers or judges nor be educated outside of Ireland. They couldn't carry guns, serve in the army, or even own a horse valued at more than five pounds. Catholic churches could not have steeples or crosses. Priests were prohibited from wearing clerical clothing and were required to take an oath of loyalty. Catholics also paid a tithe to support the Anglican Church of Ireland. They found this so infuriating that the Tithe War broke out across the country when Maurice was ten.

The Act of Union in 1800 removed any hopes of Irish autonomy. It disbanded the Irish Parliament in Dublin, subsumed Irish political affairs into English affairs in London, and tethered the Irish agrarian economy to the burgeoning industrial one in England. Granted, Maurice would have witnessed the easing of many of these penal codes as a result of the Catholic Emancipation Act in 1829, and a handful of Irish Catholics had been elected to Parliament by the small fraction of Irish Catholics who met the 10-pound property requirement to vote in county elections.[7] But by then, pathways to social mobility were effectively closed off to young Catholic men like Maurice. Plus, there was hunger on the horizon— again—precisely at a time when the island had more mouths to feed than ever before as a result of a dramatic population boom in the first half of the nineteenth century.

Irish historians Terrence McDonough and Eamonn Slater describe Maurice's situation as a non-inheriting son as a kind of "economic bondage that could only be broken by emigration."[8] In keeping with the grafting metaphor, it was better that he sever himself from the withering rootstock of Ireland than to die on its vine.

As I imagine it, Maurice was invited to come to America by William Donovan, his future brother-in-law. William had emigrated from Lisgoold sometime in the early 1840s. Maybe his letter came addressed to Maurice and his older brother Nicholas. Or maybe William had tucked a short note to Maurice into the folds of a longer letter to his family that his youngest sister, Margaret, who eventually married Maurice, ran down to him. Either way, things were about to change. Maurice was America-bound. I wondered how the Connells covered the three pounds for his passage, which Catholic historian Jay Dolan estimates to be the equivalent of a young cow or a year's rent.[9] Or maybe William sent money back for Maurice, as he did for the rest of the Donovan clan, a kind of Celtic chain migration that funneled one million pounds back into Ireland in the decade following the famine. However Maurice managed to pay, at some point in 1842 he found himself sailing west.

His belongings were few, but he was likely weighed down by what Dolan calls "a long tradition of political involvement."[10] After all, Maurice had grown up on tales of how the Connells in Cork were also kin of the great orator and parliamentarian Daniel O'Connell, known as The Liberator. I cannot help but think that Daniel O'Connell's stances about Irish emancipation from the British served as the grafting knife that finally severed Maurice from Ireland. In addition, Maurice likely heard O'Connell's unapologetic condemnations about American slavery, which he began to sound as early as 1829 in Quaker-friendly territory like Cork. O'Connell drew an easy parallel between the inherent contradictions in the British answer to the "Irish question" and the American answer to their "Negro question." He was part of the English Parliament's vote to end the English slave trade in 1833 and slavery itself in the West Indies in 1838. He linked his aversion to slavery to that of St. Patrick himself, who O'Connell called the first abolitionist. "Unless [Americans] abolish slavery," he said in a fiery speech in 1831 condemning the hypocrisy of slave owning in America of all places, "they must write themselves down as liars, or call a general convention of states and blot out the first sentence of their Declaration of Independence."[11] He raged against racialized social inequality and those who did nothing to abolish the chattel slavery that perpetuated it. Historian Angela Murphy notes that at a 1838 rally, O'Connell called out slave-owning George Washington, "the symbol of the contradictory nature of the American republic."[12]

In late March 1842, the year Maurice departed Ireland, Daniel O'Connell signed a petition drafted by the largely Protestant Hibernian Anti-Slavery Society imploring Irish émigrés in America to join the abolition movement there. O'Connell's unquestioned popularity among Catholics in Ireland emboldened Irish Protestants to gather signatures after Sunday Masses outside of churches around Ireland. It is quite possible that with all this on his heart and the desire for America's liberties stirring his soul, Maurice Connell was one of the seventy thousand Irish to sign the petition, named "Address from the People of Ireland to their Countrymen and Countrywomen in America."

"NONE CAN BE NEUTRAL . . . ," it stated. "Irishmen and Irishwomen! Treat the colored people as your equals, as brethren . . . Tell every man that you do not understand liberty for the white man, and slavery for the black man; that you are for LIBERTY FOR ALL, of every color, creed, and country."[13]

I cannot help but wonder if refrains from the petition reverberated in any part of Maurice's being as the west coast of Ireland disappeared from his view in 1842. "CLING BY THE ABOLITIONISTS—and in *America, you will do honor to the name of Ireland!*"[14]

THE CAMBIUM: THE LIBERATOR AND THE BLACK O'CONNELL

At no point in Maurice Connell's lifetime—nor perhaps in the lifetimes of the generations of O'Connells he helped to propagate—did he have more in common with Black men in Philadelphia than when he made his way across the Atlantic in 1842. He carried with him an acute sense of what it felt like to be considered inferior and economically dependent. Irish were typically stereotyped as lazy, intellectually and morally deficient. Maurice had experience with being overly surveilled because people assumed he was inherently criminal and violent by nature. And God forbid he ever spend time with a group of other young men without being seen as a traitorous agitator. His body knew what it meant to subsist under the thumb of a wealthy empire whose only desire for him was to be a "productive, untroublesome asset."[15] I wondered, could he have grafted into the abolition movement once in America?

I found some clues in historian Tom Chaffin's depiction of the transatlantic exile of another son of Ireland—although in his case it was an eastbound speaking tour. In August of 1845, American abolitionist Frederick Douglass published an autobiography that increased the bounty already on his head. He, too, was likely of Irish descent, thanks to his paternal lineage in a prestigious Maryland family. He was also familiar with the cause of Irish freedom since he had learned to read with a collection of speeches and had been especially taken with one on Catholic emancipation. Before his departure, Frederick Douglass ironically noted that he would be sailing from "American republican slavery, to monarchical liberty."[16] "The change of circumstances . . . is particularly striking," Douglass wrote to his sponsor for the trip, his friend the American abolitionist William Lloyd Garrison. "I can truly say," he wrote to Garrison, "I have spent some of the happiest moments of my life since landing in this country, I seem to have undergone a transformation, I live a new life."[17]

I wondered if it was Douglass's own experience with oppression that enabled him to recognize it so easily among Catholics in Ireland. He found extreme poverty amid abundance and often recoiled from what he called the "human misery, ignorance, degradation, filth and wretchedness" he witnessed as he traversed the length of the island.[18] He was struck by the ambivalence of the Protestant upper class, who appeared more concerned with the benevolent support of American abolition than with rectifying the abhorrent conditions of fellow Catholic countrymen. "Was there not an underground railroad that every Irishman would gladly board to get away from the tyranny of England?" he asked himself, perhaps in disbelief.[19]

In 1845, Douglass met Daniel O'Connell at a Repeal meeting in Dublin. The Liberator had just concluded a seventy-five-minute oration, which Douglass recounted in his next letter to William Garrison. "I have been assailed for attacking the American institution, as it is called—negro slavery. I am not ashamed of that attack—I do not shrink from it . . . ," said O'Connell. "My sympathy with distress is not confined within the narrow bounds of my own green island—no, it extends itself to every corner of the earth."[20] When the seventy-year-old O'Connell learned that Douglass was in the crowd, he pulled him onto the stage, called him "the Black O'Connell of the United States," and gave him the floor.[21] The next day's *Freeman's Journal* reported the highlights of Douglass's own speech, in which he "wished that some black O'Connell would rise up against his [American] countrymen and cry, 'Agitate, agitate, agitate'" and acknowledged that "with one arm the Liberator was bursting the fetters of Irishmen, with the other he was striking off the literal chains from the limbs of the negros."[22]

Together, the Black O'Connell and The Liberator identified a common denominator in Maurice Connell's and Frederick Douglass's experiences of oppression. It was not just a desire for freedom that ran through Maurice's and Frederick's veins, but rather freedom from Anglo-Saxon superiority. This powerful myth animated England's empire-building engagement with peoples beyond its borders and was predicated on the false assumption that the English were descendants of a Germanic tribe, the Saxons, whose defeat of the Roman Empire at the end of the first century was attributed to their untainted bloodline and form of government.

Scholars Kelly Brown Douglass and Theodore Allen helped me find similarity between Maurice's and Douglass's experiences at the hands of the myth of Anglo-Saxon superiority. The Anglo-Saxons in Ireland imposed penal laws at the same time as their Anglo-American counterparts developed racialized slave codes in England's American colonies.[23] Both solidified racial-religious difference as the most important feature of society and denied ascendancy of groups racialized as *other*. They destroyed cultural identities by erasing distinctions among those in the otherized groups. Allen notes there was virtually no difference between Catholics who once owned land and those who never did, or free Black people and enslaved Black people. Neither Irish Catholics nor Black Americans could own land or marry those who did, learn to read, or get the same wages for their labor as those with Anglo-Saxon heritage. Both were denied civil rights like owning a gun, serving on juries, or holding public office. Violence against Irish or Black women went without prosecution, and Anglo-Saxons were likely to be acquitted of murder charges if their victims were Irish or Black. In 1723, the Anglo-Americans in Virginia revoked African Americans' right to vote, and four years later the Anglo-Irish revoked the same right from Catholics in Ireland.[24]

Maurice Connell and Frederick Douglass might have noted any number of parallels in their respective experiences. To access liberties awarded "free" men, both needed official papers, Maurice attesting to English ancestry or conversion to Protestantism in Ireland, and Douglass to manumission in America. Both men lived in close proximity to the minority who denied them freedom in the lands of their birth. For Maurice, this was a middleman or executor of the estate the Connells lived on, as well as the tithe collectors who were always pressing in on the family to make the rent. For Douglass it would have been the overseer who did the master's bidding. Their status as Christians didn't offer any protection from this dehumanizing treatment. Catholic conversion to Protestantism was not encouraged in Ireland, and in 1667 the Virginia colony enacted a law that separated baptism from manumission.[25] In other words, enslaved people were granted freedom from the bondage of sin but not that of chattel slavery. Both men also lived in fear of vigilantism. In Ireland the Orange Order maintained social control, and in America a network of slave catchers ensured that no Black people truly felt free. Historian Steve Garner suggests they both were targets of Anglo-Saxon fascination in the mid-nineteenth century, epitomized by a book called *The Races of Man*, which asserted "the superiority of the Anglo-Saxon, contracted as reflective, reforming, and masculine in contrast to the rash, childish, rebellious and feminine Celt and the indolent, feckless, and barbarous African."[26]

So why didn't shared resistance to Anglo-Saxon culture flow between Irish and Black citizens in America? Douglass had the answer, and it pointed to the rootstock to which Maurice was about to be bound. "The Irish, who, at home, readily sympathize with the oppressed everywhere, are instantly taught when they step upon our soil to hate and despise the Negro," he said. "They are taught to believe that he eats the bread that belongs to them."[27] I am taken with Douglass's assessment of Philadelphia, where Maurice was headed: "There is not perhaps anywhere to be found a city in which prejudice against color is more rampant than in Philadelphia."[28] I can't help but wonder if it had something to do with the city's growing concentration of Irish Catholics just as my great-great-grandfather arrived.

THE ROOTSTOCK: AMERICAN ANTI-BLACKNESS

Like many Black people, Douglass had no difficulty naming anti-Blackness as a distinct dimension of Anglo-Saxon superiority in America. "Negro slavery consisted not in taking away *any* of the rights of man," he said in explaining the difference between Irish Catholic oppression in Ireland and Black oppression in America, "but in annihilating them *all*—not in taking away a man's property, but in making property of him . . ."[29]

When I continued to unpack Maurice's emigration story, I began to see more clearly how Irish Catholics like him tapped into the rootstock of American anti-Blackness to build immunity to the pathogen of anti-Catholicism, which American Catholic historian Maura Farrelly explains was at an all-time high in the middle of the nineteenth century when Maurice arrived, especially in Philadelphia.[30] The fledging nation was undergoing an identity crisis spurred by population growth and land acquisition. With the War for Independence and the struggles of nation-making behind them and those who lived through them dying off, who or what would sustain the national ethos? How would America maintain its exceptional status? Most agreed that Catholicism was both an antithesis of and a threat to that exceptionalism. After all, Protestantism made America a city on a hill and nurtured American virtues of freedom, individualism, and moral courage. Catholicism, with its Old World mind-set—monarchical, antiquated, feudal—was the antithesis of American republicanism. More specifically, Protestant Americans perceived Catholics as being "mastered" by Rome and therefore subservient, soft, and dull, incapable of the reasoning and individuality that American liberty required. This was particularly true of Irish Catholics, who had long been portrayed as an uncivilized people best suited for colonization rather than self-determination.

Moreover, the majority of the immigrants pouring into American cities in the middle of the nineteenth century were Irish Catholics. Andrew Little arrived with roughly 6,000 Irish during the 1820s, while Maurice is one of 200,000 who left Ireland during the 1840s. In Andrew's day, most Irish immigrants had been Protestant and dispersed into rural areas. Those in Maurice's generation, however, were mostly Catholic; they were incredibly poor and remained concentrated in America's eastern cities. Catholics became the single largest Christian denomination in America in 1850, sparking fears that they would dilute American values. Protestant denominations—divided over issues such as abolition and prohibition—were increasingly convinced that uncivilized Irish Catholics would only hasten the moral demise of the nation. If "democracy is political Protestantism," as a Philadelphian Presbyterian claimed in 1843, then popery and the outsiders pouring in from Ireland who espoused it were a threat to America.[31]

Digging into the context of Philadelphia, the cradle of American exceptionalism and port in the storm for Irish immigrants, I learned what made Philadelphia such a tinderbox: a surge in population and a lack of housing and jobs. Between 1830 and 1850, the city's Irish population boomed from 35,000 to 170,000. Seventy new parishes were created, most under the direction of the diocese's Irish-born Bishop Francis Kenrick. Kenrick's conflicts with lay trustees in parishes like Christ's Church, who were suspicious if not defiant of his edicts to end their trusteeship of parishes, reinforced Protestant concerns about Rome's reach into American affairs.

In 1842, fifty Protestant clergy established the American Protestant Association in Philadelphia and, along with the city's active publishing industry, helped to spread concern about popery and Romanism. This propaganda fueled speculation as to why Kenrick asked public school officials in 1843 if Catholic students might read from a different Bible than the King James version required by the state legislature in 1838. Some viewed it as a challenge to the newly founded public school system charged with shoring up the ethos of the nation. Others interpreted it as an affront to Protestantism or evidence of traitorous Roman overreach. Either way, it became an excuse for violence. Riots broke out in May of 1844 in the Kensington district of Philadelphia, then again in July in South Philadelphia. The former destroyed three Catholic buildings and several homes; the latter killed twenty people, injured more than a hundred, and required four thousand militia and volunteers to restore order.

This anti-Catholicism may well have served as both impetus and cover for Irish Catholic anti-Blackness. For one, the nativist riots resulted in an insular parochial school system in Philadelphia, the largest of its kind in the US by the 1950s, through which Catholics not only segregated themselves from Protestants but also, and with far more fervor and longevity, from Black people. Also, historian Noel Ignatiev notes that the riots were the catalyst for creating the city's police force, whether in the name of the Protestant desire for law and order or the Catholic demand for self-protection. He notes Irish Catholics on the city police "marked a turning point" in the Irish becoming white, since it meant "the Irish would be officially empowered (armed) to defend themselves from the nativist mobs, and at the same time to carry out their own agenda against black people."[32] But even more than the anti-Blackness that accompanied the establishment of a racially segregated school system and racialized police force, I found evidence of Catholic anti-Blackness in Maurice Connell's options for maintaining his *Catholic* identity as he became a white man in Philadelphia.

Historians Angela Murphy and John Quinn explain that one way he could have remained unapologetically Irish and Catholic would have been to continue to support the Repeal movement back in Ireland, which sought to overturn the Act of Union of 1800 and reestablish Ireland's parliament in Dublin. Murphy notes that in supporting Irish autonomy from Britain, Maurice could also publicly espouse the very values and capacities that Protestant Americans, including the Protestant Irish who arrived before him, assumed he lacked: a commitment to the American values of liberty and fortitude against tyranny.[33] Irish Americans established Repeal Societies, first in Boston in 1840 and then in New York and Philadelphia before the year was out. Quinn points out that on St. Patrick's Day of 1841, the head of Philadelphia's chapter sent a $200 check to "O'Connell's headquarters in Dublin" along with the names of the 900 residents who contributed.[34] On the Fourth of July that year, 2,000 members of the Philadelphia Repeal Association, the largest chapter, marched through the city's streets. It is not a coincidence these societies chose Philadelphia as the site for their first National Repeal Convention in 1842 on the anniversary of George Washington's birthday. By 1843 there were Repeal Societies in every major city, although I found none in West Chester's historical record.

It is no wonder that abolitionists in Ireland saw American Repeal Societies as a potential wellspring for their cause. The earlier iteration of this movement, which predated Ireland's Act of Emancipation in 1829 and was called the Friends of Ireland, had linked the causes of Catholic freedom in Ireland with Black freedom in the United States. Toward the end of his life, Daniel O'Connell only became more ardent in his calls to former countrymen in America to reject slavery. But O'Connell's Irish Address of 1842—calling upon all Repeal Societies in America to also demand the repeal of slavery—was met with resistance. Although Philadelphia Repealers were the only ones to mount to a defense of O'Connell's proslavery stance, its Repeal Society, the largest in the country with more than 2,000 members, splintered over the issue of slavery.[35] The Repeal Society in Pottsville, Pennsylvania, in Maurice Connell's own diocese of Philadelphia, issued a series of resolutions insisting on the natural inferiority of Black people, their subsequent fitness for slavery, and continued segregation as the only viable way forward in America.[36] According to the Irish Catholics of Pottstown—the first to add a "racial argument" into objections to the Irish Address—slavery wasn't the problem, abolitionists were. Slavery contributed to the happiness of fifteen million white Americans, they said, and the Irish were among them.

In exploring this disconnect between Irish Catholic and American Black emancipation, I discovered how Irish Catholics in America, following the lead of prominent bishops, used the Repeal Societies to pivot to anti-Blackness to assert their Americanness, particularly in the eyes of the pro-slavery Democratic party with which many Irish Catholics were aligned. If Daniel O'Connell made it difficult for the Irish in America to turn their backs on Black people, then the US Catholic leadership made it easy for them to separate themselves from O'Connell and likewise their shared Irish heritage of resistance to racialized oppression. Quinn notes that Bishop Hughes of New York—formerly a priest in Philadelphia, an editor of its first Catholic newspaper, and early sympathizer of abolition—insisted that regardless of its content, Irish Americans had a duty to reject the 1842 Address because its source was a foreign power.[37] Perhaps to obeying O'Connell's mandate to reject slavery would only reinforce stereotypes of Irish Americans as parochial rule followers who could not think for themselves. Hughes also resented that the Irish specifically were being targeted with a particular responsibility to solve the slavery problem. Irish Catholic newspapers in a number of cities shifted the blame for the growing conflicts around slavery on abolitionists, whom they saw as political extremists and heretical in their Christianity.

The Liberator was distraught. "Come out of such a land, you Irishmen," he lamented after reading a similar rejection letter from his brethren in Cincinnati in 1843. "Or, if you remain, and dare countenance the system of slavery that is supported there, we will recognize you as Irishmen no longer."[38] His threat had an opposite impact. At the first national convention of Repeal Societies in Philadelphia in 1842 delegates passed a resolution to remain solely focused on Irish emancipation rather than take up the divisive slavery question. Northern chapters prioritized maintaining the Union, which meant ignoring the slavery question for as long as possible, while those in the South pulled out of the movement entirely.

I am struck by the contradictions Maurice negotiated in grafting onto the rootstock of American anti-Blackness. On one hand, he had clear messages from an Irishman he revered, questioning his integrity if he did not advocate for the emancipation of and liberty for *all* people. On the other hand, he heard from some Catholic leaders that strident abolition, and even the emancipation of enslaved Black people, could further fracture the Union and therefore jeopardize the future he had left Lisgoold in search of. I have no idea where Maurice stood, but I can surmise the strategic lessons he would have heard about putting white America first—even before a source of cultural pride like Daniel O'Connell.

Maurice likely also realized that despite anti-Catholic rhetoric and even organized violence, oppression in the United States actually had very little to do with religious identity. It was all about race. Irish Catholics could ease out from under the weight of oppression by ensuring that it remained firmly on the shoulders of Black Americans. And they could do that by deflecting everything said about and done to Irish Catholics onto Black people. For example, Maurice Connell would have noticed that Irish arriving in Philadelphia with him not only seemed to despise Black people but also wanted their jobs and their homes. Irish Catholics claimed that Black people undercut them in the labor force or forced them out of their neighborhoods when, in fact, as Garner suggests, in cities like Philadelphia the opposite was true: "the attainment of whiteness above all meant the banishment of blackness."[39] Irish Catholics in antebellum Philadelphia took Black jobs and pushed freed Black people out of the neighborhoods to which they had been relegated, not the other way around. Garner notes that in the realm of politics, Irish Catholics quickly fueled city political machines that gained power by denying the vote to Black citizens, since "the color line would only work to the advantage of the Irish if every member of the subjugated group had a lower status than the lowest member of the dominant one."[40] Irish Catholics and Black people seemed locked in a struggle to prove their worthiness in the minds of people dead set against both of them. The "ideological struggle" in which people like Maurice and his wife, Margaret, were engaged "did not involve throwing the rule book out the window, but honing skills and playing better than those from whom they learned the rule in the first place."[41]

Finally, Irish Catholics amplified a culture of acceptable violence against Black people, which only underscored the lack of Black freedom. Between 1834 and 1849, there were nine major mob attacks against Black citizens of Philadelphia, usually at sites of Black achievement or upward mobility or on dates that commemorated Black freedom.[42] While relatively few people participated in the violence, the collective silence about it ensured its effectiveness as a form of social control. Daniel O'Connell himself condemned one such outbreak against Black people commemorating West Indian independence in August of 1842, noting, "Philadelphia has disgraced itself to the blackest extent . . . Where were the Catholic priests? Why didn't they raise their voice against this iniquitous proceeding?"[43]

I didn't have to look much further than Maurice's own bishop in Philadelphia for an unsettling answer.

THE CHURCH WINDOW: THE ST. PATRICK OF PENNSYLVANIA

I assume horticulturalists call the uncovered portion of the scion—the plant that is being grafted onto the rootstock—the church window because the open wound looks like an arched window. Even more than the name, I'm struck by the analogical fit of its purpose for making sense of my family's experience of becoming American Catholics in the 1840s and 1850s. The church window facilitates a callousing or hardening around the spot of fusion between two different plants, especially on the scion itself. This hardening stabilizes the graft and ensures growth. The American Catholic Church calloused the wounds created when Irish Catholics joined the rootstock of American anti-Blackness. Like an effective church window, the Catholic Church stabilized that fusion and ensured growth, primarily for itself.

I can easily imagine the psychic pain of Maurice and Margaret's emigration odyssey. They severed familial ties, jettisoned comforting cultural and spiritual practices, worried about American anti-Catholicism, and witnessed violence against Black people. But how did they deal with all of this? How did they tend these wounds? Rather than heal them, I think the Catholic Church in America calloused hearts in two ways. First, it refused to heal the national wound of slavery, in fact leaving it exposed by condoning it. Then the Church calloused hearts that might otherwise have been sympathetic to Black suffering, especially those of newer immigrants like the Connells. I was stunned to discover the pivotal role of yet another Irishman in executing this strategy: Philadelphia's own Bishop Francis Patrick Kenrick.

Kenrick was born in Dublin in 1797. As a contemporary of Daniel O'Connell, he knew the violent oppression of Anglo-Saxonism. He became a priest in Rome and was quickly dispatched to teach in one of the new American seminaries in Bardstown, Kentucky, where he distinguished himself as a public defender against anti-Catholic polemics. In 1830, he was appointed bishop-in-waiting of the disorderly diocese of Philadelphia and took official control in 1842, the same year Maurice Connell departed Cork. His jurisdiction entailed the entire states of Pennsylvania and Delaware and parts of southwestern New Jersey. His most challenging territory proved to be the obstinance of the trustees of several parishes in Philadelphia.[44]

Kenrick's visitation itinerary in his massive diocese rivaled Daniel O'Connell's speaking tours.[45] Both men traversed a vast and often hostile territory, trying to shore it up against anti-Catholicism by bringing people in line behind a shared vision and cause. In Kenrick's case, the cause was yielding to Roman ecclesial authority. He was called "The St. Patrick of Pennsylvania," given his efforts to grow the faith in his diocese and to liberate it from lay trustees. Between 1830 and 1850, he grew the number of parishes from 22 to 92, increased priests from 35 to 101, and expanded his flock from 35,000 to 170,000. He was a powerful disciplinarian whose ideas carried significant weight, particularly those about slavery.

I suspect those ideas about slavery made Bishop Kenrick nervous as he sailed back across the Atlantic for a European tour in 1845, a few months ahead of Frederick Douglass. There was a chance he would cross paths in Dublin with The Liberator, who was rumored to refuse to shake hands with slave-owning Irish Americans. Kenrick did not own anyone, but his brother, Peter, did. Peter Kenrick's slave-owning status was significant because he, too, was a bishop, in St. Louis in America's newly acquired

Louisiana Territory.[46] But I suspect it was his last stop that could have tied Kenrick's stomach in knots. He had a private audience with Pope Gregory XVI, who in 1839, a year after Frederick Douglass escaped from slavery, banned the global slave trade. "No one hereafter may dare unjustly to molest Indians, Negroes, or other men of this sort," the Pope exhorted via his edict *In Supremo Apostolatus*. "Or to spoil them of their goods; or to reduce them to slavery; . . . or to exercise that inhuman trade by which Negroes, as if they were not men, but mere animals . . ."[47] For all of their Romanism, Kenrick and his brother bishops balked at this exhortation.

Kenrick knew that the American capitalist economy—and likewise the financial viability of the American Church—depended entirely on both the free labor of enslaved people and the market value of their enslaved bodies. According to sociologist Matt Desmond, enslaved persons were the most valuable commodity in antebellum America and their combined value "exceeded that of all the railroads and factories in the nation."[48] Ending slavery was not only impractical but also a financial death wish. Ecclesial stances on slavery were a public death knell too. The Catholic bishops watched—perhaps with smug satisfaction—as schisms over abolition fractured many Protestant denominations in America.

Kenrick and his brother bishops walked a moral high wire to shield their defense of slavery.[49] Some argued that Catholic interference in the slavery issue violated the constitutional separation of church and state. Bishop John England of Charleston, South Carolina, insisted that the Pope's slave trade ban did not apply to the trade of people *already* enslaved. Bishop John Hughes of New York, who by the time of the Civil War was the "de facto spokesperson for Catholics and the Irish," rallied Catholics behind the Union—but not to end slavery, which he found to be legitimate.[50]

As Kenrick was geographically sandwiched between English and Hughes, with the line between freedom and slavery defining the southern border of his diocese, I wondered what he discussed with the Holy Father during that audience in 1845. Maybe he mentioned how the bishops found themselves in a balancing act in a charged political atmosphere. Maybe he highlighted how committed they were to ensuring that at the very least enslaved Black people were treated charitably by their Catholic slave owners and manumitted whenever their freedom did not present a threat to the common good. Or maybe he mentioned how they exhorted Catholic slave owners to protect their slaves' rights to spiritual goods by educating them in the basics of the faith, keeping families intact when the need for sales arose, and ensuring access to a priest who could save their otherwise heathen souls.

My biggest shock about Kenrick, however, had to do with how he squared *his* particular contribution to the bishops' pro-slavery high-wire act. From 1841 to 1843, he published an extensive three-volume moral manual for the American clergy, *Theologia Moralis*, which he said was motivated by a "desire to give practical moral principles and aid to priests dealing with slaves and masters."[51] He wrote it in Latin and in a Thomistic style—instructive questions with answers that referenced biblical texts, church teaching, the Doctors of the Church, or American civil law where appropriate. One of these three volumes focused on slavery and provided the theology to support "the status quo," which Kenrick himself reflected. He was "tolerant of slavery, anti-abolitionist, anti-immediate emancipation, pro-colonization of freed blacks and pro-fugitive slave laws."[52] Since an English translation has yet to be published—yet another telling detail about American Catholic anti-Blackness—I had to rely on analysis of the first and only American scholar to unpack his Latin treatise: Joseph Brokhage, who did so in 1955.[53]

Brokhage suggests that Kenrick's clerical experience in Northern and Southern dioceses made him "eminently well-qualified to understand both sides of the problem of slavery."[54] Kenrick's granular familiarity with the moral conundrums of Catholicism and slave owning disturbed me. While he advised against the many excesses of slavery—zealous overseers, abducting and selling freed Black people, sales of individuals to buyers who were not "humane and just" Catholics, and cruelty in punishment—to my mind, Kenrick's detailed moral parsing about even these matters reflected a heart calloused to the social death of slavery.[55] Building upon the theological premise that enslavement was not contrary to the natural law, he condoned a variety of practices that normalized the dehumanizing violence of slavery. For example, he concurred that mothers determined "the title of nativity," meaning their free or enslaved status determined the status of their children.[56] He advised that "[m]asters should give to the slaves work that does not exceed their strength or ability, lest they be given the occasion of idleness."[57] In addition, "those who are an evil disposition are to be subdued by labor; but those of a milder disposition are to be more mildly and kindly treated."[58] Should an enslaved person be killed, he advised that monetary restitution be awarded their master.[59] I noticed that obedience with love was Kenrick's central rule for enslaved people. Enslaved people who refused to do the work given them did not sin against justice or fail to uphold their end of the slave contract but instead violated the loving relationship that Kenrick believed bound them to their master and vice versa. I was particularly horrified by his ideas about the sacraments and slavery. He obligated Catholic slave owners to baptize the people they owned, even if against their wishes.[60] Enslaved Catholics had the right to marry, he instructed, but only if it did not interfere with the work they owed their masters. Priests could administer the sacrament of marriage to enslaved Catholics who didn't have their master's blessing only if doing so did not contradict state law.[61] He rejected the separation of families as a sin, except in cases where owners were "led to the sale by grave reason," such as death of the owner.[62]

When it came to confession in particular, Kenrick not only concluded that slaves lived in "a necessary condition of sin" that required regular absolution but he also implied that there was something inherently criminal about Black people.[63] For example, if slaves were not working they would be idle, and "by idleness they could easily fall into crimes," especially in Southern states where Kenrick acknowledged that fear of "uprisings and slaughters" was a "grave reason for permitting work on Sunday."[64] In what was perhaps a harbinger for the American Church's obsession with sexuality and sexual activity, as well as historical evidence of the persistent sexualization of Black female bodies, I noticed that Kenrick viewed enslaved women as sources of temptation for white Catholic men.[65] He advised his priests to recall that men can sin "not from affection toward a certain woman, but from an insane lust that he desires to satisfy with any woman." He thought it best, therefore, to remove the temptation and apply "opportune remedies . . . for allaying the lust, before the master is admitted to the sacraments."[66]

Through the third volume of *Theologia Moralis*, Kenrick literally wrote the theological book on American Catholic slave mastery, albeit anchoring it in the Church's less contextualized historical teaching on the legality of slavery in general. "It can be questioned whether the masters are permitted to keep in slavery those whose ancestors seem to have been taken by injustice from Africa," he granted on the pressing question of whether or not *American* slavery was morally permissible. "It seems to us that it must be answered in the affirmative."[67] According to Kenrick's reasoning, while "the slaves had been taken unjustly from Africa" at the outset, enslaved people in the South had been in bondage so long they could no longer lay claim to the title of their freedom.[68] Plus, since they were often "ignorant persons, without any property, and without sufficient protection, and with slavery having become the foundation of the whole social order," emancipation would only endanger them and society.[69]

Kenrick's concerns about the dangers of emancipation compelled him to advocate as early as 1820 for expatriation to Africa as the optimal means of emancipation, given the threat he saw freed Blacks posing to the common good. He pointed to failed experiments in Black freedom as proof that Black people were inferior, incapable of self-governance, and therefore at great risk even in places like Philadelphia. His assumption that slavery was a balm for Black anxieties about emancipation only reinforced his stance that returning enslaved people to Africa was the only solution. He was an ardent supporter of the American Colonization Society (ACS), a rare ecumenical and North–South alliance in the antebellum period. Charles Carroll, the slave-owning Catholic signer of the Declaration of Independence, served as the second president of the ACS from 1830 to 1832, by which time 15,000 manumitted people had been sent back across the Atlantic. Kenrick committed precious resources to the endeavor, most notably sending his close friend Edward Barron as a missionary to the Cape Palmas colony in Liberia 1841. Barron later became the rector of Philadelphia's St. Charles Borromeo Seminary, which Kenrick opened in 1832. Prior to his audience with the Pope, Kenrick received a note from Barron stating that not only had the mission failed, but also that several American families wished to return to the US. The fervor of one Black man by the name of Brooks stood out. "He and his five children ought to be with you in Philadelphia," Barron wrote Kenrick.[70] Whether or not they returned remains unclear.

THE BIND AND THE GREENHOUSE: THE CIVIL WAR IN ST. AGNES PARISH

Even with the church window stabilizing the graft between their Irish and American identities, Maurice and Margaret needed something to bind them to the rootstock of American anti-Blackness as well as a greenhouse to cultivate growth. Here's where I learned how the Civil War and St. Agnes Parish in West Chester merge in their story, under a giant American flag.

By 1861, Fr. John Prendergast had been pastor at St. Agnes Parish for just over a decade. He was born in 1821 in Tipperary, Ireland, just a few months before Maurice Connell. He was ordained in 1851 at Philadelphia's St. Charles Borromeo Seminary and then his bishop, Francis Kenrick, immediately sent him to Christ's Church in West Chester. The parish was no longer under the control of lay trustees and needed a permanent pastor.

Fr. John made his home in a small rectory, from which he oversaw "a poor scanty parish," which was already sixty years old, "with four outlying mission stations."[71] He got to work building an extensive infrastructure. He razed the original church building and planted the renamed St. Agnes in its place, with a brick edifice and three arched entrances. Given that southeastern Pennsylvania was still largely Catholic mission territory, Fr. John oversaw the construction of three adjoining Catholic parishes in Chester County. He served alternating Sundays in the various parishes under his canonical jurisdiction. In the midst of it all, he performed the marriage of Maurice Connell and Margaret Donovan in 1856.

Fr. John may not have consulted the third volume of Kenrick's *Theologia Moralis* since he didn't minister to Catholics bound to one another through the relationships of slavery, but as an immigrant priest he nevertheless modeled for his flock in West Chester the callousing against Black Americans he surely received in Kenrick's seminary. As I noted in the previous chapter, much like Kenrick's extensive visitation log, I could find no trace of Black people in the historical record of St. Agnes during Fr. John's tenure there. What's more, from what I can tell, Fr. John also embodied his superior's distrust of abolition. Under his leadership, West Chester's Catholics did not participate in the array of anti-slavery activities swirling around them, including discussions of colonization, which their bishop publicly supported.

But perhaps most importantly, as war loomed, Fr. John embraced a dramatic pro-Union stance that was consistent with what Northern bishops modeled for him. I was taken with the description of his fervor for the Union from St. Agnes's centenary history book: "When the dark spirit of treason permeated a portion of our land in 1861 and the greatest fratricidal war of history was inaugurated, when many were doubting the ability and debating the right of the loyal States to suppress the rebellious, Father John was an earnest champion of the cause of the Union."[72] Surely this man was a source of pride. And yet, the silence about Black people in the same historical record suggests to me that for all of his fervor, Fr. John was not necessarily anti-slavery or pro-emancipation. In fact, according to historian Randall Miller (who was one of my college professors), Catholics were in fact intentionally not anti-slavery in their support of the Union. This was to combat three things that threatened their own survival in America: nativism that questioned their Americanness; anti-Catholicism that questioned their loyalty; and sectarian divisions that could fracture Catholics as they had other denominations.[73]

Miller helped me see how Fr. John, like his predecessors, embraced the "church's public prose," which attempted to prove—in word and symbols—that "Catholics were, and must be, good citizens."[74] To that end, he "preached a patriotic sermon every Sunday."[75] He joined an aid society for soldiers' families. And most notably, he raised funds from his parishioners to buy a forty-by-sixty-foot American flag, the largest the borough had ever seen, which he hung across Gaye Street in front of St. Agnes. The St. Agnes choir sang the national anthem the day it went up. It remained on display for the duration of war, a public statement that Fr. John, and ideally all of his Catholic parishioners, "had sworn to support the constitution of the United States and as an adopted citizen would defend the flag or die by it."[76] "With such displays," which Miller suggests point toward the Americanizing tendency of Irish Catholicism, "Catholics showed their true colors while they simultaneously claimed their own space in American history."[77] Prendergast's 1871 obituary pointed to the success of this endeavor: "As a citizen Father John was full of public spirit . . . When our government was in danger, Fr. John was the first to inspire his spiritual children with the spirit of patriotism, and with his blessing send them forth to fight for the land of their adoption."[78] But Prendergast did not rally his people to fight for the freedom of all people living in their adopted land—and thus he rallied them behind a half-truth, if not a full lie.

The possibility for all Americans to fight for freedom, however, brought Frederick Douglass to West Chester on July 14, 1863. He was on yet another speaking tour, this time seeking recruits for colored regiments in the Union Army. Douglass remained confident that military service would earn Black men the full rights of citizenship. My mind reels with the thought that Maurice and Frederick may have actually been in each other's presence in a crowd of Black and white citizens in Horticultural Hall that summer. "You are a member of a long enslaved and despised race," Douglass had written in an article in the *Douglass Monthly* that laid out nine talking points that peppered his stump speech.[79] Given their shared history with Anglo-Saxon superiority, the ethos that ran through American slavery and anti-Catholicism, to my mind Douglass could have been speaking to the Irish men in the crowd as well as the Black men. I wondered if in fact he was.

Even though Maurice was too old to enlist and his four sons too young, Douglass's message would have been appealing, since only Irish Catholics were more self-conscious of their tenuous American identities than Blacks in antebellum America.[80] "Men have set down your submission to Slavery and insult to lack of manly courage," Douglass wrote. "They point to this fact as demonstrating your fitness only to be a servile class. You should enlist and disprove the slander and wipe out the reproach."[81]

In the end, Douglass's stop in West Chester was a success. According to accounts in *The Village Record*, there had been a great turnout, especially among Black citizens. The audience had been enthusiastic and peaceful. Several men registered. His national campaign was also a success—180,000 Black men served in the Union Army, including two of his own sons and sixty Black citizens of West Chester.[82] This enlistment of course also led to immense sacrifice, including 40,000 who died, all while discrimination and prejudice continued. In fact, before departing West Chester in July of 1863, Douglass received a telegram from a janitor at his next venue in Lancaster County advising him to postpone his speaking engagement there the following day. Rumors of a mob came to fruition, but Douglass had already heeded the warning.[83]

Fr. John was a successful pied piper as well. I now believe that at least one of my family members marched behind him under the St. Agnes American flag. Private John Little, Andrew and Catherine Little's second oldest son, had joined the E Company, also known as Mulligan Guard, a mostly Irish brigade in West Chester's 97th Infantry. Fr. John may have been at the head of John's column in September of 1861 on his way to training outside of Washington, DC. His parents and siblings would have been among the other parishioners and residents of the borough there to see him. John Little saw much of the Deep South in his tour of duty— South Carolina, Georgia, Florida. He was wounded in a picket skirmish on James Island in South Carolina in June of 1862, promoted to corporal a year later, and then, after being reduced in rank in July of 1864, deserted at some point after the Union defeat at Deep Bottom along the James River eleven miles southeast of Richmond.

ROUNDING ST. AGNES: RACIAL MERCY AND UN-SUTURING

I was a week into my research in the Chester County archives when Ash Wednesday arrived. I took a break from reviewing yellowed newspaper clippings and walked the three blocks from the Historical Society to St. Agnes Parish for the noon Mass. I arrived early and meandered around a bit, looking for evidence of my family. The interior had a somber reverence—dark wood-paneled ceiling, polished flagstone flooring, stained glass in deep blues and greens. While most of those in my family tree had moved away from West Chester by the time the current structure was built in 1920, I hoped for a familiar surname on one of the memorial plaques in the vestibule or in the stained glass windows. I found traces of the Donovans, my great-great-great-grandmother Margaret's tribe, but no O'Connells, whose story is more familiar to me.

I settled into a pew more than halfway up the aisle and tried to quiet my mind enough to catch lingering remnants of my ancestors in the ether of the place. As the pews filled around me, I could only ruminate on all I had learned about Chester County, West Chester Borough, and St. Agnes. It was an ugly history, and parishioners' relative absence from the extensive historical record housed just blocks away brought me no comfort. As the cantor began the classic Lenten hymn "Hosea, Come Back to Me," it dawned on me that the first of my ancestors to have their foreheads marked with ashes in America had done so on this very spot nearly two hundred years ago. Given everything that was happening around them in West Chester, for what had they atoned? Given everything happening around me, for what should I atone? The answers were murky but the summons was clear: racism is a sin requiring repentance.

Joseph Barndt, however, suggests that when it comes to racism, it's critical to operate with an accurate notion of sin. The more familiar understanding of sin as rebellion—deliberate choices of individuals arising from our individually sinful humanness and atoned through seeking repentance from a God who desires sacrifice—is insufficient. It implies that "racism is a sin freely chosen and able to be freely rejected" and that the rote formula of "act of contrition, repentance, confession and absolution" can do the trick to free the individual soul from its snares.[84] Clearly, two hundred years on, we need a different approach. Instead, Barndt suggests we think about the sin of racism in terms of a "collective imprisonment" by an oppressive force that overpowers and compels our active and collective submission. He says that "evidence of that captivity is manifested unmistakably in the isolation, separation, hostility and mistrust between white churches and churches of color."[85] It leaves us unable to understand the structural oppression that people of color experience and therefore likely to respond only with charity, if we respond at all. And it leaves us unable to "perceive, understand, or deal with our own spiritual, social, or political bondage."[86] We become collectively calloused, unable to see that our "church is being held captive by the very system of racism it helped to create."[87]

Approaching racism as a "sin of captivity" requires that we change our standard operating procedures when it comes to repentance. Individual repentance is not enough. To Barndt's mind it requires "rescue, liberation, healing and rebuilding."[88] To that end, racial mercy involves a desire to become undone, to shave away the calluses, to sever the bind that keeps us attached to the rootstock of American anti-Blackness. Philosopher George Yancy calls this "un-suturing," or a metaphorical state of "opening [myself] up, to speak to, to admit to the racist poison that is inside of [me]," which will require that I "let go of [my] white innocence" in order to "enter into a battle" with myself to take responsibility for the ways in which my comfort in a society created for me is linked to Black pain.[89]

My family members had access to figures who modeled both vulnerability and impenetrability across the color line. Frederick Douglass did not shield himself against the suffering of my people's compatriots in Ireland. "I am not going through this land with my eyes shut, ears stopped, or heart steeled. I am seeking to see, hear and feel, all that may be seen, heard and felt," Douglass wrote. "I believe that the sooner the wrongs of the whole human family are made known, the sooner those wrongs will be reached."[90] Philadelphia's own Bishop Kenrick, by contrast, not only advocated for the literal bondage of Black people, but also held white Catholics captive to economic, political, and religious values and systems that justified that bondage. He advocated for law and order, as well as the rights of states to defy national anti-slavery legislation. He admonished priests to work within the parameters of state laws when it came to literacy and freedom of movement of enslaved people. "Such is the state of things, nothing should be attempted against the laws, nor anything done or said that would make them [read: Black people] bear their yoke unwillingly."[91] His words of caution when it came to working within that evil system certainly calloused the hearts of my ancestors and disempowered any desire for liberation they may have brought with them from Ireland. Where Douglass is part of the long tradition of Black Americans who perfected democracy, Kenrick is part of a tradition of white Americans who perverted it and Christianity as well.

Racial mercy summons me to a particular kind of confession—not the private exchange with a vowed religious person in a solemn holy place, but a public acknowledgment of what has been holding me and my people captive. This seems to be a critical step in the process of undoing the knots—choosing to face and reckon with situations of suffering that challenge what we think we know about our pasts. In the case of the West Chester O'Connells, it means facing what Yancy calls the poison of racism that is laced through *my* entire Catholic experience, because it was spread by white Catholics like herbicide into the very soil in which my family's roots began to take hold. Racial mercy suggests that calloused hearts that tolerated the suffering of first becoming and then being anti-Black generation after generation can become undone—un-sutured—by all of that suffering, past and present, if we publicly acknowledge it. Bryan Massingale calls this stance "lamenting" and suggests that it plays a critical role for white people in making a confession: "For the beneficiaries of white privilege, lament involves the difficult task of acknowledging their personal and community complicity in past and present racial injustices."[92] Racial mercy helps me see that my release from captivity is an act of liberation, certainly for me but also for the people harmed by my refusal to be set free from my whiteness. Racial mercy is essential if we want to be grafted into movements for racial justice.

CHAPTER FOUR

MANUFACTURING

St. Charles Borromeo

IN 2019, the four hundredth anniversary of the arrival of enslaved Africans to the American colonies sparked a national examination of conscience. The arresting articles and podcasts curated by the 1619 Project in the *New York Times Magazine* simultaneously validated my desire to write this book and admonished me for being surprised at what I'd taken so long to discover.[1] I found myself wrestling with the significance of August 20, 1619, for Catholics in America. If, as contributors contended, that date was as significant to American history as July 4, 1776, then what's the equally disturbing analogue for November 8, 1960, when the first Catholic president was elected, which some hail as the most significant date in American Catholic history? Would it be sometime during August of 1513, when Spaniards first waded ashore in Florida, bringing genocide and enslavement in their wake? Or was it March of 1634 when a pair of ships sailed up the Chesapeake Bay with English Catholics on board who created a haven for Catholicism in Maryland and soon after that for slavery as well?

In the swirl of the summer of 2019—with kids in cages on the US–Mexico border, and the US Senate refusing to debate gun control legislation, and a hurricane tracing the route of slave ships across the Caribbean and bearing down, again, on islands populated by descendants of people brought there in bondage, all while a slate of Democratic presidential candidates put structural racism front and center in their campaigns—I reencountered the Reconstruction period as it was experienced by a few of my ancestors in Philadelphia. I quickly noticed what our eras shared: a bitterly divided and wounded nation, competing strategies for dealing with trauma, and a choice between making America great again by returning to the slavocracy status quo or becoming a greater America by addressing race-based structural inequalities.

I envy my people of that period—William and Mary O'Connell. He was the youngest of Maurice and Margaret's four sons, one of whom changed the family's surname to O'Connell, and she was the granddaughter of Andrew and Catherine Little. I envy them because they came of age in the ten-year window immediately following the Civil War, when Americans seemed to get behind the idea that racism was a traumatic and structural reality that had wounded everybody, and that structural change and healing was both necessary and possible. But I want to rail at my people too. In the thirty years that followed, William and Mary joined most white Americans in an about-face, reconciling with Southern whites by recommitting themselves to the anti-Blackness that had promised white progress since 1619. In his relatively shortly life of forty-seven years, William O'Connell lived through both moments. What he learned and how he practiced his citizenship and Catholicism in a parish in South Philadelphia surely impacts me on the brink of similar choices about the future in the summer of 2019.

TO RECONCILE OR RECONSTRUCT?

William O'Connell was born on April 12, 1864—exactly three-quarters of the way into the Civil War, a year and a day from its conclusion, which also means a year and three days before Lincoln's assassination. In other words, William came of age during what historian Carol Anderson calls a crossroads in America history "between its slaveholding past and the possibility of truly inclusive, vibrant democracy."[2] The path the nation chose was both familiar in its anti-Blackness and new in what it required of white Americans, particularly Catholics.

The aftermath of the war itself was staggering: more than 600,000 dead and 1.5 million casualties; widows seeking federal assistance from a welfare system unable to handle the deluge; more than a million disabled ex-soldiers adrift; and 20 percent of white Southern males "wiped off the face of the earth."[3] The nation's economy was crippled: 80 percent of gross national product in 1860 was tied to slavery. "By the eve of the Civil War, the Mississippi Valley was home to more millionaires per capita than anywhere else in the United States," explains sociologist Matt Desmond. "New Orleans boasted a denser concentration of banking capital than New York City."[4] Infrastructure—railroads and bridges—had been destroyed; fields lay fallow and barren.

While war did not harm the O'Connell men—Maurice was too old to enlist and William's oldest brother, John, was too young to serve—they surely knew less fortunate neighbors and likely contributed to the St. Agnes aid society to support families of soldiers and veterans. They also experienced the economic and political tumult even in idyllic West Chester. Occupations such as farming and small business ownership were being replaced by work in large factories, labor that did not always achieve the standard of living residents hoped it would.[5] This was already happening in West Chester given its close proximity to two steel towns—Coatesville and Phoenixville—which fueled the construction of railroads, the arteries of industrialization. Small industry came to West Chester along with the arrival of railroad lines. There was a planing mill, an agricultural machine shop, a massive brickyard, and the Sharpless Cream Separator Works. The hotel industry picked up to accommodate an uptick in visitors, including one for people of color run by a mixed-race citizen, Moses Hepburn Jr.[6] Black people made up roughly 10 percent of the Northern population and 8 percent of Chester County in the years immediately following the war.[7] Chester County historian Robert Bussell notes that figure was higher in West Chester itself both before and after the war; Black residents constituted 14 percent of the borough in 1850 and nearly 25 percent by the turn of the century.[8] Their presence sparked divisive political attitudes and determined party affiliations.

To the aftermath of war and industrialization was added the biggest disruption of all, one that brewed a national conundrum and a forced-choice exercise between reconciling or reconstructing that would shape most of William O'Connell's life: What to do about formerly enslaved Black people and their freedom? Even in the midst of the destruction of life and infrastructure, the end of the Civil War brought tremendous possibility for a national rebirth given the simple fact that the main binary that had shaped the American ethos was broken open, at least temporarily. The transition of four million formerly enslaved people into citizens splintered the dominant racial frame, which relied on certitude about Black inferiority and white superiority. For example, some Northern whites saw Black people as more deserving of and fitting for citizenship than their traitorous white

Southern counterparts, which created cracks in the edifice of white superiority. Disentangling skin color from freedom status, at least theoretically and temporarily, created what Reconstruction historian Edward Blum calls "another titanic struggle, not to save the nation but to determine who constitutes the 'nation' and who did not."[9] With familiar categories for making this determination negated, the Reconstruction period was an unparalleled moment in American history to move away from narrow racial frames that had shaped individual and collective self-understandings toward something more just, more equitable, and more humane.

But without the concept of white supremacy to orient a population traumatized by war, anxiety mounted as the country tried to figure out how to put the Union back together with emancipated Black people in the mix. This kicked up the debates that led up to the war in the first place: to either save the Union or to make it more perfect by ending slavery. Those passionate about the former prioritized reconciliation between Northern and Southern whites. Those who fought the war to end slavery wanted to reconstruct the country's economic and social systems to ensure the freedom of newly emancipated people.

The choice between reconciling or reconstructing—between smoothing things over in the name of social order and stability or further upending that social order to right a deeply embedded wrong—was a profoundly religious question. The nation was already wading into its Christian theological traditions to both make sense of tremendous suffering and discern a path forward. Lincoln himself set that theological tone, noting in his second inaugural address, shortly before his assassination, that God wanted the offense of slavery removed one way or the other and if God willed it so, it would continue "until all of the wealth piled by the bondman's two hundred and fifty years of unrequited toil shall be sunk, and until every drop of blood drawn with the lash, shall be paid by another's drawn with the sword." He also wished that this necessary atonement would be followed by healing: binding of wounds, caring for veterans, tending to widows and orphans to "achieve and cherish a just and lasting peace among ourselves."[10]

Frederick Douglass on the other hand, who had stumped in West Chester just a few years earlier to recruit Black soldiers for the Union Army, named the real choice that the end of the war presented. "The thing worse than rebellion is the thing that causes rebellion," he wrote in *The Atlantic Monthly* in December of 1866. "What that thing is, we have been taught to our cost. It remains now to be seen whether we have the needed courage to have that cause entirely removed from the Republic."[11]

These American icons point to two critical dimensions of a path toward healing and justice: acknowledging trauma, both personal and collective, and resolving to identify and fix trauma's root causes. Given what I had already learned about American white Catholics, especially those in West Chester, I wondered where they stood on the reconcile–reconstruct continuum and if they were ready to walk that path to which Lincoln and Douglass pointed. Once again, I learned that the Catholic hierarchy had been planning for this post-war crossroads since before the war began. Their answer formed the O'Connells of the Reconstruction era and subsequent generations when it came to redressing the trauma of racialized inequality and violence.

UNITY THROUGH UNIFORMITY

In March of 1866, Bishop Martin John Spalding of Baltimore sent out an invitation to his brother bishops for a plenary meeting, only the second of its kind in the country's history. Pius IX had written to them that the "welfare of the emancipated Negroes was 'of the utmost necessity'" and several acknowledged as much, recognizing they may have missed an opportunity for evangelization.[12] It had been fourteen years since their last gathering. During those tumultuous intervening years, the Catholic hierarchy in the US had practiced what I can only describe as a head in the sand strategy. The long-term survival of the institutional Church, with Catholics and Catholic infrastructure on both sides of the Mason-Dixon line, was their primary goal. The Church "tolerated disunity in political matters so that it could concentrate on achieving ethnic unity in religious ones," summed up historian Randall Miller.[13] Moreover, many Catholic bishops saw the Civil War as a way to combat anti-Catholicism, which they perceived as the biggest threat to Catholic well-being. The war interrupted nativist violence and also fractured many Protestant denominations. What's more, Catholic loyalty could hardly have been questioned in light of what an early historian of Catholics and the Civil War called "the singular spectacle of Catholics in the front ranks for Federal and Confederate armies, with their respective spiritual leaders, priests and bishops, encouraging them in what all believed to be their duty."[14]

Spalding summoned his nearly fifty brother bishops to Baltimore with a number of purposes: to "present to the country and the world a striking proof of the strong unity with which [Catholics] are knit together"; to bring the "collective wisdom of the Church in this country" to the task of determining "what measures should be adopted in order to meet the new phase of national life which the end of the war had just inaugurated"; and to "discuss the future status of the negro."[15] The urgency of that last matter was both corporeal and spiritual: "Four millions of these unfortunate being are thrown on our charity," Spalding wrote to his brother bishops, "and they silently but eloquently appeal to us for help."[16]

Having studied my fair share of bishops' statements, I scoured the Pastoral Letter of 1866 expecting to perhaps find early roots of American Catholic social teaching that tried to apply Catholicism to the lived reality of the day. After all, this was the first document after the most traumatic experience in American history. How would the bishops face the horrors of the war? Did Lincoln's call for atonement resonate? Would they follow Douglass's advice that "the right of the negro is the true solution of our national troubles"?[17] Certainly there was ample evidence of Protestant denominations that did both.[18] I had high hopes for finding language of atonement, healing and reconciliation, or even redemption. What I found instead was an approach to trauma that I can recognize as distinctively Catholic in light of subsequent Catholic responses to national traumas around race since, including my own.

First, the bishops ignored the past. Never once did they directly mention the Civil War—its causes, horrors, or aftermath. It was as if it had never happened, as if tens of thousands of Catholic lives had not been lost on both sides. Then, it took them a full eleven sections of discussing their ecclesial authority, the relationship between the Church and the state, and day-to-day matters pertaining to priests and the laity, before they turned their attention to the "emancipation of the immense slave population of the South."[19] Picnics, excursions, and fairs received a more direct condemnation for the ways in which such activities "cover up a multitude of sins in the name of charity" than the conditions in which newly freed people found themselves in 1866.[20] In the two short paragraphs in which they did address what they called "the sudden liberation of so large a multitude, with their peculiar dispositions and habits," the bishops appealed to "Christian charity and zeal."[21]

In these two short paragraphs, the bishops otherized rather than empathized, degraded rather than advocated, drew back rather than pulled close. While the majority of Northern Christians and Black people themselves considered newly emancipated people ideal American citizens (compared to the Confederates) in their willingness to serve the country and their desire for work, the US bishops did the opposite. The bishops managed to call freed people slaves; they complained that their emancipation had not been more gradual; they questioned their ability to use their newly found freedom; they made them targets of charitable education, particularly in the area of moral restraint "which they so much stand in need of"; and, invoking fears of anti-Catholicism, they played the victim card by bemoaning limits imposed on Catholic education that might impede evangelizing efforts.[22]

Second, the bishops put the well-being of the institutional Church above that of suffering people who were not Catholic—at least not yet. Under Spalding's leadership, the bishops subsumed the "future status of the negro"—the most pressing political, economic, cultural, and religious question of the day—into the "golden opportunity to reap a harvest of souls" in the "new and most extensive field of charity and devotedness" that emancipation "opened to us."[23] And they did so precisely—and intentionally—at a time when the Protestants were caught scrambling to reassemble their denominations in the wake of the war. Paired with adherence to a set of decrees to promote doctrinal and ritual unity among American Catholics, the bishops were confident that bringing these newly emancipated Black souls into the Catholic fold before they could be lured into Protestant churches would ensure the primacy of the Church in America.

Third, they implied that diversity—even among an ethnically diverse and yet increasingly culturally homogenous American Catholic Church—opened a dangerous door to deviation from normative frameworks of understanding and and ways of relating. I was struck by the symbolism of their decision to end the document with a call "to enact such decrees as will tend to promote uniformity of discipline and practice among us."[24] Uniformity—not unity, or reunion, or reconciliation, and certainly not reconstruction—was the path to Catholic primacy.

Ultimately, when it came to facing the trauma of war and alternative ways forward, the Church opted to keep battling for its own supremacy in the American Christian landscape rather than do their part to further decenter white supremacy. For example, the bishops could have required

Confederate Catholics to atone for the sin of slavery rather than simply ask for their conformity to doctrine and ritual. They could have advocated for the full humanity of newly emancipated Black people rather than simply edge out Protestants in the race to convert them. They could have bolstered Christian calls for America to embody more fully its promises of liberty and justice for all, or Lincoln's call for a just and lasting peace through binding wounds—both of which might have extended the life of the movement for reconstruction. But the Church chose institutional advancement instead, or what I was coming to recognize as a preferential option for the institutional Church. The Catholic bishops prioritized converting Black souls rather than reconstructing conditions that continued to oppress their bodies. They prioritized reuniting Union and Confederate Catholics by continuing to manufacture a defensive posture against Protestant discrimination and insisting on doctrinal orthodoxy rather than engaging in the hard work of truly reconciling a deeply wounded nation. The American Church defiantly declared its authority over the people of its flock rather than humbly standing with them in calling for atonement.

SO WHAT DID WILLIAM AND MARY O'CONNELL learn during this traumatic period when they came of age? Listen, do not speak; accept, do not challenge; follow, do not seek to lead; keep your head down, do not ask questions. I have no way of knowing whether this suited them. Even if it didn't, William could work it out on the job, which was how most white American Catholics dealt with the trauma of it all. Historian Heather Cox Richardson discovered a perspective from the *Philadelphia Inquirer* shortly after the war indicating that Northerners desired "a reunion of the people North and South—a reunion of hearts and a reunion of hands" to build "the prosperity of our people and the glory and honor of our common country."[25] But it was shifts in Northern white attitudes about Black laborers—from the industrious ideal to the welfare-usurping antithesis—that she identifies as one of the main causes of the death of Reconstruction.[26]

WILLIAM O'CONNELL IN THE MANUFACTURING WORKSHOP OF THE WORLD

Aside from being the youngest of Maurice and Margaret O'Connell's four sons, I don't know too much about my great-grandfather William. The

1880 census reported that he was "at school," and Maurice deceased. In 1888, William married Mary Emily Carroll—granddaughter of Andrew and Catherine Little, also from St. Agnes in West Chester—in St. Charles Borromeo Parish in South Philadelphia. I can only conjecture how the two of them migrated there and shrugged off expectations that they be married in St. Agnes, especially since upon their deaths undertakers shipped their bodies back there by train for burial. But I suspect the pull of Philadelphia's industrializing economy had something to do with it. It was the Workshop of the World by the time they arrived.

Philadelphia boasted a strong economy for most of the nineteenth century. From the start it was a port for agricultural products grown in the verdant farmland of surrounding counties and across the Delaware River in New Jersey. In the mid-1800s it became the heart of the nation's growing railroad industry, linking the anthracite coal found in Pennsylvania's northeastern counties with foundries and steel mills whose smokestacks spiked above neighborhoods across the landscape.[27] The Civil War acted as a "great stimulant when it came to manufacturing everything from cigars, dental implants, cutlery, rugs, and Stetson hats. Manufacturing plants grew from 600 in 1840 to 6,467 in 1860 to 8,262 in 1870."[28] By the turn of the century, Philadelphia was the largest producer of wool, silk, and cotton textiles in the world.[29]

William O'Connell exemplified the typical Philadelphia worker in a number of ways. First, as a molder or metalworker —a skill he identified in the earliest census of his adult years that I could find—William was part of the groundswell of industrial workers who, in 1880, outnumbered agricultural workers for the first time in the nation's history. As such, he and Mary joined a generational migration of young people from small family farms to big cities or land in the West, much to the dismay of their parents who clung to the American ideal of work that provided economic and political stability: close to the land, close to family, and close to the means of production.[30] Moreover, William's trade was in demand in Philadelphia, since metalworking was at the heart of the industrial boom.

I suspect young William first honed his craft at the Hoopes Brothers and Darlington Wheel Works, owned and operated by the same family who employed his father and older brothers in the nursery. I am not sure why he went into molding rather than agricultural work, especially since his older brother, Andrew, had plans to open his own nursery one day. Maybe there was no more room on the crews for another O'Connell, or maybe William wanted to go his own way. Regardless, the Wheel Works was more than a safe bet. Shortly after opening in 1867, it quickly became one of the country's leading manufacturers of wheels. William likely served his time in more labor-intensive positions like stoking furnaces, shoveling ore, and carrying ingots before moving into a management position in one of the ten iron factories located throughout Philadelphia. His southwest Philadelphia neighborhood in St. Charles Borromeo Parish was just blocks from Washington Avenue, a hub for metalworkers. I was astonished by the variety of goods flowing out of South Philadelphia when the O'Connells moved there: wallpaper, gas lamps, metal beds, furniture, sash doors and blinds, barrels, sewing machines, wagons and coaches.[31]

William's eventual seniority by the 1890s—in work experience and citizenship status—gave him a leg up in the tumultuous labor scene in Philadelphia. The Reconstruction period in Philadelphia saw an influx of European immigrants as well as Southern Black migrants who competed for unskilled labor with the same levels of violent competition that many experienced in the places they had left. As second-generation Irish, William was part of a growing class of professional workers—clerks, bookkeepers, plumbers, grocers, and policemen—in occupational roles that neither their parents nor the newer arrivals from Europe could have imagined. Even though only a few may have owned their own businesses or factories by the 1870s, "they had begun the process of penetrating [Philadelphia's] economic structure" in niches in the marketplace that promised security for them and that could be handed on to their children.[32]

Cox Richardson helps me understand how Philadelphia was in the midst of changing attitudes about Black people, particularly the Black worker, when William arrived. In the years immediately following the Civil War, most Northerners considered Black laborers the ideal, especially compared to Confederate traitors who remained noncompliant even after the war. Black people were hardworking, committed patriots, eager to take up the task of restoring the economy. West Chester newspapers paid a variety of tributes to newly freed citizens throughout the 1880s, reporting on their harrowing experiences as enslaved workers in the Deep South. But by the time William was fully ensconced in the Philadelphia labor scene at the turn of the century, Black people were depicted in a dramatically different light. They were described as easily manipulated and therefore a threat to political stability, as well as lazy, shiftless, idle clamorers for government handouts. In 1904, William's hometown paper in West Chester bemoaned that "the old type of negro" known for their humor, kindness to children, and "semi-industrious ways" were "passing away" and presumably replaced by those who "steal" and "make a living by begging."[33] Why the change?

William and Mary marinated in the emerging dynamic in American culture that created a tie between racial identity and the kind of work one did. If whites were no longer the definitively free race, then something other than slavery needed to be the foil for whiteness. Whites clung to certain forms of work to stay on top of Black people as the racial hierarchy, briefly interrupted by the ten years immediately following the war, got reinscribed. "No longer did [the color line] coincide with the distinction between freedom and slavery," explains historian Ignatiev. "It now came to correspond to the distinction between free, wage labor and unfree, semi-feudal labor, and between those who had access to political power and those who did not."[34] As a free laborer, William was better positioned than new immigrants or Black laborers to determine the variables related to the work he did: his employer, pay, hours, conditions. He could get honorable work, empowering work.

However, it was only of value if others could be kept out. In short, wherever and however William labored in South Philadelphia, his work reflected the primary way of redrawing the color line in the decades immediately following the war. The abolition of slavery had blurred it temporarily by eliminating the lack of freedom as a permanent marker of Blackness, but labor redrew it—manufactured it, if you will—by connecting race with forms of work. If enslaved work was unfree work and associated with Black people, then free Black people were still associated with unpaid or low-paying work. Therefore, workplaces became spaces where racial identities were both shaped and contested, especially in industrializing places like Philadelphia, where free Black people had already been laboring for generations and refugees from the emerging violence of Jim Crow were arriving every day.

Catholics make a big to-do about Catholic social teaching, officially inaugurated in 1891 with Pope Leo XIII's encyclical *Rerum Novarum* on the dignity of work. Certainly it is a document worth touting. Through it, the Church faced outward, demonstrated concern for more than just its own members, and articulated the framework for what would become a robust Catholic tradition on human rights. In all of my scholarly engagement with this document as a Catholic social ethicist, I always envisioned the Pope advocating for the newly industrialized European worker—English or German or French—toiling in factories in Manchester or Berlin or Paris. Why is it that I never considered workers in Philadelphia, my own family members? If William even heard excerpts of this social teaching, how did he square the Pope's words about the right to work, to a wage that could sustain a family, to form unions, with the discriminatory practices he certainly witnessed if not enforced? More to the point, why were my imaginary laborers never Black? Who did the US bishops and priests envision when they read that document, especially in light of a conclusion that William Edward Burghardt Du Bois, a pioneer in American sociology, would shortly come to about workers in Philadelphia?

WILLIAM DU BOIS IN THE 7TH WARD

At the same time my great-grandfather William encountered all of this in the 30th Ward, another William just four years younger than he also arrived in South Philadelphia, with the hope of making a name for himself as a sociologist. Yet again, I am struck by the geographical proximity of one of my ancestors and a famous Black American, and by my William's proximity to his counterpart's observations about the structural cause of "the Negro problem" in Philadelphia: no access to meaningful work.

As the first Black person to earn a PhD from Harvard University, W. E. B. Du Bois struck a group of white social reformers in Philadelphia as an ideal person to "investigate the Negro problem" in the city to develop what they hoped would be effective solutions to it. "Ostensibly [they were] very interested in the plight of the Philadelphia Negro," explains sociologist Elijah Anderson, but Du Bois sensed deeper motivations, which he laid bare in his autobiography: "The city was 'going to the dogs' because of the crime and venality of its Negro citizens."[35] Du Bois accepted the position, since in his estimation, "after the war and emancipation, great hopes were entertained by the Negroes for rapid advancement, and nowhere did they seem better founded than Philadelphia."[36] Moreover, the gig came with an affiliation with the University of Pennsylvania—although not a faculty position, a racist snub to be sure.

Du Bois agreed to study Philadelphia's 7th Ward, home to one-third of the city's Black population, who constituted roughly 4 percent of its one million people. The 45,000 inhabitants of this "city within a city" were not entirely Black nor entirely assimilated into American culture. "And yet," Du Bois wrote at the outset of his landmark study, published in 1899, "in the case of the Negroes the segregation is more conspicuous, more patent to the eye, and so intertwined with a long historic evolution, with peculiarly pressing social problems of poverty, ignorance, crime, and labor, that the Negro problem far surpasses in scientific interest and social gravity most of the other race or class questions."[37]

Reading my family history through the lens of Du Bois's *The Philadelphia Negro* reveals my familial entanglements in anti-Black dynamics at a historical moment that determined the economic trajectories of white and Black Philadelphians for generations. William, the Black researcher of Black life in Philadelphia, laid bare the negative impact that William, the white worker, had on Black people in Philadelphia. "The slave went free; stood a brief moment in the sun; then moved back again towards slavery," Du Bois wrote later, certainly reflecting on the data he gathered in Philadelphia.[38] Looking at his evidence, I am faced with the fact that it wasn't so much that Blacks *moved* back toward conditions of unfreedom; rather, they were *pushed away* from freedom. And not just by Southerners with their segregating Jim Crow laws and vigilante lynchings, but also by white Americans in Northern cities—Americans like William and Mary O'Connell—motivated by what American social historian Jacqueline Jones calls a fear that "whatever enhanced the opportunities of black workers must limit the opportunities of white workers."[39]

First, Du Bois makes clear to me that William was likely aware of if not actively engaged in manufacturing anti-Blackness in the workplace, which Du Bois identified as the root cause of the host of problems facing Black citizens in Philadelphia. "Every one knows that in a city like Philadelphia a Negro does not have the same chance to exercise his ability or secure work according to his talents as a white man," Du Bois noted.[40] Perhaps for William O'Connell this played out in the context of a network of relationships that he tapped into when he moved to Philadelphia for work—whites looking to hire other whites like him, whether in entry-level or management positions, rather than equally or more qualified Black workers. Du Bois noted that native Black workers did not have similar networks in industries across the city, since at critical points in Philadelphia's history whites had pushed them out of the viable positions they held—whether as artisans, dockworkers, or machinists. Instead, they worked menial service jobs that were less dependable and reinscribed an association between Blackness and servitude in the minds of white Philadelphians.

Also, while I am not certain which Southwest Philadelphia foundry employed William, Du Bois's work assures me that it is unlikely he worked with Black laborers, since "the carpenters, masons, painters, iron-workers, etc., [had] succeeded in keeping out nearly all Negro workmen by simply declining to work with non-union men and refusing to let colored men join the union."[41] Even if not unionized, William may have watched managers bring Black workers in on a temporary basis to increase competition among newly immigrated white workers. Either way, Du Bois revealed evidence of whites gatekeeping industrial work as well as its devastating impact on Black Philadelphians and negative side effects for workers like William who refused to challenge the color line. "In other words," explains Du Bois, "one of the great postulates of the science of economics—that men will seek their economic advantage—is in this case untrue because in many cases men will not do this if it involves association, even in a casual and business way, with Negroes."[42] Despite a booming industrial economy, Black laborers comprised only 10 percent of the industrial workforce.[43] Du Bois concluded that "[Blacks'] economic rise is not only hindered by present poverty, but also by a widespread inclination to shut against them many doors of advancement open to the talented and efficient of other races."[44]

Through interviews and conversations with more than five thousand residents of the 7th Ward, Du Bois documented the ripple effect of this shutout. There was the psychological toll on the workers themselves. "When one group of people suffer all these little differences of treatment and discriminations and insults continually, the result is either discouragement, or bitterness, or over-sensitiveness, or recklessness," he observed.[45] Lack of viable work and wages strained families too. Black families were relegated to substandard housing that was often more expensive, so many took on boarders to defray costs, leading to precarious overcrowding. Low wages also separated families. Black women frequently lived away from the home in domestic service in white households in more affluent neighborhoods, while Black men performed sporadic day labor in and around the 7th Ward, and children remained with grandparents somewhere in Virginia or Maryland. Finally, he noticed the communal impact of lack of meaningful work: higher rates of death and disease among Black residents of the 7th Ward and higher rates of criminal activity. In an article summarizing his key findings, Du Bois claimed that Black Philadelphians "do not share the full national life because there has always existed in America a conviction—varying in intensity, but always widespread—that people of Negro blood should not be admitted to the group life of the nation no matter what their condition might be."[46]

I'd like to think that evidence of the "Negro problem" would have only been apparent to a specialist like Du Bois, but I know that William, Mary, and their children saw these inequalities too. The O'Connells lived in close proximity to Black people dealing with the fallout of anti-Blackness in the workplace. Unlike other cities that concentrated industry in particular quadrants, manufacturing plants and foundries were scattered across Philadelphia, which meant that Philadelphia was a walking city. Moreover, as access to work in those factories ebbed and flowed with the tides of immigrant arrivals, Philadelphia's neighborhoods were defined by clusters of ethnic groups on a block-by-block basis, including African Americans. In this era, the O'Connells bumped into racial and ethnic difference on a far more regular basis than did any members of my family in any generation that followed.

Because my family was so close to the economic precariousness of Blackness, their proximity may have reinforced their participation in pushing Black people back into the unfreedoms that persisted after slavery ended. Du Bois warned that Northern whites' refusals to accept that Black disadvantages in work—what he saw as the catalyst for similar disadvantages in housing, in crime, in health—were a detriment to *everyone* in Philadelphia would come at their own expense. "Such discrimination is morally wrong, politically dangerous, industrially wasteful, and socially silly," he concluded. "It is the duty of whites to stop it, and to do so primarily for their own sakes. Industrial freedom of opportunity has by long experiences proven to be generally best for all."[47]

Given that whites seemed only too willing to compromise their own financial well-being by denying Blacks entry to the workforce, Du Bois was convinced that something else compensated them for that sacrifice. While it took him thirty years to name this dynamic in his book *Black Reconstruction*, and even though he primarily studied Southern workers in doing so, I suspect Du Bois picked up hints of what he later called a "public and psychological wage" during his time in Philadelphia's 7th Ward. To this mind, this wage of whiteness drove "such a wedge" between "white and black workers" that "there are probably not today in the world two groups of workers with practically identical interests who hate and fear each other so deeply and persistently and who are kept so far apart that neither sees anything of common interest."[48] In short, despite the stress and tumult of a changing economy, whites could find some respite from their own anxieties about downward mobility in the fact that they were not Black. Du Bois noted that a social deference afforded to whites, regardless of their economic status, compensated for the economic losses they experienced in racially segregated workplaces.

I wondered which psychological wages of whiteness the O'Connells cashed in on. Key points in Du Bois's longer description of the payoffs of whiteness made that clearer. For example, people like William and Margaret were "admitted freely with all classes of white people to public functions, public parks, and the best schools."[49] Their schools were always located in optimal places and invested "twice to ten times as much per capita as the colored schools."[50] The growing city police force "were drawn from their ranks."[51] Had the need arisen, the O'Connells would have received lenient treatment at the hands of courts, since judges needed their votes to get appointed. They could read news that "flattered" people like them in the newspapers and only come across Black people in stories about "crime and ridicule."[52]

Long before the term *white privilege* became common parlance, Du Bois identified the privileges that flowed back onto white people when they exercised their power to maintain predominantly white institutions, neighborhoods, and workplaces. The catch? They could only cash in on those privileges as long as Black people couldn't access them, as long as Black people were denied both assimilation to whiteness and social advancement on their own terms. Regardless of what they might lose in the midst of economic uncertainty or even in the face of threats of downward mobility, historian David Roediger notes that doubling down on racial divisions ensured that white people "could never lose their whiteness."[53]

Unexpectedly, Du Bois also helped me discover the other source of the O'Connells' public and psychological wage of whiteness—the spiritual wages of white Catholicism doled out by their parish in South Philadelphia.

ST. CHARLES BORROMEO: THE SPIRITUAL WAGES OF WHITE CATHOLICISM

The diocese of Philadelphia became an archdiocese in 1875 and among James Wood's top priority as Philadelphia's first archbishop involved manufacturing parishes—in his case, out of increasingly dense and ethnically distinct neighborhoods. He took his job seriously. Before his death in 1883, Wood had completed construction on Philadelphia's Cathedral Basilica of Saints Peter and Paul, as well as a new seminary on more than 130 acres at the base of what would become Philadelphia's Main Line. Even with the separation from what became the Delaware and Scranton dioceses in 1868, he still oversaw 76 parishes, 42 schools, and 200,000 souls. My exploration of two parishes that Wood helped make in South Philadelphia—St. Charles Borromeo and St. Peter Claver—reveal that the power to draw parish boundary lines also involved the power to make the people within them.[54] This boundary-making power was the wellspring of the spiritual wages of white Catholicism, by which I mean the psychological benefits white Catholics received—then and now—in a racialized Catholic Church.

Wood purchased the acreage for St. Charles Borromeo Parish in 1866, at the outset of Reconstruction, and opened the parish two years later. He dedicated it in the summer of 1876 as the nation celebrated its centennial. St. Charles Borromeo was the third largest of the 131 parishes in the archdiocese and was called the Cathedral of the South. It was a parish befitting the Workshop of the World and US bishops' preoccupation during the period immediately following Reconstruction. "The right-minded American nowhere finds himself more at home than in the Catholic Church," they declared, almost defensively, at the outset of their third plenary council document in 1884.[55] They claimed that being American required embracing "individual rights and popular liberties."[56] Although they didn't explicitly map out how those rights and liberties applied to Black people, beyond "Christian instruction and missionary labor," the bishops provided a familiar formula that demonstrated the alignment of American values with those of the Church. "The spirit of American freedom is not one of anarchy or license," the American hierarchy cautioned in 1884. "It essentially involves love of order, respect for rightful authority, and obedience to just laws."[57] What better place to work out an obedient, orderly, and subservient approach to rights and liberties—particularly in increasingly ethnically and racially mixed urban places—than the Catholic parish?

Despite St. Charles Borromeo's Italian namesake and interior architectural style, Archbishop Wood founded it for the city's growing Irish population in the southwest. According to a parish souvenir history book, this "Irish 'ghetto,' was not an area for newly arrived immigrants, but rather home to a more stable segment of the immigrant population who had achieved a moderate degree of success."[58] The Irish in the southwest pockets of the city tended to be both native born and skilled craftspeople, drawn to the sector's abundant factory work. William O'Connell fit that bill when he and Mary, a daughter of a successful hotelier, arrived at some point in the late 1880s. They were lace curtain rather than shanty Irish, as they say, when they married there in 1888. The local census records for 1890 aren't extant, and the archdiocese didn't have extensive materials for St. Charles Borromeo in its archival collection, so I can only speculate about William and Mary's life somewhere in and around 19th and Christian Streets. "The community they were joining was stable," one parish history assured me. "The neighborhood was safe and convenient to work; and the local parish was pre-eminent in the diocese."[59] If they owned their home, it is likely they bought it "on trust" for about $1,000 with the help of burgeoning homeowners' loan corporations. "Block after block of brick row houses was built in St. Charles Borromeo's neighborhood in the 1870s and 1880s, filling the need for supply of cheap, concentrated housing for workers in the nearby industries."[60]

The O'Connells reaped the benefits of the interplay of two kinds of boundaries in St. Charles Borromeo: symbolic and social. Symbolic boundaries are "conceptual distinctions made by social actors to categorize objects, people, practices, and even time and space."[61] In the case of St. Charles Borromeo, the archbishop drew the parish's boundaries according to ethnicity and class. I'm struck, for example, by the way the newly arrived O'Connells met the description of the typical parishioner at St. Charles Borromeo: native to America, Irish, a cohesive family unit orbiting a skilled wage earner, and relatively affluent. Rituals, parish and liturgical calendars, nods to a shared Irish heritage, and reverence for their Irish pastor inculcated in the O'Connells a sense of communal identity bound by a shared religious framework that gave their lives meaning and purpose.

Symbolic boundaries generated group membership and identity, especially in the midst of Philadelphia's increasing cultural diversity and in opposition to its Protestant elites. They also incubated social capital or relational goods like networks of acquaintances and access to employment opportunities or people of influence. In particular, the O'Connells experienced "bonding social capital," since most parish networks were inward facing and focused on helping those in the parish get by, initially in an overtly hostile Protestant climate and later in an alien industrializing American economy.[62]

However, it appears that parishioners weren't entirely ready to extend that bonding social capital to Black Catholics in South Philadelphia. A parish history made note of the 1,789 Black people tallied in the 30th Ward during the 1890 census, mostly "clustered at the northern edge" of the parish along Bainbridge Street.[63] This preoccupation with the number of Black residents points to the parish's *social* boundary, a physical manifestation of the ways social goods were distributed between in- and out-groups. White Catholics had long shared a sense that certain goods were limited, such as freedom of religious expression, housing, schooling, connections for employment, and public safety, especially during anti-Catholic and anti-immigrant periods in Philadelphia's history. These goods needed to be protected, particularly from Blacks citizens, who had been reconceptualized as a drain on the nation, as liabilities. Although usually invisible, the social boundaries of St. Charles Borromeo Parish were determined by the parish's actual territorial boundary of Bainbridge Street, which served as "the dividing line between white and black residents."[64]

It's unclear to me whether the archdiocese's plan for Black Catholics eased or heightened white perceptions of Black threats to material and immaterial communal goods. Just five years after the O'Connells married in St. Charles Borromeo in 1888—and only ten blocks to the northeast— Wood's successor, Patrick Ryan, approved Philadelphia's first Black parish. It struck me as notable that he didn't found or fund the parish; he simply gave permission for others to do so. For all of the parish-making happening everywhere else in the latter half of the nineteenth century, anti-Blackness ensured that despite the presence of African Americans in parishes across South and even North Philadelphia during the Post-Reconstruction period, the "one Catholic Church in the City designed especially for Negro work," to use Du Bois's description in *The Philadelphia Negro*, happened to get planted in the 7th Ward.[65] The future of St. Peter Claver, what would become the mother church of Black Catholics in Philadelphia in the coming century, was determined by Catholic anti-Blackness in the previous one.

White Catholics had sidelined Black Catholics since before the Revolutionary War when, according to Philadelphia archivist Stephanie Morris, "they worshipped in Catholic churches as whites did," in Philadelphia's earliest parishes like St. Joseph's or Holy Trinity or St. Augustine's. "But not with them," she qualifies.[66] Black Catholics were not given seats in the pews and were forced to the back of Communion lines. If, like their newly arriving European counterparts, they sought pastoral support to meet their particular liturgical needs, they were entirely dependent upon the whims or availability of already overtaxed diocesan priests. Few of these white priests had experience with or a taste for Black Catholicism. Black Catholics could rely on white religious orders with emerging commitments to marginalized Catholics, but these orders operated without the institutional support of the archdiocese. When funds ran out or congregational priorities changed, religious orders were forced to pull out.

For example, the seeds of St. Peter Claver were first planted in 1863 as a school for Black Catholic children, who were not any more welcomed in Catholic schools than they were in public ones. Wood opened the school at 4th and Lombard Streets and outsourced the work (with little if any financial assistance) to the Oblate Sisters of Providence, the nation's first Black order of religious sisters, who were headquartered in Baltimore. Not only were the Sisters dependent on fundraising from the Motherhouse, but they also endured public insults from white Philadelphians. The Oblate Sisters later closed St. Peter Claver School in 1871. Between 1878 and 1882, the School Sisters of Notre Dame made two failed attempts at catechetical instruction for African American girls in homes along Lombard Street.

Eventually, in 1886, Black Catholic parents affiliated with St. Mary's Church in what is now Philadelphia's Old City petitioned the pastor to open a school for their children. Philadelphia heiress Catherine Drexel (who later changed her name to Katharine), on her way to discerning a vocation as a vowed religious, used her largesse to purchase a 4-story house on the corner of 9th and Lombard for the school, and soon a chapel, rectory, and parish offices.[67] In that same year, the pastor of another of the city's oldest parishes, Holy Trinity, "invited" Black Catholics to form the St. Peter Claver Union. The group met in people's houses to pray for a few years before petitioning Wood's successor, Patrick Ryan, for a permanent home. Claiming he had no priests for the work, Ryan stalled. He put out a call to the Holy Ghost Fathers, who had built a reputation ministering to Black Catholics in Pittsburgh. They responded positively in 1889. Ms. Drexel funded the operation at 832 Pine Street. The school, a refuge from the anti-Blackness in Philadelphia's public and private schools, eventually gave birth to the parish, which likewise became a refuge from Catholic anti-Blackness in parishes across the city. At some point in the early 1890s, Drexel supplemented a bequest by an Irish Catholic named Patrick Quinn so that the Peter Claver Union could purchase the Fourth Presbyterian Church at 12th and Lombard, in the heart of Du Bois's 7th Ward. What was once a Union became a parish. It was distinct not only for its Blackness but also for the fact that it wasn't the geographical boundaries that contained its people but rather their Blackness. The determining factor for membership was Parishioners' addresses but their skin color.[68]

The Black Catholic experience of parish boundaries in St. Peter Claver was quite different from that of their white counterparts. First, the parish itself really didn't have boundary lines, other than the social boundaries of every other parish around the archdiocese that relied on racial difference to deny Black Catholics the social capital their white counterparts took for granted. Certainly the parish provided much-needed bonding capital among Black Catholics—a chance to build relationships, to experience Catholic ritual collectively if not necessarily in a culturally distinct way, a decent and affordable education for their children. It enabled them to experience linking capital as well, as St. Peter Claver became enmeshed in the social fabric of the 7th Ward, which would become an incubator for Black culture, entrepreneurship, and leadership. By the 1930s, Black residents were the majority in the 30th Ward in part because of its proximity to the 7th: "Here, along South and Lombard Streets, [Black residents] patronized butchers and produce markets which sold familiar Southern food, clothing stores and barber shops that catered to their needs, and theaters, restaurants, and nightclubs that featured black performers."[69] And yet because they were segregated in everything—liturgy, schooling, and even housing—adding a Catholic parish to the social goods that the 7th Ward had to offer helped to contain Black people and, to some extent, Black Catholicism there too.

To my mind, it was the dividends of social capital generated within tightly regulated parish boundaries that generated the spiritual wages of white Catholicism, or the privileges awarded by the Church to white Catholics simply for being "not-Black." For example, practicing their faith in a uniform and ready-made spiritual context instilled in my ancestors a sense that their experience was normative and therefore uncontestable. As a result, they experienced little cognitive dissonance or challenges to the assumptions they had about God, themselves, or other people. The grandeur of St. Charles Borromeo alone reflected their self-understanding as upwardly mobile American Catholics. Since they could see themselves in the priests, statues of saints, depictions of the life of Christ in St. Charles

Borromeo's frescoes, William and Mary O'Connell could also see themselves in the Divine. That brought significant assurance, particularly to a
family like mine navigating a new urban context. Moreover, it protected
them against disquieting thoughts about the treatment of others, since not
seeing people who were different from you in your sacred space—in the
pews, on the altar, or depicted in statues or art—suggests that those other
people were somehow less like the Divine and maybe even less human in
some way. Moreover, the ecclesial resources so readily available to white
Catholics—the purchase of land and start-up cash, a steady flow of priests
to run the parish and nuns to run for the elementary schools, access to the
archbishop, pathways to the high school—surely became goods to which
white Catholics assumed they were entitled. Surely they experienced a
sense of mutual trust with the Church hierarchy, who made their upward
mobility a priority. In other words, white Catholics could operate with a
sense that there was something so inherently deserving about them that
such resources were available to them and not to Black Catholics, who had
to agitate to have their basic sacramental and educational needs met. One
group had to be more worthy.

Perhaps most significantly, white Catholics experienced bridging capital across closely regulated parish boundaries, including those that defined the national parishes—parishes that initially served other than Irish
immigrant groups. *Bridging capital* refers to networks of relationships or
connections that enable people to cross boundaries that might otherwise
contain them and to get ahead through relationships of exchange outside
the normal in-group. For example, during William and Mary O'Connell's
lives, the staunch boundaries between Italian, German, and Polish parishes became porous as those communities assimilated into Irish American Catholic whiteness. This established fruitful connections and access
opportunities in employment or education.

But Black Catholics remained contained in the national parish designated specifically for them. By World War I, St. Peter Claver had grown
to a network of six such Black parishes across the archdiocese. Although
Catholics were not officially proscribed from worshipping in each other's
churches, anti-Blackness ensured that only white Catholics really did so,
revealing yet another spiritual wage of white Catholicism: a sense of belonging anywhere in the archdiocese. For example, the O'Connells were
not contained in St. Charles Borromeo, since my grandfather, Maurice,
the eighth of William and Mary's nine children, was baptized in 1906 in

St. Agatha Parish in the affluent "Cork City" neighborhood of West Philadelphia. White parishioners' ability to belong anywhere was amplified by the fact that Black Catholics were not. Where the parish boundaries of St. Charles Borromeo created a chrysalis of social mobility that metamorphized into generational wealth, those of St. Peter Claver contained Blackness in specific parishes in the archdiocese, in which generational inequity gradually metastasized as federal, municipal, and ecclesial resources were reallocated to whiter neighborhoods and parishes by the middle of the century.

These spiritual wages of whiteness were gratifying enough to incentivize white Catholics to prefer the pre-Reconstruction racialized status quo so familiar to Philadelphia—and the nation—rather than participate in the more difficult task of transforming institutions and systems that perpetuated anti-Blackness. It is not difficult to name some of the psychological and spiritual payoffs that William and Mary O'Connell banked on: William's ability to work where and when he wanted; the confidence of moving their family to whatever neighborhood they wanted and paying the fair market value for that property; the security of sending their children to the school they preferred; the relief of personal connections to public servants like cops or judges, or at least knowing somebody who knew somebody, who gave them the benefit of the doubt. Ultimately, they experienced a deep-seated satisfaction that emanated from a simple fact reinforced in every sphere of their lives in South Philadelphia: they were not Black. Black problems were not only a source of their forward mobility, but they were also not *their* problem. In the words of historian Edward Blum, "Forgetting and abandoning commitments to racial justice were essential to the remaking of the white republic."[70] They were also essential to maintaining a white Catholic Church.

ROUNDING ST. CHARLES BORROMEO: RACIAL MERCY AND RECONSTRUCTION

Rev. William Barber III, co-director of the Poor People's Campaign, claims, "Nothing less than a Third Reconstruction holds the promise of healing our nations wounds and birthing a better future for all."[71] It has many of the elements of the previous one that I discovered William and Mary O'Connell lived through in St. Charles Borromeo Parish: religious leaders invoking moral visions that can reorient America toward its yet unfulfilled promises, calls for "fusion coalitions" to span the chasms dividing us, demands to dismantle the structures of racialized social inequality, blueprints constructing more just alternatives. I can't help but hope that we are on the brink of this Third Reconstruction. If so, then I face similar options to William and Mary when it comes to the white Catholic response: should I support movements that aim to bring back political and economic stability enjoyed by so many white Catholics before the upheavals of the last few years, or should I get behind movements that envision something radically different for all Americans when it comes to racial equity? Should I reconcile with white people who see the world very differently than I do, or should I support more comfortable, centrist policies promising gradual change, even if doing so leaves much of the structural racial inequity around us unchanged? Or should I be part of far more left-leaning movements that seek to overhaul structures and systems of American life that currently deny freedom to so many? Should I reconcile myself with returning to the status quo or commit myself to reconstructing it? And what about my wages of whiteness, especially the spiritual ones, that I've both inherited and then accrued on my own? Will I continue to use them as a safety net that allows me to put my own social mobility above racial justice, or will I invest them in the shared work of dismantling the very systems that created these benefits in the first place?

Racial mercy—the desire to enter into the chaos that racism has created—invites me to conduct an audit of these earnings and to consider divesting whiteness in order to lend my privilege and power to building integrated and inclusive communities instead. In particular, racial mercy calls me to pay close attention to a particular spiritual wage of whiteness I receive: the rewards when I opt for easy reconciliation rather than reconstruction in my various Catholic communities. How do I express and exercise that preference for reconciliation? I prefer reconciling over reconstructing when I fail to situate incidents of racism or racist policies into a deeper historical context of pain. When I move too quickly to assess racism as a sin of individual rebellion. When I appeal to good intentions— either my own or those of others—in order to be absolved from participating in cultures of white supremacy. When I place too much confidence in the conversion of hearts as the reasonable or palatable solution for racial injustice. When I want to move too quickly to ask forgiveness of people of color or to offer it (as if I could) to my fellow white people. When I avoid the fear of the unknown by advocating for reforming the status quo or when I seek compromises that don't evenly distribute burdens.

What are the spiritual wages or rewards I receive? I advance professionally. I'm viewed as trustworthy by people in positions of power and influence. I get to feel good about myself because I think I'm one of the "good" white people. I can move through the day largely impervious to others' traumas or pains and with a largely untroubled conscience. Perhaps most importantly, in the words of Catholic ethicist Bryan Massingale, "my comfort level determines the limits of racial justice" in the groups in which I'm working.[72]

Racial mercy moves me past a desire for racial reconciliation and toward racial reconstruction, which is more demanding but in the end potentially more just. Referencing Eric Yamamato's work in interracial reconciliation, Massingale calls racial reconstruction "the active steps of healing the psychological and social wounds caused by racial injustice."[73] Certainly the trauma of racism has been primarily borne by communities of color, particularly Black communities. And yet, in her book *White Fragility*, Robin DiAngelo helps me see that it has created a "collective moral trauma" for white people, who have carried significant guilt "over what we have done and continue to do" and "our complicity with the profound torture of Black people from past to present."[74] In contrast to racial reconciliation, racial reconstruction mines history to name these traumas and their root causes so that we can free ourselves from guilt, which only keeps us trapped in the status quo. Reconstruction understands racism as a sin of captivity that can only be rectified when we liberate ourselves from systems and structures that dehumanize Black people. Therefore, it makes clear the limits of personal conversion in responding to that kind of trauma and points the way for re-visioning those systems and structures instead. This is the work to which white Catholics are called to contribute.

CHAPTER FIVE

MANEUVERING

St. Stephen's

MY MUSE GOT THROUGH to me about writing this book at 13th and Erie. I had grown up hearing about how my mother's family, the Hargadons, got their start at those coordinates in North Philadelphia. But the chance to see a three-story community mural on the side of a row home that now serves as a halfway house for formerly incarcerated women reentering society finally lured me there. The mural tells the story of a teenager named Kevin who was paralyzed from the neck down by peers who shot him in 2003 for his Allen Iverson jersey. Rather than adhere to the code of the street, in which respect demands responding to violence with violence, Kevin chose a different strategy. He forgave his assailants in court. The mural also depicts his mother's story. Janice watched over the interactions among incarcerated boys and men who honored her son's countercultural choice by painting the mural, titled *Forgiveness*, after he eventually died from his injuries.[1]

Forgiveness is saturated with color, texture, and theological significance, and it soon became a regular stop on the mural pilgrimages I often lead. I reflect on how forgiveness can liberate us from the stranglehold of retribution or from being defined solely by our failings. I point out subtle visual references to Rembrandt's famous sketches of the prodigal son. The poetry of adjudicated boys Kevin's age and lifers who will never be let out to see this masterpiece humanize the staggering statistics I rattle off about rates of gun violence, incarceration, and recidivism in Philadelphia. As women come and go from the house on which it is painted, maneuvering the many pitfalls of reentry into the community, I mention the viability of the arts in responding to the vortex of problems connected to gun violence.

But on one particular visit, as I stood with my back turned to the mural so I could speak to the upturned white faces in front of me, my muse interrupted me with the sudden realization that this wasn't just my great-grandparent's neighborhood. It was their intersection. Edward and Belinda's home stood on the opposite corner. I had been coming home to this neighborhood for several years without fully realizing it.

With *Forgiveness* behind me and my eyes darting to the Hargadon side of the street, I was overtaken by the sensation of belonging to this space. I felt as if I were standing downwind of the familiar people who filled the sepia-toned photos my mother displays on an antique table in her living room. I caught glimpses of the Catholic immigrant lives that unfolded from this very spot: Edward walking home from the corner grocery store he ran just down Erie Avenue, the younger Hargadon boys playing, Belinda sweeping the porch, my grandmother jumping on the 56 trolley to get to St. Mary's Academy up on Broad Street, the bells of St. Stephen's church just two blocks away reminding them of the code of Catholicism that structured their whole lives. As pride welled up, I suddenly had a new respect for 13th and Erie.

And at the same time, I knew just as viscerally that I was an outsider. My family was no longer here and I did not belong in or to this place. I got the sense that current residents knew more about why and how my family detached themselves from this block than I did. I sensed that I was disrespecting them with my curious troupes of nervously smiling white interlopers. As we loaded back on our bus, I noticed that my great-grandparents' home was literally gone—1313 was now an empty lot, a gap in the row of once stately three-story brick dwellings. That felt telling for a reason I couldn't quite put my finger on.

Looking back over my shoulder at the mural, I wondered who the real prodigals at 13th and Erie are and what elements of our departure from the people who live here now need forgiving.

WHEN NICETOWN WAS A GHETTO OF OPPORTUNITY

Philadelphia historical lore traces the origins of the Nicetown neighborhood to a 187-acre plot that William Penn gave to either a French Protestant named John Neisse or two Dutch settlers with the last name of de Neus, depending on which of Philadelphia's trendy websites I perused.[2] Development was slow in coming because the five-mile trek from the center of the city along what would become Germantown Avenue was often impassible. The road that intersected Germantown Avenue and connected two Quaker communities both founded in the early 1680s— Germantown to the west and Frankford to the east—was called Nicetown Lane and later became Hunting Park Avenue.

One of my favorite family tall tales from sometime in the early 1920s involves some maneuvering my great-grandmother did in the Nicetown–Tioga ecosystem at Broad and Erie. It reveals that my family was on the move and describes the conditions that made their upward mobility possible.

Ireland had offered Edward Hargadon and Belinda Dempsey little economic or social opportunity, so each sailed separately to Philadelphia in the slipstream of older siblings. Edward arrived in 1902 from Sligo and Belinda in 1904 from Mayo, with only a rabbit sandwich to her name as family lore goes. She was part of the female exodus from Ireland, as half of Irish émigrés at the turn of the twentieth century were women. Both Belinda and Edward were absorbed into a network of Dempseys and Hargadons with extensive social and economic connections. Two of Edward's brothers were chauffeurs, and he immediately landed a job as bartender in a taproom on the 1500 block of Opal Street in North Philadelphia. It is unclear when or how Edward and Belinda reconnected in America— apocryphal family history has them meeting at a dance back home—but they married in 1909 in the Jesuit's Church of the Gesu, an Irish enclave within an enclave since so many parishioners hailed from County Mayo. They initially rented 1826 Seybert Street amidst a sea of two-story brick row homes just two blocks north of the eight-story parish church. In quick succession they baptized the first of their babies at the Gesu and then moved east across Broad Street and into St. Edward's Parish. They finally became homeowners on the 1300 block of Erie Avenue in St. Stephen's Parish sometime in the early 1920s. Their three-story brick row home had bay windows on the first and second floors, a sizable front porch, and a postage stamp of a front yard with a three-foot ornamental iron fence separating it from the busy street.

My favorite story about them goes like this. One evening, Edward made an offhand comment to Belinda about her appearance—something to the effect that she had lost her girlish figure. Belinda had every right to be put off. In addition to managing a household of eight children—all boys except my maternal grandmother, Catherine—she was Edward's right hand at the bar he managed down the block on Erie Ave. She was the first up every morning, getting her brood fed and out the door to school. She'd wake Edward by 10 a.m. and help with the lunch rush. Then she'd walk home, put on her nightgown, and climb back into bed for an afternoon nap. Upon waking, she'd take a bath, dress, then prepare dinner for the family. In short, the figure that mattered most to Belinda was on the bottom on their monthly balance sheet. A woman who preferred the long game, she likely offered no immediate response to her husband's barb. But before letting the sun go down on her anger, she had concocted a plan. She politely asked Edward if they might "stroll the Avenue" the following day.

Germantown Avenue was the economic and social spine of their predominantly Irish and Catholic Nicetown neighborhood. McCarthy's Imported and Domestic Groceries fed families while Hobson's Grain, Hay, Feed, and Straw fueled their horses. Ladies perused the latest fashions for themselves at Mrs. Lynch's Millinery Hats and for their husbands at L. Moore's Men's Shirts, Underwear, Neckwear, and Hosiery. For medicines there was Wolfer Pharmacy. Frick's Dry Goods and Notion Bazaar was ideal for sundries. Of course there were some German and Polish outliers—Riedinger's Hardware and Housefurnishings or Dorbranski's Dry Goods, for example. But at least they were also Catholic. Even Bernstein & Sons Jewelers catered to a predominantly Catholic customer base, advertising "fine rosaries" in emerald, garnet, and amethyst during Mary's month of May. Reading through the advertisements in St. Stephen's monthly calendars (predecessor to today's parish bulletin), I could not help but wonder if the preponderance of restaurants claiming oysters or deviled crabs as their specialty had anything to do with a mandated Friday fish diet for most of their Nicetown–Tioga clientele.[3]

Edward complied with Belinda's plan. The Hargadons put on their Sunday finery and walked barely a block to the intersection of Erie and Germantown. As they crossed Erie Avenue, dodging the trolleys and newfangled automobiles, Belinda suggested something out of the ordinary. She wanted Edward to walk *behind* her rather than by her side. The milder of the two, he dutifully obliged. The Hargadons hadn't gone more than a few blocks on Germantown Avenue before Edward noticed that the men walking toward them were ogling Belinda as she walked by. Some even stopped dead in their tracks to watch her pass. Outwardly, Edward took umbrage. The nerve! Inwardly, he was awash in panic. Had he misjudged his wife's attractiveness? How easily could Belinda have belonged to another man?

He reached for her hand and turned her around to face him. "Belinda," he pleaded, "let's go home." Feigning surprise, Belinda agreed and took his arm. A few weeks later, Edward presented her with the diamond ring he could not afford when they married in 1909, a contrite reminder that his affection endured even if her waistline had not. He never knew that as she walked in front of him on Germantown Avenue, Belinda had been sticking her tongue out at every man who caught her eye.

In addition to being taken with my great-grandmother's feistiness, something she relied on after Edward's sudden death a few years before the Depression, I find that diamond ring interesting, especially when I consider Nicetown then and now. It signaled the upward mobility that Nicetown's parochial enclave of opportunity awarded the Hargadons.[4] Edward was financially secure enough to afford that ring and lavish the family with other luxuries from time to time. I can see their upward mobility in a 1924 family photograph. Eight staid children are strategically arranged around taciturn parents. The youngest child, Martin, is propped on Belinda's knee, likely wearing his white christening gown and strategically angled away from the long strand of pearls wrapped twice around her neck. Edward wears a suit, his tie tacked by a pin filled with small diamonds that his sons would later appropriate for engagement rings. Belinda's ring, the talisman of their ability to finagle a different future than the one that faced them in Ireland, went to Catherine and eventually her oldest daughter, my mother. The tips of everybody's shoes shine.

But Nicetown wasn't a ghetto of opportunity for everyone and didn't remain as such for too much longer. The Hargadons arrived in Nicetown between 1920 and 1930 when the number of Black residents in Philadelphia grew from roughly 135,000 to nearly 220,000 as a result of the Great Migration.[5] Between 1922 and 1924 alone, 20,000 Black migrants arrived in Philadelphia, overwhelming the city's Black districts like the 7th Ward in South Philadelphia and moving into neighborhoods in North Philadelphia that were hardly receptive.[6] In fact, I cannot help but wonder if Belinda and Edward moved on from their original parish—the Gesu in the Fairmount section on the west side of Broad Street—because in 1909

Mother Katharine Drexel opened the city's second parish and school for Black Catholics, Our Lady of the Blessed Sacrament, a few blocks away on Broad Street. Looking into the archival history of the Gesu, I was dismayed to learn that a Jesuit there was among the first to map North Philadelphia by race. This was an effort to maneuver Mother Katharine Drexel's desire for what he called "an ebony mission" on a "principle street" central to "as many colored districts as possible" but "far away from the Gesu Church," the Hargadons' original parish. "I would rather open five hundred colored missions, than select the site for one in one of our large cities," Emerick reported. "By far the most difficult thing was to keep the site out of the Gesu Parish."[7]

Black laborers found work at Atlantic Refining in the Point Breeze section of South Philadelphia; at Franklin Sugar Refinery on the Delaware River in Old City, which controlled 90 percent of the country's sugar production; and at the US Naval Shipyard just down the river in South Philadelphia. In the Hargadon's North Philadelphia, Black residents worked at Midvale Steel in Nicetown, one of the country's biggest producers of steel for guns and armor. I initially assumed that all of this work would allow Black families to achieve the same financial stability as the Hargadons, but not so. Black workers earned less than their white counterparts while paying more for their housing, which they were more likely to rent than own. Perhaps most importantly, possibilities for Black business ownership were restricted to particular districts across the city. By the time they could wrangle their way into Nicetown, it had already begun to morph from a "communal ghetto," which launched white families like the Hargadons into the upper-middle class into a "hyperghetto," which mired Black families in a lack of opportunity as a result of economic and social marginalization.[8]

As I dirtied my hands sifting through the extensive archival materials for St. Stephen's in the Catholic Historical Research Center of the Archdiocese of Philadelphia, I discovered a critical role that Catholics played in engineering who experienced Nicetown as a catalyst and who experienced it as a container.

SCHEMING IN PRE-REVOLUTIONARY ST. STEPHEN'S

According to one account of its origins in the 1840s, "The original St. Stephen's was a mere chapel, located up a country lane and surrounded by an old graveyard." It was the ninth parish when Bishop Kenrick founded it in 1843, "hidden away, as if ashamed to show itself to the public eye."[9] But Catholics had been in the Nicetown vicinity for almost a century at that point, in part thanks to a "young Irish lady" named Elizabeth Mc-Grawley. According to John Watson, one of Philadelphia's earliest historians to put oral histories to paper, McGrawley built a "Roman chapel" in an "inconvenient space, as if in secrecy" on her property on Nicetown Lane as early as 1729.[10] The chapel—along with a priest whom Watson supposed she brought with her, as well as "a number of tenantry" from Ireland—was incognito due to Protestant distaste for Catholics, even in Penn's Philadelphia.[11] In his description of McGrawley's chapel, Watson included reference to a missive that Penn sent back to the colony at some point, indicating that the Crown was scandalized that Mass was publicly celebrated in Philadelphia.[12]

While Catholic historians in the nineteenth century seemed preoccupied with whether or not Ms. McGrawley did in fact have a chapel on her property—since doing so might prove that Nicetown was home to the earliest Catholics in Philadelphia—I couldn't help but marvel at this single Catholic Irish woman who prepared the soil in which my people would be planted two hundred years later. She was savvy enough to manage indentured people to work land she owned and devout enough to entice a priest to minister to members of her household and her neighbors. I found myself drawing comparisons between Elizabeth McGrawley and Belinda Hargadon, another feisty Irish woman who helped build the Catholic Church in Nicetown. In 1929, Belinda donated funds for the candelabra over the main altar at St. Stephen's as part of a $275,000 renovation (worth $4 million today). She did it in memory of Edward, who had recently died.

The parish may not have been incognito in 1929, but Protestant disdain lingered. In his dedication of the renovation in March of 1929, Cardinal Dougherty dismissed comments by outsiders that the church's windows, frescos, furniture, and vestments were an "empty and wasteful extravagance." So, too, were the oils and perfume that the woman used to wash Jesus's feet, he assured St. Stephen's faithful.[13] I wondered if these words comforted Belinda. In light of all that loomed ahead of her on the eve of the Great Depression, I felt as though this widowed mother, who lost a son just six months before her husband's death, had been taken advantage of in the scheme to establish Catholic dominance in Nicetown. My suspicion was only amplified when I discovered the names of two other women in the archival material connected to St. Stephen's pre-Revolutionary history who offered a different kind of sacrifice in the name of Catholic ascendency in Philadelphia. Their names were Christina and Hanna and both were owned by a colonial Irish Catholic on Nicetown Lane—Dr. John Michael Browne—to whom St. Stephen's was beholden.[14]

Browne and his wife, Sara, came to Philadelphia in the late 1730s or early 1740s by way of Barbados, where they were part of a mix of entrepreneurial and indentured Irish capitalizing on the trade in sugar, rum, and Black people. Browne was an Irish-born physician trained in France, so it is not entirely clear to me how he amassed the 850-pound fortune— just under $2 million in today's dollars—that he used to buy nearly three hundred acres in North Philadelphia, which spanned parts of what would become Nicetown–Tioga, Hunting Park, and Frankford. However, I suspect the five Black people he owned and entrusted to another Catholic upon departure from Barbados, as well as the three he is known to have owned while in Nicetown, had something to do with it.

The diocese—still part of Baltimore, the nation's first and only diocese at that point—benefited from the wealth these people helped Browne accrue, since forty acres of his land were eventually bequeathed to the archdiocese for the New Cathedral Cemetery, in which some of my family are buried. His reputation as a gentleman farmer, particularly among the Lenape with whom he was friendly and who visited his orchard grave for decades after his death, lent gravitas to Philadelphia Catholics contending with Protestants who didn't like them. By 1848, nearly a century after Browne's death, Catholics in Nicetown honored the lore of his priestly status and insisted that his body belonged on church property at St. Stephen's first location, also on land he once owned, at Lycoming and Elser Streets.

I was struck by the respect a historian behind St. Stephen's fiftieth jubilee in 1893 paid to Browne. He was a point of parish pride, this colonial Catholic who was so devoted to his faith that he bought vestments and a chalice for priests to use when he turned his home into a chapel for their random visits to Nicetown. Similarly, I found it telling that Catholic historians in the nineteenth century were more preoccupied with disputing whether or not Browne himself was a priest rather than the more unsettling historical fact, at least to my mind, that Browne was a slave owner. By now I recognized this maneuver as an intentional sleight of hand, a kind of historical and even spiritual bypassing on the part of white Catholic communities reluctant to face our pasts. So I was determined to figure out how Christina and Hanna's story interrupted that whitewashed hagiography of St. Stephen's. Who were they and what of them lingered in the soil in which the Hargadons put down their roots? What of their story did the mural *Forgiveness,* also on Browne's land, convey?

In the spring of 1744, an itinerant priest (meaning he served a number of Catholic communities in the region) named Fr. George Schneider, who was based in the Catholic mission region of Goshenhoppen to the west of Philadelphia, made his usual stop at the Brownes' home for Mass. Dr. Browne provided vestments and a chalice for visiting priests, which made his house church quite a respectable place and likely contributed to the rumors among Protestants that he was a priest. According to Schneider's sacramental records, he baptized Christina, an "adult negress slave of Dr. Browne."[15] The good doctor and his wife served as Christina's godparents. By now I had learned that sacramental sponsorship of enslaved people was not uncommon among Catholic slave owners and established a kind of racialized sacramental kinship I found troubling. Catholic ethicist Katie Walker Grimes suggests that for enslaved people, baptism was a kind of rebranding that amplified "that they belonged no more to their families and communities of origin but only to the culture and kin group of their new masters."[16] Put another way, it underscored the fact that Christina belonged to the Brownes materially and spiritually, that she would remain in childlike dependence on them in perpetuity. Grimes notes Christina's baptism instilled in her white Catholic owners a sense of their own beneficence and moral goodness in the eyes of God. It was a godlike power that they exercised over her—to bestow the gift of eternal life through baptism and to sanctify her social death by slavery.

The same priest who baptized Christina returned a few years later as the first of three executors of Dr. Browne's estate upon his death in 1750. Hanna's name appeared atop the inventory of Browne's possessions, second only to a younger enslaved man, Tom Thum, who also came with the Brownes from Barbados.[17] Likely due to her age, Hanna was worth 30 pounds ($7,000 today) to Tom's 35 ($8,000 today). Either way, they were both more valuable than his vestments and chalice. Some slave-owning Catholics, such as America's first bishop, John Carroll, freed their enslaved people upon their deaths. But not Browne. He willed that Hanna be sold so that his beneficiaries could reap a bigger windfall. She died in 1752 while awaiting arrangements for her "sale at Vendue," a French colloquial term for a slave auction house. Expenses for her funeral were paid out of Browne's estate, although I could not tell if this included a funeral Mass. Nor could I identify the location of her interment. Attempts were made to sell Tom in 1753, but the executor could "not make the title."[18] After that, he, too, disappeared from the Catholic historical record. What became of him, I wondered? I asked the same question about Christina. She did not appear at all in Browne's will, leaving me to wonder if sometime before his death Browne had sold her or if she had run away. Assuming that Hanna and Tom were baptized at some point in Barbados, I got the sense that the Brownes brought to Nicetown Lane their Catholic strategy of maneuvering around the moral conundrum of slavery by treating Black people with sacramental niceties. Like other ways of being Catholic, these ploys were codified by the time the Hargadons moved onto what was once the Brownes' land, and they were especially employed during the Golden Age of American Catholicism.

ST. STEPHEN'S CODE OF CATHOLICISM

By the 1920s, St. Stephen's was certainly an ideal place for becoming respectable Americans. The parish encompassed one of the city's many "red-brick row-house neighborhoods" that were "strongholds of Victorian Catholic family life."[19] St. Stephen's was already about seventy years old and two thousand members strong by the time Belinda and Edward joined the parish. Like its original five hundred parishioners in 1843, most were Irish. The parish grew so rapidly in those early decades that by the 1880s its Irish-born pastor was compelled to look for a larger and more prominent location befitting of his community. In 1884, McLoughlin bought a brickyard on Broad and Butler Streets and constructed buildings "not surpassed by any parish in the city."[20] His was a vision where "order and grandeur reigned where then there were disorder and neglect."[21] Within a decade he completed the church, school, and convent and, just as the Hargadons arrived in Philadelphia, he built two towers, one with a clock and the other with a two-thousand-pound bell made in New York City. The towers may have burdened the parish with $3,200 in debt (roughly $1.7 million today), but the clock chimed the hour and half-hour, and the bell rang for Masses, the Angelus at noon, and the De Profundis each evening. They reminded all in Nicetown that through its beauty and orderly influence over the lives of Catholics surrounding it, St. Stephen's was indeed a parish to contend with.

Edward and Belinda played distinct roles in orienting their community and their family unit toward upward mobility by cultivating a communal ethos that reinforced a sense of identity and belonging deeply rooted in their connection to their parish neighborhood. Running a taproom rooted Edward in an Irish tradition of the *shebeen*, Gaelic for *mug*, one of the few enterprises that would have been available to Catholics in his native Ireland. Edward's bar was likely an important site of neighborhood affiliation and civic engagement as well as a place of respite and kinship. According to Philadelphia historian Dennis Clark, "In the immigrant areas where work was hard, housing inadequate to outrageous, and accessible entertainment limited, the saloon was a powerful resort for men torn from their native environments and cast into American cities."[22] Perhaps most importantly, for Edward and Belinda, the taproom provided what Dolan called "a stepping stone into the middle class."[23]

As the head of a busy household of eight children, which only became busier when she took on boarders after Edward's death, Belinda played her own respectable part. She was constantly harangued by missives in the monthly parish calendar about her duties as a Catholic mother—that her prayers, "silent and gentle, can never miss the road to the throne of God," or lessons on the importance of patience and tact, or how to "train a boy" in a way that fostered the American and human dimensions of his character, or how to keep her sons from "rubbing elbows" with Protestant boys during the week, or ways to hold the nonnegotiable line with Catherine when it came to only dating "good practical Catholic" boys.[24] It was her job to ensure that proper materials were on hand for the sacrament of last rites should a priest need to be called to the house and that Friday and Lenten fasts were kept. She would have been the one answering the door to Mary Gallagher, the head of the parish block collection. Belinda likely handled the family contribution to the parish's annual collection for the seminary. Cardinal Dougherty practically equated respectability with the parish's ranking in that most essential fundraising effort. And it was her job to ensure that everyone walked the few blocks to Mass each Sunday.

American Catholic historian John McGreevy describes parishes like St. Stephen's as the organizers of the "local life" of the community and spaces where "dense social networks centered themselves around an institutional structure of enormous magnitude."[25] The Hargadons were expected to be unquestioningly committed to the distinctive features of their faith tradition: the authority of Pope, cardinal, bishop, and priest; the centrality of public devotional practices; a sacramental imagination that infused the material reality with the extraordinary presence of the Divine; a preoccupation with inventorying and confessing sin. Like most parishes in the first half of the twentieth century, St. Stephen's bound "Catholics to the institutional Church by providing them with a demonstrative, emotion-packed religion distinguished by its emphasis on the practice of religious rituals, communion with a heavenly host of saintly relatives, and devotion to a suffering savior, all of which was mediated through a sacramental system controlled by the clergy."[26]

For immigrant Catholics, respectability not only required devotion to Church but also to America. Catholics in Philadelphia like the Hargadons submitted to an ecclesial hierarchy still on high alert for anti-Catholic sentiment and opportunities to prove its patriotism. In parishes like St. Stephen's during the "Golden Age of American Catholicism" in the 1920s and 1930s, immigrants like the Hargadons became thoroughly Catholic Americans without much tension between these two dimensions of their identity. The Hargadons were dedicated to the evolving American experiment, with its values of fierce independence and industriousness, duty to family and neighbor, the expansion of democracy and capitalism, and fervor to reform social ills.

Their cardinal, the indefatigable Dennis Dougherty, demanded nothing less. He wanted Catholics, especially the 800,000 under his direct supervision in Philadelphia, to belong in America. To that end, he led the charge in the US bishops' conference to close "national" ethnic parishes— German, Polish, Italian—in order to assimilate immigrant Catholics into "American" parishes run by American-born and trained priests, the vast majority of both—parishes and priests—having Irish roots. He financially tethered Catholics to their parishes with building campaigns for rectories, convents, and schools, as well as endless fundraisers for archdiocesan-wide initiatives, from support of the seminary to the annual Peter's Pence collection for the Vatican. The latter was of great importance to Dougherty, since he also wanted Philadelphia's Catholics to belong to Rome. He embodied and demanded strict adherence to a set of cultural norms that tethered Catholics to his vision of an American Roman Church: "emotional and sexual restraint, the deference to clerical authority, the insistence on order, the theological rigorism, all overlaid with Roman pomp and splendor." His primary focus was his archdiocese and he saw tyrannical rule of it as an "expression of a message, a mystery, a mystique, a revelatory wind blowing through the millennia from Rome, from Christ himself."[27]

To that end, St. Stephen's, like most parishes across the city, "had become an agent of Americanization rather than a promoter of ethnic identity."[28] For example, as I turned the pages on yellowing parish calendars, I noticed that by the time the Hargadons arrived in St. Stephen's, the parish was no longer pastored by Irish-born priests who made intermittent trips back to their native soil, returning with stories, pictures, and mementos that kept their flocks tethered to the Ireland they left behind and to the Catholicism they practiced there. Their pastors were American-born Irish. Nor did I find evidence that St. Stephen's honored feast days or rituals that would have been sacred in the Celtic Catholicism of the vast majority of its parishioners. The Hargadons and their fellow parishioners were not looking back. Instead, according to McGreevy, "Philadelphia's Catholics enjoyed a comforting sense of rootedness, while the Church's constant emphasis on discipline, order, and family responsibilities ensured steady, if unspectacular, economic progress."[29]

What's more, Dougherty had little time for nostalgia, since he was preparing for the biggest display of American Catholicism the country had ever witnessed, just as America experienced a spike in white supremacy that targeted Black people and Catholics in the run-up to its sesquicentennial in 1926. To my mind, this was a chance to angle for solidarity among these two targeted groups, even if Dougherty was motivated by the bishops' scheme to outgrow the Protestants by converting lapsed Black Christians to Catholicism. But I soon got the sense that he was more interested in *white* Catholic dominance.

THE CARDINAL AND THE KKK

In June of 1926, a few months after he dedicated the renovations at St. Stephen's, Dougherty received a letter from Fr. Thomas Nolan of St. Thomas Aquinas parish in Croydon, which had opened just four years earlier. Fr. Nolan, like many of his fellow priests who dutifully asked Dougherty for permission to do anything in their parochial fiefdoms, inquired if he could begin some work on the parish property. The reason for these efforts, however, was unusual. A shrine to St. Theresa of the Little Flower had been burned down.

"The evidence shows that the doors were forced open and pulled down, with large letters 'KKK' painted on the doors," Nolan reported.[30] He included a pamphlet the arsonists had posted on the door to the parish school "announcing an indignation meeting on the 'KKK'" to be held outdoors in Croydon a few days later. In addition to introducing "all white, gentile, Protestant Americans" to the "truth and principles of this wonderful organization," participants would "hear the answer to the recent remarks made by the Bishop speaking at the dedication of the parochial school at Cornwells Heights."[31]

To some extent, I can't imagine that Dougherty was surprised by this turn of events. He was of the opinion that "the Catholic church here is ridiculed, scoffed at, despised and persecuted; not by sword, but by hatred and opposition."[32] Moreover, as the most Roman of his brother bishops in the US, Dougherty was a lightning rod for the Klan. He clearly irked the head of Philadelphia's Klavern, Paul Meres Winter, a Lutheran from the suburban town of Narberth. In Winter's Christmas letter to the membership in 1924, a copy of which I came across in Dougherty's correspondences, he demanded, "What are you doing to stop the vitriolic utterances of a paid emissary of the 'Champion Bead Rattler' on the Tiber? Is the faith of your fathers not worth fighting for?" Acknowledging the Klan's growing political clout around the country, Winter went on to say, "Let us build a mighty and effective machine in the City of Independence, which will forever crush the ambitions of the Papal Hierarchy. Man-power means votes."[33]

Prior to reading Winter's letter, I had no real sense of the Klan's vitality in Philadelphia. I was stunned to learn the city boasted twenty Klaverns in the 1920s in its industrial hubs and growing suburbs. More than half had at least twenty members. "The Klansman of 1926 was as likely to be a Pittsburgh steel worker or a Manayunk shop keeper as he was to be a Mississippi cotton farmer."[34] Winter's missive reflected a growing sentiment shared by the five million Klansmen around the country who were increasingly politically active. Now that the Great War was over, threats to the American experiment were no longer external but internal. The Klan's main objection to Catholics was political. Catholics were autocratic, refused to assimilate to American culture, indoctrinated their children in parochial schools rather than public ones, and handed over their freedom of conscience to papist priests. On that score, Winter and his

Philadelphia Klaverns had met their match in Dougherty, who ruled the city's Catholics as the "infallible head of a state-within-a-state."[35]

Winter invigorated the Philadelphia Klaverns at a meeting in West Philadelphia in January 1925, perhaps to build enthusiasm for a Klonvocation in Washington, DC, in August of that year. Philadelphians were among the tens of thousands of Klanspersons who arrived from around the country for that fully hooded march down Pennsylvania Avenue. The event was such a success that they planned a reunion the following summer at the nation's sesquicentennial celebration, a world's fair–scale extravaganza to be held in Philadelphia and referred to as the "Sesqui." According to historian Thomas Keels, the Klan met no opposition from the Sesqui Planning Committee headed by Philadelphia's mayor. "The Klan," Mayor Kendrick said, "like the Shriners or any other civic or patriotic group, will receive the same courtesies during their convention that we accord to all."[36]

Certainly, Cardinal Dougherty had the looming Sesqui Klonvocation on his mind as he read Nolan's letter in June of 1926. His real estate advisor and confidant, Albert Greenfield, was a member of the Sesqui planning committee. Their friendship was not just the fruit of a mutually beneficial business relationship but it was also forged in their shared status as outsiders among Philadelphia's Protestant elite. Greenfield had likely informed Dougherty just days after the violence in Croydon that the Sesqui planning committee had succumbed to growing public pressure to revoke permission for the Klonvocation. Outrage at that decision would surely be forthcoming. Dougherty treaded lightly with Fr. Nolan. He thought it best to "allow the bigoted elements some time in which to repent and be ashamed, rather than dare them to perform a fresh act of vandalism."[37] Plus, this skirmish only reinforced Dougherty's constant message to his flock: Catholic values remained under assault and the time had come for Catholics to demand the respect they deserved. Most importantly, the cancellation of the Klonvocation left a significant hole in the Sesqui program that only a skilled autocrat could fill on such a short notice. Dougherty began plotting.

To my mind, the Klan's targeting of both Black people and Catholics presented an opportunity for Catholic solidarity across the color line during that sesquicentennial moment when the country recalled and recommitted itself to the values that inspired its founding 150 years earlier. But Dougherty had something else in mind. He would beat the Klan at their own game. Doing so required holding the line on anti-Blackness, which he did in various ways during the country's sesquicentennial celebration in Philadelphia.

BLACK AND CATHOLIC EXHIBITS AT THE SESQUI

The impetus for the Sesqui was not only to remember the original signing of the Declaration of Independence or to demonstrate the country's growth in the intervening 150 years. Philadelphia's business elite also wanted to maneuver Philadelphia to the top of the list of cities worthy of national and even international respect. The city's most respectable businessmen mounted the effort, which brought roughly ten million visitors to fairgrounds in South Philadelphia between May and November of 1926. The Sesqui's pageantry—massive theatrical productions, re-creations of colonial streets, sporting events, public addresses, visits by international dignitaries—was significant in a decade rife with tensions about precisely what America was trying to be and, even more importantly, about who counted as an American. The Sesquicentennial Exhibit Association (SCEA) was composed largely of the city's Protestant and Republican elite—aside from three of the Philadelphia's most successful Jewish businessmen, including Cardinal Dougherty's partner in real estate, Albert Greenfield. They vetted proposals for a number of groups who saw participation in the fair as a chance to make a public case that they were thoroughly American.

I was struck by the religious undertones of the entire affair. Philadelphia's Mayor Kendrick said that visitors to the fairgrounds—and I imagine the Hargadons among them—would experience the deep spiritual values at the foundation of American prosperity and development. Those spiritual values, however, did not include Catholicism. In his opening address, President Coolidge made clear that the religious wellspring of this spirit rested with New England Puritanism. "Democracy is Christ's government in Church and State," he said, quoting a lesser-known Puritan preacher. "Unless the faith of the American people in these religious convictions is to endure, the principles of our Declaration will perish."[38]

Dougherty was not the only one angling for the respect of his countrymen by proving Catholics' commitment to those principles. So, too, were Black American, particularly in Philadelphia, where their numbers were second only to New York. "This is to be the one big chance for the

Philadelphia Negro to prove to the world by deed well done just how he stands in the outward march of events," said a *Philadelphia Tribune* opinion piece in 1921 in an effort to build excitement in Philadelphia's Black community.[39] This clarion call was familiar to Black people. As early as the mid-1700s, exceptional Black people had been trotted out in front of largely white audiences as evidence that they could assimilate into white culture, easing white anxiety about the future of racial integration and white guilt about the treatment of Black people assumed to be less exceptional than those on exhibit.[40]

However, Keels details how Black enthusiasm for the Sesqui was lukewarm at best.[41] Not only did the SCEA delay as long as possible in establishing a Committee on Negro Activities but it also dramatically underfunded it. Black people, including veterans, were prohibited from marching in Sesqui parades or performing in its massive chorus. Organizer and activist A. Philip Randolph was invited at the last minute to offer remarks on the Opening Day but his name was left off the program. A replica of a "negro hut" and watermelon patch, complete with costumed "pickannies," refuted the story that Black citizens were attempting to tell about themselves in their exhibit space in the Place of Agriculture and Foreign Exhibits—which was not given to them until a week before the event opened. Many Black people considered it little more than "a Jim Crow sideshow" that demonstrated "all too clearly" that the event was another "Nordic showcase."[42] One of the founding editors of Philadelphia's *Tribune* reflected that the sesquicentennial was a painful reminder that "America has reached a point where it is impossible to think clearly on the issue of race."[43]

Dougherty chose a similar tactic with the Black Catholics in the archdiocese. On April 15, just weeks before the opening of the fair and the KKK violence in Croydon, he received a handwritten letter from three women of St. Peter Claver, Philadelphia's first Black parish. Rosa White, M. Gertrude Palmer, and Clara Baptist-Jones informed him that they had been "selected to represent the Colored Catholics at the Sesqui Centennial Exposition."[44] I could not determine if they hoped to bring a dimension of the Black experience to the Catholic exhibit put up by the archdiocese—which featured a "City of Charity" that displayed in miniature a variety of Philadelphia's Catholic social welfare institutions and a collection of embroidery made by Catholic pupils in the Philippines—or a Catholic dimension to the Black exhibits that displayed Black success from a variety of angles. Either way, Rosa, Gertrude, and Clara knew they needed to finagle the "blessing, advice, and approval" of the cardinal. In their letter they offered to meet with him at his earliest convenience to "receive the necessary advice and counsel."

As was the case for all Black people navigating the power dynamics of the Sesqui, the response from those in charge—in this case Dougherty— was tepid at best. A faintly penciled note at the bottom of the St. Peter Claver ladies' initial note in April 1926, in the hand of Dougherty's executive secretary, indicated the cardinal's unequivocal position. "Note: these people are to be told that the Archbishop does not intend to take a hand in this matter."[45] Dougherty dictated this same response to a follow-up inquiry the women sent a week later, this one typed, perhaps hoping a more formal presentation of their request would prompt a response. Again, in pencil appeared the same words: "These people are to be told that the Archbishop does not intend to take a hand in this matter."[46]

I was once again struck by white Catholic behaviors toward Black women. *These* people. *This* matter. What exactly was it that Black Catholics were hoping to do at the Sesqui that Dougherty wanted no part of? What larger strategy could their presence have threatened? I could find no further traces of the three women from St. Peter Claver in any of the archdiocese's holdings. If what mattered to them as Black Catholics didn't matter to Dougherty in 1926, then their affairs likely didn't matter to official archdiocesan recordkeepers either. I extrapolated their response from discussions about racism at the Sesqui in Philadelphia's Black press. "There is something wrong with this whole Sesquicentennial business," the *Philadelphia Tribune* opined in May of 1926. "The colored participation has been sidetracked, switched off, and discouraged."[47]

I can't help but speculate about two possible reasons why Dougherty would have refused to meet with the women of St. Peter Claver. The experience of people like Belinda and Edward at the Sesqui illuminates both.

First, the Sesqui was no less racially segregated than any other space the Hargadons would have moved through in Philadelphia in the 1920s, implicitly reminding them that whites naturally belonged at the Sesqui—and in Philadelphia and America—in a way that Black people never fully would. There were no Black servicemen in the opening day parade. Black singers were initially rejected from the five-thousand-member Festival Chorus, who entertained as part of Coolidge's presidential visit on the Fourth of July. They would have encountered no Black visitors at any of the concession stands or restaurants. While only formally banned from restaurants, Black visitors were made to feel so uncomfortable that most ate at the cafeteria funded and staffed by the Federation of Colored Women's Clubs, which didn't even appear on Sesqui maps. If little effort was made to ensure that Black people belonged on their own terms at the Sesqui, then Dougherty would have felt no particular compulsion to ensure that Black Catholics belonged there either.

Second, eugenics, which was in vogue in the '20s and turned the Sesqui into an "unwitting battlefield for warring factions who sought to dictate who did and did not belong in the United States," may have given Dougherty an out.[48] This ideological movement sought to improve the nation's progeny in a time of melting-pot race mixing. Relying on a racist reading of Darwin's evolutionary theories, as well as pseudo biological and social sciences, eugenicists stoked Americans' desire to "believe that the racial, ethnic, class, and gender hierarchies in the United States were natural and normal."[49] They insisted that behavior was hereditary and therefore certain races were superior because they had inherited superior behavioral traits.

Eugenics was on full display at the Sesqui. Edward and Belinda may have encountered an exhibit by the American Eugenics Society, who asked, "How long are we Americans to be careful for the pedigree of our pigs and chickens and cattle and then leave the ancestry of our children to chance or 'blind' sentiment?"[50] Visitors to the exhibit picked up a "catechism," an instructional method familiar to Catholics like the Hargadons, for avoiding the mongrelization of the American race. The eugenic science of the time could have appealed to Belinda and Edward, as Catholics, since it provided a justification for the sorting of people they experienced upon arrival in Philadelphia. They may not have been as "committed" to the "essentialized hierarchies" associated with racial and ethnic groups, but like their Catholic peers, they could have used eugenics to explain and uphold the ethnic and racial segregation that was part of their Catholic experience in Philadelphia.[51] That the Catholic exhibit was in the same Palace of Education and Social Economy as the eugenics exhibit suggests a proximity of thought if not necessarily of practice.

But I really think Dougherty denied his support to the three Black Catholic women from St. Peter Claver because whatever it was they planned to undertake might dilute or even detract from his plan to fill the void in the Sesqui left by the Klonvocation cancellation. Dougherty was plotting to pull off the biggest exhibit of them all, the exhibit that mattered. It all went down on a Sunday in October of 1926, and since it involved 250,000 Catholics across Philadelphia, I have good reason to believe that Edward and Belinda Hargadon, as respectable members of one of the city's most respectable parishes, were part of it.

WHITE AMERICAN CATHOLICS OUTMANEUVERING THE KKK

Culling from extensive coverage in scrapbooks at the Archdiocese's Catholic Historical Research Center, I imagine Dougherty's Catholic exhibit on October 3 unfolded something like this for the members of my family who may have participated.

Edward and his older sons—Edward Jr. and John—would have jostled among the throng of fellow St. Stephen's parishioners who, by 8:15 a.m., were packed onto Bainbridge Street on the east side of South Broad Street. Cassocked priests perched at the top of the intersections along South Broad, fishing the men from their parishes out of the stream of Catholic humanity walking south to the Sesqui Stadium. There were veterans in military dress, and parish bands decked out in red, white, and blue played familiar religious melodies. Men dressed in their Sunday best clustered under banners representing their fraternal organizations, with some members of the Holy Name Society even sporting morning suits and top hats.

Meanwhile, at City Hall a mile north on Broad, at precisely 8:45, the marshal shot the red flare, signaling that the Main Division, which had formed at the Cathedral up on the Parkway, was stepping off. Edward would have heard the buzz of parish regiments in similar staging areas on blocks to his north, readying themselves to fall into formation behind the Main Division. When it was St. Stephen's turn to fold in, the men stood shoulder to shoulder—sixteen across—with others from the parish, who funneled onto Broad from the east, where they eventually joined another sixteen men from St. Elizabeth's parish who had formed up on the west side of Bainbridge. Meeting in the middle, both lines turned sharply south for the final twenty-five blocks of the four-mile march to the Sesqui fairgrounds. Edward would have become part of what Dougherty described as a "moving solid"—80,000 formally dressed Catholic men walking in lockstep toward the Sesqui Stadium for the Solemn Pontifical Mass of Thanksgiving for American Independence.[52] The *Catholic Standard & Times* called it a "mighty host of stalwart Catholic men."[53]

It all "went off like an oiled machine," Dougherty bragged the next day in a letter to his nieces.[54] Catholic men from more than 130 city parishes, the 12 newer "country" parishes from Philadelphia's suburban counties, and even a smattering from Dougherty's native central Pennsylvania flipped the script on the KKK and marched down Philadelphia's most iconic street. I marveled at the logistics of this maneuver. The weekend before the event, a half a million copies of an instruction manual for the day's festivities had been printed and distributed in every parish in the archdiocese. More than 400 additional trolley cars were put in service and 2,600 police lined the streets and joined 500 firemen in managing the crowds at the stadium.[55] Many were members of the Catholic Police, Firemen Park Guards and Peace Officers of Philadelphia League of the Sacred Heart, "worthy Catholics" and "guardians of the city."[56]

But logistics paled in comparison to the pageantry. As Edward and the older Hargadon boys would have passed under the sixty-foot replica of the Liberty Bell that spanned the entrance to the fairgrounds, Belinda and Catherine would have had the little ones by the hand in the sea of Catholic humanity streaming into the Sesqui Stadium, which had been transformed into "an unroofed Cathedral" for the Mass.[57] They were lucky to get into the stadium itself before the police closed the entrances at 10 a.m. Tens of thousands milled about outside, while thousands of others waited on street corners across the city as trolleys, buses, and taxis filled to capacity passed them by. Dougherty was also prepared for this eventuality. He had tapped St. Stephen's own pastor, Fr. McCollough, to offer a concurrent Mass adjacent to the stadium for an overflow crowd estimated to be 130,000 strong.

Inside, the fanfare was glorious. In keeping the Sesqui's replica theme, the altar was modeled after the high altar in St. Peter's in Rome, complete with an ornate *baldachino*, a ceremonial canopy, sixty feet high and twenty-five feet wide. The dais alone had reserved seating for 5,000 people. There were 20,000 colorfully dressed school children assembled in the stand under the watchful eye of nuns, who must have been roasting in their habits. The men packed in, still shoulder to shoulder, in the standing area, "the old and the young, the rich and the poor."[58]

The pep rally atmosphere quickly turned to one of reverence as trumpets heralded the beginning of the procession. An honor guard of fraternal organizations in formal costumes—Knights of Columbus, Ancient Order of Hibernians, League of the Sacred Heart, and Men of Malvern—lined the final stretch of the center aisle. Behind the cardinal (actually, behind his train) followed two rows of clergy arranged in descending hierarchical order: bishops, monsignori, priests, seminarians. With the help of a new-fangled amplifier system, the voices of the 300-member seminarian choir magically wafted across the stadium with hymns arranged especially for the occasion. It was nothing short of a Catholic spectacle of "incomparable grandeur," captured in both the assemblage of "the princes and ministrants of the church, garbed in medieval beauty of brilliance of clerical vestments" as well in the sheer number of the faithful who had gathered.[59] A reporter from the *Philadelphia Record* called it "the most magnificent religious spectacle the new world has ever seen."[60]

Dougherty's message was clear, even if it was delivered by Monsignor Whitaker of Our Lady of Mercy parish who offered the homily. Catholics were American, Catholics belonged in America, and Catholics were essential to the past and future success of the nation. In short, Catholics demanded respect. In his sermon, printed in full by the end of the week in the *Catholic Standard & Times*, Whitaker called Philadelphia the Holy City of our country, "because it was the 'sacred' birthplace of our freedom and tender cradle of our nation."[61] Like other religious leaders who had taken to the stage throughout the Sesqui, he bemoaned the growth of irreligion in the midst of luxury. Catholics could ensure against it precisely by being distinctively Catholic. This "holy sacrifice of the Mass," Whitaker reminded them, was "being offered up by a Prince-Priest of the Church of Jesus Christ in public thanksgiving to Almighty God" who had given "the priceless boon of political independence . . . to our beloved country."[62] He called for a renewal of "spirit of high and holy patriotism," to which the massive congregation responded with applause—yet another first.[63] The Mass ended with "Holy God We Praise thy Name" and the national anthem.

"No confusion, no hitch, no delay," Dougherty bragged to his nieces. Nevertheless, Dougherty noted how Catholics commanded respect, which I suspect was his ultimate goal: "The multitudes expressed their astonishment at the feat."[64]

I cannot help but think that Dougherty was intentionally gaslighting the Klan with this Catholic spectacle. He unapologetically performed the very characteristics the Klan reviled and feared most about him and the Catholics who adhered to his every word in Philadelphia: autocratic control and a lockstep mentality. What's more, in putting on the biggest event of the entire Sesqui celebration, he practically stole the Klonvocation game plan: a well-disciplined march of men through the heart of the city that went off with military precision and culminated in an emotionally charged rally that integrated religious and patriotic values. Dougherty also stole the Klan's anti-Black strategy to become more respectable in the eyes of the Protestant elite. I could find no evidence that there were any Black Catholics on that dais, nor among the fraternal organizations that lined the center aisle. There was no mention of the Knights of Peter Claver, founded in 1909 just after the ordination of the first American Black priests.

Granted, Black Catholics did participate in the Catholic pageantry that Sunday. The men of the "colored" parishes marched in the parade and were greeted enthusiastically when they arrived in the Sesqui Stadium. But since Dougherty did not allow Black Catholics to participate in the Sesqui on their own terms, their presence in the Catholic parade was just as orchestrated by whites as it was everywhere else in the Sesqui celebration. While Philadelphia's six Black parishes were alphabetically integrated into the public listing of parishes and staging areas in the *Catholic Standard & Times* the day before the Mass, Dougherty had in fact segregated them at the event itself. Internal planning documents show at least four of these parishes marked with a "c" for "colored," a designation that was significant in light of the fact that in 1926 Dougherty had eliminated all of the other national ethnic parishes by which the Black parishes were classified.[65] While they were considered "national" parishes, Christian ethicist Katie Walker Grimes notes that "in truth they operated much more like ghettos."[66] The white hierarchy created these parishes and ministered to Black people in them on white terms; Black Catholics were confined to them. Even more troubling to me was the fact that Dougherty didn't integrate Black Catholics into the 70,000 marchers. Rather, he corralled Black parishioners together onto Ellsworth Street, which essentially placed them toward the back of the parade and the standing section in the stadium.

The Catholic pageantry at the Sesqui was a chance to exhibit a Catholicism that transcended the racist boundaries so embedded in American culture. It was a chance to include Black people in Dougherty's conviction about Catholic belonging: that Black Catholics fully belonged in the Church and so in America as well. Had Dougherty integrated Black congregations in his lineup of parishes on Broad Street, Edward could have walked near, if not shoulder to shoulder, with men from St. Peter Claver, or Our Lady of the Blessed Sacrament, or St. Ignatius. Belinda could have witnessed the pomp of Black fraternal organizations or watched Black and white schoolchildren frolic in the stands, or heard messages of unity among Catholics or calls to make the freedoms of the Declaration of Independence real for *all* in the Catholic community. Instead, Black Catholics' token participation reinforced the racial boundaries the KKK also wanted to keep intact by burning Catholic churches in Northeast Philadelphia or wanting to march down Market Street themselves. Dougherty's grand exhibit did not repudiate the Klan's hate for Black people, Catholics, and Jewish people—just white Catholics. In performing their Catholic identity in such a grand fashion to command the respect of the city and nation, Philadelphia's white Catholics proved themselves no less anti-Black than the other white Americans they were obsessed with becoming.

ROUNDING: RACIAL MERCY AND COURAGE

Rounding St. Stephen's afforded me the opportunity to cover significant chronological ground connected to that particular parish. Here Catholics went from belonging in secret to one of the first Catholic chapels in Philadelphia served by itinerant priests in the decades before the Revolutionary War to parading in public at the biggest event of the nation's sesquicentennial celebration, led by a pastor who celebrated Mass for the overflow crowd of 130,000 who could not get inside the stadium for the main event. The parish's unprecedented growth in size and power required some serious maneuvering. From Irish-born Dr. Michael John Browne to second generation Irish immigrant Cardinal Joseph Dougherty, St. Stephen's rise in respectability and influence involved tactical maneuvers to gain economic and political power. The power afforded to the Brownes to baptize the people they owned was passed on to subsequent generations in the form of land, amassed through the wealth of slave owning, on which Catholic infrastructure in Nicetown was built. Likewise, the power Dougherty exercised to deny Black Catholics meaningful participation in a triumphal display of Catholic patriotism, despite requests from three Black women that they be permitted to do so on their own terms, was passed on to subsequent generations who struggle to see Black people as both Catholics and Americans or to hear demands from Black people that their experiences matter.

I'm also struck by the fact that my people experienced this exercise of Catholic power in the context of the rise of the KKK in the 1920s, which still looms large in white consciousness as the epitome of anti-Black racism. Perhaps it was here that Catholics learned the good/bad or mean/nice binary that we use to examine our consciences or confess our sins where racism is concerned. If being racists means acting like the KKK, then most of us are off the hook. The KKK, with their overt acts of bigotry and violence, became the foil for racism at the expense of racism's more insidious systemic and structural forms. As a result, most Catholics, even today, believe that refraining from acting like the KKK is all that is required to avoid the label of "racist." But preoccupation with white supremacists distracts us from the dynamics of racism as an expression of power—the power to deny the full humanity of certain people and to create rituals, cultures, and churches that reinforce that power. Dougherty exercised Catholic white supremacy at the Sesqui. He may not have publicly slandered Black Catholics, but he refused to recognize white Catholics' commonality with them, knowing full well that doing so was considered un-American in the eyes of the Klan. Instead, he exercised power to deny Black people their claim to the American experiment and the American Catholic Church, and in so doing he reinforced a sense of white supremacy and entitlement for those for whom he was building American Catholicism.

Finally, all of this anti-Black power was masked in niceties, which is fitting for a parish community in Nicetown. After all, Dr. Browne and his wife were *nice enough* to go to the lengths of baptizing their enslaved people; Dougherty was *nice enough* to permit Black parishes to march down Broad Street; the Hargadons and other white Catholics in the Sesqui Stadium were *nice enough* to cheer enthusiastically when the Black contingents arrived for the Mass. Catholics were not racist like those mean Southern slave owners or the KKK. If we were—if we *are*—nice then how can we be anti-Black? Niceness is what most white people like me assume is the answer to racism, since we tend to think about racism as animosity between individuals based on racial identities. We rely on niceness to communicate that we are one of the "good white people." We rely on niceness to avoid taking responsibility for abuses of white power while we nicely maneuver away from Black people. Niceness may be something that we extend to Black people as an indicator of our respect for them, but since it does not transform the power imbalances that so negatively impact Black people in the first place, niceness actually aligns us with systems and cultures that sustain white dominance. According to Robin DiAngelo, "To continue reproducing racial inequality," like the kind reproduced in St. Stephen's, "the system only needs for white people to be really nice and carry on."[67]

Racial mercy, or the ability to enter into the chaos of racism, summons me to pay attention to my preference for niceness. Doing so can help me recognize my own fragility, or what DiAngelo calls our inability to deal with "racial stress."[68] By this she means moments when our racial equilibrium—so perfectly calibrated by generations of distancing ourselves from Black people and absolving ourselves of responsibility for the injustices they face by insisting on seeing racism primarily in terms of badness or meanness—gets disturbed by the presence of Black people who call that false binary and our innocence into question. Becoming aware of these moments of racial stress can help me be more intentional with how I react to them. To that end, racial mercy invites courage. If niceness either keeps us on the periphery of the chaos of racism because we're afraid to jump in or conditions us to react defensively in a way that only amplifies our power over others in racially charged situations, then courage presents different strategies. I think some of the responses DiAngelo offers as alternatives to fragility are expressions of courage: "reflection, listening, processing, grappling, engaging, believing."[69]

When I think now of *Forgiveness*, the mural in Nicetown across the street from where my great-grandparents lived, I encounter the courage in its story. Kevin and Janice, impacted by in the violent dynamics created and sustained by white supremacy, saw forgiveness as the most meaningful way to transform their personal situation. This wasn't a gesture of niceness, but rather a difficult and countercultural choice rooted in the deep conviction of their own worth as well as that of others. They refused to capitulate to a culture and criminal justice system that said Kevin's perpetrators were somehow less human or beyond redemption and decided instead to risk a new relationship with those who had been separated from them by gun violence, itself a violent expression of racism. This choice was not about being nice, nor was Janice's agreement to do the mural after Kevin's death some kind of public performance of their virtue. It was simply a courageous choice to maneuver closer to their pain and fear to bridge a chasm none of them created in the first place, and then another choice to courageously paint—with the permanently rejected men serving life sentences—their story without words. The next time I take pilgrims there, I'll ask the white members of the group to reflect on how their family maneuverings might have created similar chasms, or what pains and fears we might need to courageously draw close to in order to move beyond our "but I'm not racist" niceties, and how we might do the work of building racial equity without all of our performative gestures.

CHAPTER SIX

DEFENDING

The Church of Gesu

THE RACKET from the street became too much to ignore as I sifted through the archival history of Catholics of the Gesu Parish. I was on the fifth floor of what was once a massive rectory at 18th and Thompson Streets. In its heyday a hundred years ago, the building housed fifty-four Jesuit priests who buzzed around this North Central Philadelphia Catholic hive servicing the massive twelve-story Church of the Gesu, five thousand parishioners, and three schools, elementary through college. Today, the former rectory is the bustling appendage of St. Joseph's Prep High School where one of my former elementary school teachers is on the faculty. He had heard about my project and thought I might find some of the school's historical records interesting. I was starting to agree with him, but the clamor was distracting me.

I walked over to a north-facing window to investigate. Immediately behind the building, on a block of Seybert Street where Belinda and Edward Hargadon had lived after they married in the Gesu in 1909, two construction crews worked on what I assumed were former empty lots that pocked the block. Similar crews banged away on other blocks.

"That's the sound of gentrification," said a teacher also trying to work quietly in the office. And indeed, a 2019 report from the National Community Reinvestment Coalition found that Philadelphia is the fourth-fastest gentrifying city in the country, with fifty-seven census tracts reversing their racial and economic makeup between 2013 and 2017 alone.[1] More than eighty years after a massive white exodus from this once fashionable

Fairmount neighborhood, the Gesu finds itself towering once again above white hustle and bustle.

The correspondences I was reading on the fifth floor of that converted rectory—between Jesuit priests here and in DC, among parishioners, between members of a parish committee and politicians of all sorts—told a gripping story of the catalytic role that Catholics played in the cycle of investment, disinvestment, and reinvestment unfolding in neighborhoods like this one across Philadelphia. And once again, my people were there, on the westernmost block of the parish, trying their best to be Catholic and learning anti-Blackness as it all went down.

THE HARLEM OF PHILADELPHIA

I didn't have to read between the lines of his letters to realize that by late summer in 1936, Fr. Thomas Love had had it with the rumors. On August 8, he retreated to his desk in the six-story Jesuit residence and dashed off two letters to possible informants in his Jesuit network in the Maryland province.

First, he wrote Fr. Raymond Cosgrove, on a silent retreat at the Jesuit seminary in Maryland. "I have heard a rumor about the house that pamphlets are being distributed in Washington urging colored people to move to Philadelphia to the Forty-seventh Ward. The rumor says that you are the source of this information."[2] Awaiting response, Love turned his attention to Fr. Laurence Kelly of St. Aloysius Parish, one of the oldest in the nation's capital, in a missive with a less amiable tone.

"We are making what best effort is possible to us to prevent this neighborhood from being submerged by colored," Love punched out in his first sentence. The next read with telegram-like precision. "I have heard it said that pamphlets are being distributed in Washington, D.C., urging colored people of Washington to move to Philadelphia to the Forty-seventh Ward. This is our territory."[3]

Full stop.

Digging a bit deeper, I discovered that Philadelphia's 47th Ward had been Jesuit territory since they had first scouted it out in 1866. Fr. Felix Barbelin, then pastor of Old Saint Joseph's, the Jesuits' first parish in Philadelphia, was concerned about declining enrollments at the fifteen-year-old Saint Joseph's College. Barbelin thought it best to follow the Catholic families migrating to parts north and west of the city center. What's more, the Jesuits needed a plot strategically positioned amidst the emergent development "up town" to lay the foundation for what they hoped would become Philadelphia Catholic University. So he dispatched one of his colleagues, Fr. Villiger, to survey open land in the northern and western fringes of the city.

Villiger decided on Green Hill, a parcel on the northern slope of a hill a mile north of the city center in the "fashionable area around 17th and Styles Street" just west of Broad Street.[4] In 1866, he bought an entire city block for $45,000, putting $15 down with the help of a loan from Archbishop Wood. Within two years, the Jesuits had built New Saint Joseph's chapel, reflecting the outpost's tether to the Jesuits' initial stake in Philadelphia, and a residence for two priests. Villiger promised a "magnificent basilica" in twenty years' time.[5] He did not disappoint. After opening a new school in 1870, he turned his attention to the church, whose cornerstone was laid in 1879. Even then, the three thousand parishioners—most from County Mayo in Ireland—wondered if the plans for "an edifice as great as a cathedral" were warranted.[6]

In the Jesuit "go big or go home" style, the church was modeled on its namesake in Rome and stood twelve stories high when completed in 1895. The foundation stones were twelve to fourteen feet thick, so no interior columns were required to hold up its ninety-five-foot ceiling. The main altar alone reached five stories high. There were eight side altars, two transept altars to St. Ignatius and St. Francis Xavier, and four Doric columns framing five massive entrance doors. The two towers held five bells. "When it was finished, it was claimed that there was no parish church, or to put it another way, no non-cathedral church, in the country as large as this."[7]

It became clear to me that the founding impulse of the Gesu— claiming permanent territory in the midst of urban development and migrating populations—remained a constant theme of its story. For example, a 1929 *Philadelphia Evening Bulletin* commentary marking the fiftieth anniversary of the laying of the Gesu's cornerstone noted the Jesuits' "complete occupation of the block"—with a school hall, auditorium, library, rectory, residence, and church—while also suggesting that "the changing character of the neighborhood" was having "some effect."[8] I noticed how central the whole idea of home was to the Jesuits' strategy. "This is a house of God," Archbishop Ryan preached at the dedication Mass in 1888, "and so it functions as a house: to contain the

Real Presence of God; to contract business but in this case the business of the sacraments; to entertain friends . . ."[9]

But by the 1920s, just who counted as "friends" was keeping the Jesuits in the Gesu compound up at night. African Americans leaving densely populated southern wards for northern territories like the Gesu was enough without having to worry about a targeted marketing campaign in Black wards in other cities. Down in Maryland in the summer of 1936, Fr. Cosgrove responded to Love's note within a day.

"I was told that the colored in Washington were 'being invited' to come and settle in the 47th Ward of Philadelphia as it was to be made the 'Harlem of Philadelphia,'" Cosgrove carefully explained. He further underscored his innocence in the whole affair. "Whether the 'being invited' meant that pamphlets were being distributed or that the inviting was being done by word of mouth—I don't know." He referred Fr. Love to Fr. Kelly, and then signed off saying, "In the meanwhile I'll keep my ear to the ground and I'll try to find something according to any opportunity."[10]

The trail goes cold here in the Gesu archives housed in the very building from which Fr. Love sent those letters more than eighty years ago. But perhaps that's because more aggressive strategies in the parish to address the "Harlem of Philadelphia" situation were heating up.

COUNTRY CATHOLICS TO CITY CATHOLICS

My father's maternal grandparents, George and Sophie Yeager, moved into the Fairmount neighborhood from Reading, a much smaller city in central Pennsylvania, sometime in the early 1920s. It is likely that George's occupation took them there. He was a typesetter and his employer, Lanston Monotype, had just opened two big offices, both a short commute from their new home. My dad remembers visiting their east-facing, three-story brick row home on N. 20th Street as a little kid, especially the ice cream parlor a block away on Fairmount Avenue. Sophie enjoyed the view of the street from her rocking chair in the front parlor while their only daughter, Georgia, practiced at the upright piano by the oak pocket doors to the dining room. They had a boarder on the third floor, which helped the Yeagers make ends meet.

Fairmount was a blue-collar neighborhood filled with ethnic whites— Irish, Polish, German—who worked in a variety of industries in North Philadelphia: iron foundries, lime and lumber mills, and breweries. The neighborhood had quite a bit going for it: public transportation, hospitals, a vibrant shopping district, and several of the city's best schools. The Philadelphia Museum of Art opened about ten blocks away from the Yeagers' home in 1928. As the Gesu parish calendar reported in 1937, the parish's "opportunities for spiritual and mental development are exceptional."[11]

I wondered, however, whether that was true for Sophie, who was a second-generation German transplant with a Protestant husband. The Gesu's Irish brogues may have disappeared, but only a smattering of Germans populated the parish. The Reicherts were the only other German Catholics on N. 20th Street. Given strict Catholic guidelines about marriage, Sophie surely endured questions from priests about whether or not George planned to join the converts' class. And then there was the Yeagers' decision to send Georgia, twelve years old when they arrived in the parish, to public school.

Although the Jesuits could still boast "complete occupation of the block," by the late '20s the tide was beginning to turn. Gone were the heady days of fifteen thousand parishioners, or the Sundays when each of the seven Masses had twelve hundred people attending, with more affluent parishioners donning top hats and tails for the High Mass at 11 a.m. Some of those fancier Catholics were enticed by ads in the Gesu parish calendars in 1929 for newly constructed homes in neighborhoods further to the north.[12] Gone too were the days when a thousand members of the Holy Name Society marched around the parish each May. Some of their number left for newly constructed homes in neighborhoods in the northern reaches of the city like West Oak Lane, Olney, and Rawnhurst. The Jesuits' decision in 1927 to move St. Joseph's College out to the western edge of the city, perched on Philadelphia's Main Line, was a harbinger of things to come.

Parishioners initially blamed real estate speculators for the decline. Men in suits went door to door assuring landlords that the arrival of Black residents into Fairmount would raise rents—either through efforts to price them out or simply because there were plenty of Black families ready to pay twice as much to buy or to rent. I noticed an initial defensive strategy that involved moving white parishioners who rented into more permanent homeownership. The Loyola Building and Loan Association, aptly named for the founder of the Jesuits, placed ads in parish calendars that promised renting parishioners an unparalleled peace of mind that came with homeownership. "You will be secure in the thought, 'I will not be forced to move from the neighborhood in which I have lived for many years, now that I own my home.'"[13] The campaign for home-ownership also took on a spiritual dimension. A parish inventory of the "favors granted during the Novena of Grace" in April of 1925 included five apartments and rooms rented, one house rented, and one prayer of thanksgiving that a house would not be sold.[14]

I guessed that Sophie handled the frequent knocks at the door in their first decade on N. 20th Street—realtors inquiring as to whether or not she and George were interested in selling. They were decidedly not, she informed them. "We're meeting expectations," she might have thought to herself after sending them on their way. At least for now. But everyone knew that the real concern was not so much rates of homeownership as much as *who* owned the homes in the parish.

JIM CROWED HOUSING IN PHILADELPHIA

The Yeagers could hardly have been impervious to the fact that their new neighborhood in the Fairmount section of North Central Philadelphia was on the frontlines of the "colored invasion," as Fr. Love called it, even in the 1920s. Their arrival at 823 N. 20th Street coincided with that of some of the first Black residents in their ward, although looking at census data I didn't find any Black families living on the 800 block when they bought their home in 1924. Like the Yeagers, Black people arriving at this time had the financial means to move into fashionable neighborhoods like Fairmount. They were not intimidated by the foreboding white-run institutions anchoring it: the notorious Eastern State Penitentiary, with its fifteen-foot-thick walls and forty-foot guard towers two blocks to the west, the fifteen-foot high walls of the legally segregated Girard College for white orphan boys just two blocks north, and the Jesuits' massive out-post at the Gesu about a quarter of a mile to the east.

But I'm not sure how much the Yeagers were aware of the workings of the government—federal, state, and city—to defend against this "in-vasion" or the way parish leaders colluded in those efforts. Nor was I before rounding the Gesu. But through his extensive examination of the causes of residential segregation in the twentieth century in *The Color of Law*, as well as in a few one-on-one conversations with me, Richard Roth-stein helped me understand three ways the government shaped what was happening in the Gesu parish and how those Jim Crow policies impacted the Yeagers.[15]

The first had to do with public housing, which was the government's earliest involvement in the housing business immediately following World War I and which set the tone for everything that followed. To address a housing shortage, the government built eighty-three public projects in twenty-six states. This early public housing initiative did not fit today's stereotype on two counts: it had nothing to do with a family's ability to pay and it initially only housed whites. Gradually, public housing units became available for Black families, but like all things Jim Crow, they were separate from and unequal to those of their white counterparts regardless of where they were built. By 1933, federal public housing reflected the "neighborhood composition rule," which indicated that new housing should "reflect the previous racial composition of their neighborhoods"— or at least what bureaucrats predicted it to be.[16] In other words, white public housing was zoned for white neighborhoods, Black public housing for Black neighborhoods. Rothstein notes these policies were so effective that they segregated communities already integrated and pushed cities like Philadelphia "into a more rigid segregation than would have existed otherwise."[17]

Then came the federal push to create American homeowners in the wake of the Great Depression. To jump-start the economy with a construction boom, a variety of New Deal programs, particularly those sponsored by the Public Works Administration, made housing more affordable. The plan was twofold: help existing homeowners avoid default, and make new homeowners. The Yeagers fell into the first camp. Up until then, home financing practices of the day required 50 percent down on a non-amortized mortgage. Buyers had only five to seven years to pay down the debt, which is likely why George and Sophie took in boarders. But with the help of the Home Owners' Loan Corporation (HOLC), their mortgage at 823 N. 20th became amortized, which allowed them a chance to build equity they could pass on to Georgia. The HOLC also lowered their mortgage, giving them a bit of breathing room with the monthly expenses and even a chance to tuck away more of George's salary each month. Their loan was likely extended from five years to ten or even fifteen years.

Black people moving into the Gesu Parish likely fell into the category of new homeowners. But since FDR had to make significant concessions to segregationist Southern Democrats to get New Deal legislation through, these programs also shored up residential segregation by ensuring new buyers avoided "incompatible ownership occupancy."[18] The government did this largely through zoning, which channeled the millions of dollars flowing to local economies for housing away from Black people and toward whites. Zoning laws at the state and municipal levels were designed "to isolate white families in all-white urban neighborhoods" and to protect property values in those zones.[19] Of course, racial zoning was not new. In 1921 President Harding's secretary of commerce, Herbert Hoover, organized an Advisory Committee on Zoning, which helped create policies that designated certain zones for single-family homes or "restricted residential districts" and legalized racialized housing covenants that either prohibited sales to Black buyers or created deeds that prevented future sales to them. Municipal governments also passed "spot zoning" that allowed small industries in Black neighborhoods, setting them up for later devaluation at the hands of government insurance appraisers.[20]

Finally, to assist with the prudent distribution of more than one million loans, appraisers with the HOLC devised a series of color-coded "residential security maps" in cities across the country meant to assess return on investment and risk of default, as well as to avoid integrated "inharmonious racial or nationality groups."[21] While rates of homeownership and conditions of existing housing stock were among the criteria used, the racial and ethnic identity of the tracts proved to be the deciding factor in whether a neighborhood was shaded green for A or red for D. The HOLC handed these maps over to its successor in government bureaucracy, the Federal Housing Authority (FHA), which initially distributed housing loans across the grades when founded in 1934. Rothstein put it very plainly: "Because the FHA's appraisal standards included a whites-only requirement, racial segregation now became an official requirement of the federal mortgage insurance program."[22]

When I went looking for the residential security map of the Gesu's Fairmount section, I found the 1936 assessment of one J. M. Brewer, an appraiser for the Met Life Insurance Company, one of Philadelphia's biggest insurance lenders. Brewer was also a map consultant to the HOLC. He shaded most of the Gesu Parish, including the 800 block of N. 20th Street, red.[23] The FHA's instruction in its 1935 *Underwriting Manual* spelled the fate for the Gesu: "If a neighborhood is to retain stability it is necessary that properties shall continue to be occupied by the same social and racial classes. A change in social or racial occupancy generally leads to instability and reduction in values."[24]

THE YEAGERS AND GESU PARISH IMPROVEMENT

From what I could ascertain from Gesu parish calendars in the mid 1930s, the tension about "undesirables" hung like a fog of incense over the Fairmount neighborhood. The number of parishioners was dwindling, evidenced by lower returns in the block collection and consolidation of Mass offerings. I could also tell from those calendars that Sophie tried to do her part. Aside from a few exceptionally tight months in 1931—in the wake of losing their savings in the first of Philadelphia's banks to close in the Crash of 1929—she set aside a dollar each month for the Church Debt Association. She always graciously welcomed a visit from their block collection solicitor, Josephine McConnell. She even made an extra contribution in the name of Mary Beely, a friend in their collection district. When Fr. Higgins made an appeal for "old gold" to repair chalices and engravings around the church's ornate altars, Sophie donated jewelry. She was even prepared to pull out the bricks in the basement wall to raid George's secret stash. He was a fool to think he could keep any of his earnings safe from her vigilant bookkeeping.

By 1936, however, it was clear that austerity measures and novenas were insufficient. In July, as she and Georgia were preoccupied with the plans for Georgia's wedding in the Gesu that September—she was to marry Maurice Andrew O'Connell from St. Agatha's in West Philadelphia—Sophie would have noticed something entirely new in the parish calendar. Amidst announcements about sodalities, card games, the Boy Scout troop, and reminders about the extra need for piety in the summer months, there was an announcement from a Gesu Parish Improvement Association (GPIA) with an extensive plan "to keep and bring into the parish respectable home-owners and tenants and to prevent the further influx of undesirables into the neighborhood."[25]

It was clear from the full-page spread that the GPIA meant business. I was struck by their organizational chart, which listed a president, Dr. Francis Stokes; a vice president each for buildings, organization, and finances; a publicity director; and their goal: stop the incursion of Black people and keep the remaining white parishioners in place. The first step required securing commitments from white parishioners not to sell to Black buyers. The second involved protecting against white property devaluation by offering financial assistance for home improvements to those who needed it. This required taking an inventory of all of the housing and seeking funding. Third, and most importantly, all parishioners were to "remain firm" by "actively 'warring' against unscrupulous speculators who seek to hasten the decline of the parish and gain financial advantage from this depreciation."[26]

As a homeowner on the edge of the parish and in the vicinity of Black residents, Sophie likely received a personal invitation from Dr. Francis Stokes on GPIA letterhead. I can imagine her reading it to George: "We feel sure that you are interested in preventing further deterioration of your neighborhood. This prevention can be accomplished only through the concerted efforts of the residents of this district . . . Help yourself by helping your neighbors save their homes from invasion and ruin."[27]

"I wonder if I should attend," Sophie may have pondered, as she rocked away in her chair in the front room, her eye on the 800 block of N. 20th Street.

By September 1936, the GPIA called all parishioners to a "PLEDGE OF ASSISTANCE." They were to attend meetings, join canvassing teams to spread the word, or take an inventory of various districts across the parish. Homeowners like the Yeagers were encouraged to inform the GPIA if they planned to sell their home and to contribute yearly dues of one dollar to support the association's work. A month into the initiative, turnout was low and men seemed particularly underrepresented. GPIA officers wondered why "the heads of the families, the lords and masters of the home, the fathers who have toiled to provide homes for their families" were missing in action. Perhaps the men didn't understand the magnitude of the situation, or worse, assumed that it was a "women's organization." "Well it isn't," was the loud and clear message.[28] I can't imagine that sat right with the Yeager matriarch on N. 20th Street.

As I read announcement after announcement in the parish calendars, I found myself wondering about my great-grandmother. Was Sophie an unnamed foot soldier in that army of women doing the bidding of the GPIA on a battlefield whose frontlines were drawn by the Federal Housing Administration? From what my dad remembers, she was the real head of the Yeager household, so the decision to be involved was probably hers to make. Did she dip her toe in and sign a petition calling for the municipal authorities to do their part in terms of neighborhood upkeep or notifying someone on the committee about a "desirable" occupant for a recently vacated property? After all, their life's savings were tied up in their home. As a homeowner on the very edge of the parish and with a handful of Black residents on surrounding blocks, was she a leader who held block meetings in her parlor to identify and shore up weak spots in the ramparts? Or, as a landlord with a tenant on her third floor, did she share intelligence about the moving plans of neighbors or the phone numbers of less scrupulous landlords? I tried to infer from Sophie and George's other choices—to send Georgia to Girls High, one of Philadelphia's prestigious public schools, for example, where I counted at least twenty Black faces smiling along with her in her senior class picture—proof that they remained on the sidelines. And yet, the internal pressure to conform was relentless. There were so many parish announcements with so much capitalization and shaming that even I could hear the shouts of the GPIA leadership coercing parishioners into action. "It is YOUR home—YOUR neighborhood—YOUR parish—YOUR gain when gain is made—YOUR DUTY TO CO-OPERATE."[29]

Once again, Christian ethicist Katie Walker Grimes's work on anti-Blackness as a vice or a bad habit cultivated in the racial habitat of the Northern Catholic parish allowed me to see how my family members were, in her words, "blighted by their strategic spacial isolation from and domination over black people." Grimes explains that although they become second nature, habits are things we choose to do in order to "maximize our ability to move ourselves in the direction of a desired end." If virtues are habits of mind and body that move us toward flourishing, then vices are habits that impede that capacity. Racialized habits of anti-Blackness, like perceiving Black people as dangerous liabilities and moving our bodies away from them—whether by crossing streets, avoiding Black neighborhoods, or living in exclusively white ones—advance whites toward the end of maintaining our power and privilege over Black people. They extend the dominating dynamics of slavery and sustain its afterlife. Grimes notes that Catholic parishes like the Gesu helped to cultivate corporate vices of anti-Blackness because they carved Northern American cities into swaths of voluntary spatial isolation or racial habitats in which individual and collective habits of anti-Blackness could go unreflected on, unchecked, uninterrupted, unquestioned. In this way, the varied and evolving strategies of the Gesu Parish Improvement Association were really an attempt to "manufacture social identity spatially, preserving racial difference through residential distance."[30]

I agree with her assessment that anti-Black vices are not innocuous, but vicious, and that in performing them we are not innocent but culpable. But where or to whom could the Yeagers have turned for more virtuous directions, especially in their Catholic tradition? The answer to that question provided little comfort.

CATHOLIC ANSWERS TO THE "NEGRO QUESTION"

From the moment her little family staked their claim on the Gesu parish boundary line, Sophie received mixed messages about what Catholics should do about the influx of African Americans into the 47th Ward. From what I could tell, she could choose from three options on the Catholic menu, all of which were unfolding at the same time in the Gesu in the late 1930s.

First, Sophie would have heard the language of human rights like that used by GPIA, which had theological roots in the newly promulgated encyclicals of Catholic social teaching. These emphasized the right to private property as critical to human dignity and to protection of the family, the basic social unit of society. White American Catholics put their own spin on Catholic rights talk. They emphasized the individual nature of human rights via patriotic appeals to American individualism. For example, Sophie would have read commentary in the Gesu monthly calendar about the democratic virtues of Charles Carroll, Catholic signer of the Declaration of Independence—albeit with no mention of his slave-owning legacy. The Catholic rights tradition also took on a defensive posture in the United States, especially in cities like Philadelphia with a long tradition of anti-Catholicism. Thanks to propaganda in the parish bulletins that kept everybody focused on lingering anti-Catholic discrimination, parishioners understood rights in the context of immunity from others' impositions to their way of life rather than obligations toward the care for others. Catholics had always had to defend themselves against Protestants, the thinking went, and so this situation with Black people was no different.

Sophie likely read a flier put out by the GPIA publicity committee, which clearly appealed to her twin sensibilities as an American and a

Catholic. In a litany akin to the rights delineated in the Declaration of Independence, the committee made references to rights and preservation of the family as the basic unit of society. They couched these rights in a language of struggle and militarism, which likely stirred memories of World War I nationalist calls to action:

- WE must obtain tenants for unoccupied homes
- WE must improve our houses to induce others to follow our example
- WE must contribute to the support of the movement of organizing to stop further inroads
- WE must get every person in every block in the Parish to become a member in order to make the voice of the people heard by those who for selfish reasons wish to lower the standards of living in this neighborhood
- WE must induce owners and tenants not to let properties become unoccupied especially in the zone of combat
- WE must be ready to sacrifice time and money in the work of restoring this region to its former grandeur
- WE must not give up our homes without a mighty struggle for our rights
- WE must consider this a battle to preserve the family as the proper unit of society[31]

IT WASN'T JUST BLACK PEOPLE who were infringing on the rights of the citizens of the 47th Ward, but also the federal and municipal government. "We assert our right to reside in this district" a petition proclaimed, "and deny that any agency of the municipality, state or federal government has the right to encroach upon this right." Fr. Maguire encouraged the leadership committee to "get any white voter to sign."[32] The petition then morphed into a personalized pledge card, which parishioners—whether "owner, tenant, or sub-tenant"—were expected to sign.[33] To my mind, it read like a Pledge of Allegiance to the white parish: "I will not sell or rent or sublet my property to any person or persons who would be undesirable to my neighbors or who would be likely to lower the standards of living in this neighborhood." GPIA leadership indicated that twelve hundred had signed pledge cards by December of 1936.[34] I have no way of knowing if Sophie and George were among them.

Sophie's second option on the Catholic menu may have glided right past her front parlor window. From her perch on her rocker, she likely spied pairs of nuns with their formidable black habits who were not canvassing for real estate but rather for the souls of lapsed and possible future Black Catholics in the hostile territory of North Philadelphia. These Sisters of the Blessed Sacrament literally embodied missionary zeal for evangelizing Black souls. Once again, the Gesu parish bulletin would have provided Sophie some context for their work. A note on the feast of St. Peter Claver in September 1924 pondered what he might do in the current day in light of "the great influx of colored people" into Northern cities like Philadelphia. "The colored race in our country is truly in need of an apostle," it said. "But until he arrives let each and every one of us prepare the soil for his labors by our prayers and by our active endeavors in [sic] behalf of the race in every capacity in which we are permitted to labor for it."[35] The disciples of Philadelphia's own such apostle, Katharine Drexel, were doing just that right there in Sophie's neighborhood. In 1909, Mother Drexel had opened a parish and school for Black Catholics at Broad and Spring Garden, at a distance far enough from the Jesuits at the Gesu to keep Black Catholics from turning up on their doorstep.[36] In the spirit of evangelization, the Sisters canvassed the blocks of Fairmount to identify lapsed or potential Black Catholics and direct them to "catechetical centers" they were running in the homes of Black Catholics in the neighborhood.[37]

Finally, had Sophie attended one of the GPIA meetings, she likely would have met Mrs. Anna McGarry, who joined the executive committee within a year of its founding. They had much in common. Although Anna was ten years Sophie's junior, they both were transplants into the parish. Both were without husbands at parish functions, since Anna was a widow. And their only children—Georgia and Mary—were the center of their respective worlds. Pulling from a few interviews Anna did later in life, it was not difficult to conjure an encounter between her and Sophie at one of the GPIA meetings in which Anna offered her a third option when it came to Black people moving into the Gesu.

Pulling from McGarry's materials in three different archives, a biographical article about her life's work in U.S. Catholic Historian, and my interview with her only surviving nephew a year before he died at age eighty-six, I imagine an exchange between Anna McGarry and my great-grandmother Sophie could have gone something like what follows.[38]

> "Real estate speculators first knocked on my door in 1923 to tell me that my rent would likely being going up," Anna confided to Sophie. "When they came back a few weeks later with an option to buy I decided to do it."[39]
>
> Anna explained that protecting the value of her $3,000 investment on Perkiomen Street wasn't her only motivation for joining the GPIA. She also wanted to shift white attitudes about Black people, particularly white *Catholic* attitudes. As an active member of the American Legion, she had witnessed ugliness from widows of white veterans toward those of Black veterans. While visiting a Josephite mission to Black Catholics in the Deep South, she saw Catholic hospitals that were racially segregated.
>
> "This was my first introduction to racial injustice," she confessed. "Negroes were being used to exploit white fears, and they, in turn, were exploited themselves."[40]
>
> Anna continued, "I believed my husband had given his life to protect democracy but here in my own neighborhood I [see] actions that nullified his sacrifice." Clearly, their unquestioned contributions to the war effort were enough to affirm once and for all Black people's fitness for citizenship. And surely Americans proved during the war years that they were capable of overcoming racial animus. "It seems as if the Lord has given me a vivid illustration of injustice. I could not put it in a package and forget it."[41]

Prior to joining the GPIA, Anna had met Fr. William Walsh, pastor of St. Ignatius in West Philadelphia, one of the Archdiocese's "colored" parishes, who had a different answer to the "Negro question." Why not bring Black and white Catholics together for conversation and fellowship? Dioceses around the country had created Catholic Interracial Councils, similar to initiatives in Protestant denominations that saw ignorance as a root cause of racial prejudice. Conversion of attitudes was the first step toward much-needed changes in policies. Anna attended a lecture in 1936 by one of the leaders of the movement, John LaFarge, SJ. He explained that "Negro and white relations" were of concern to all Americans, particularly to the missionary activity of the Catholic Church. It extended beyond the Black/white binary and was a road that all Americans would sooner or later find themselves on. So why not start to provide guidance now?[42]

LaFarge's solution, interracial justice, involved combatting race prejudice and establishing social justice. He believed interracial work required equal parts social justice to build a new social order and social charity to foster unity of hearts and minds. Catholic Interracial Councils in Northern cities brought Black and white Catholics together to address suffering and indifference. They prayed together, collaborated in ministries directed at the welfare of Black people, educated white Catholics about racial prejudice and its impact, and engaged in constructive action to remove disadvantages and violations of human rights in everything from education and housing to employment and child welfare.

Anna found the interpersonal and spiritual approach compelling. It was already underway in discrete pockets around Philadelphia. A good friend had been running informal forums for white and Black people in her home. Anna herself had attended something similar at St. Ignatius. She had returned to the 47th Ward with a fire in her heart. There was still time to turn the Gesu around. Minds could be changed. Hearts could be moved. The Catholic tradition could be better harnessed to make decisions rooted in justice rather than fear. Before the end of 1937, sixteen Black and white Catholics gathered in her living room.

"Not for cards," she smiled shrewdly at Sophie, "but for discussion."[43]

Should she save a space for Sophie and George at their next forum?

FRONTSTAGE AND BACKSTAGE RACISM IN THE GPIA

As I got lost in all of the GPIA correspondence and promotional materials, I noticed that the group took different stances toward Black people depending on whom they were dealing with. Sociologists Leslie Houts Picca and Joe Feagin call this dual mode of operation, in which white people use language and imagery in a particular social setting to shape the inclinations of other white people, "frontstage" and "backstage" racism.[44] On the more public frontstage, white people perform racism by being extremely polite, avoiding the topic of racism and people who are not white, insisting that we are not racist but rather tolerant, and using racial stereotypes to identify people of color as threats to our personal security and private property. By contrast, in the more private backstage, safe spaces where white people assume there are no people of color present, we are less vigilant about maintaining a veneer of appropriate behavior, so overt racist language and stereotypes are the acceptable and even expected norm.[45]

Since the Yeagers were either in the Gesu audience or perhaps even members of the cast on the stage themselves, the GPIA certainly taught them how to perform two-faced racism, which was anti-Black regardless of orientation or audience. In its frontstage performances—block captain meetings, the parish calendar, the announcements from the pulpit—the GPIA couched their initiative in the language of material and spiritual improvement of people and homes in the parish. For example, reports from the GPIA in spring of 1937 detailed progress toward general improvements of the neighborhood: the installation of traffic lights; blocking a new taproom from opening a few blocks away; a cost-saving workshop with a heating and plumbing expert; a lecture with the district director of the FHA on how to improve housing conditions. At first, this struck me as innocuous. But the GPIA implicitly revealed their anti-Black intent. For example, even though they didn't want any new taprooms, they backed the renewal of a lease for a state-run liquor store at 18th and Girard rather than see the property be rented to another tenant like a Black-owned business or, even worse in their minds, a Black church.

But in its more private whites-only backstage interactions, I noticed that the GPIA's racist intentions and language were on full display. Men like Dr. Francis Stokes, the new president, and Jesuits like Fr. Thomas Higgins, SJ pastor and also president from 1933–1939 of Saint Joseph's College (which was also situated within the Gesu footprint before moving to its current location straddling the boundary between the city and Montgomery County in 1927), and Fr. James Maguire, SJ the animator of the movement, used racist speech to galvanize parishioners to action. For example, in June 1936, Dr. Stokes, a physician and prominent parishioner, wrote a letter to Higgins reminding him of what was at stake with the association's first meeting the following evening.

"First of all I feel that this movement is a last ditch stand to prevent the invasion that will sweep practically all of the parishioners out of the Gesu," wrote Stokes.[46] A survey of parish real estate by the end of September 1936 was telling: sixty-five houses for sale or rent and fifteen apartments for rent. The response from the pews was frustratingly lackluster. I found that, as anxieties mounted, the GPIA became increasingly overtly anti-Black in its backstage attempts to persuade well-connected Catholics beyond the parish to lend their support. For example, in late summer and fall of 1936, Fr. Higgins pleaded with his contacts in city and state government for counsel and assistance. "You've probably heard that we here are making strenuous efforts to rehabilitate this old neighborhood and to preserve it from further inroads of the colored," he wrote Thomas Logue, secretary of internal affairs for the Commonwealth of Pennsylvania. "It stands to reason that if this locality become colored, we shall lose an investment of two million dollars, which we hold in this plant."[47]

Higgins also sought a meeting with Matthew McCloskey of the newly created Regional Planning Federation, on "the matter of the housing project for undesirables in this neighborhood," as well as the plans for the sale of the state-run liquor store at 18th and Girard to a "colored Baptist Church." This latest "menace of negro invasion threatens us," Higgins explained in his initial letter to McCloskey. "Of course, if a colored Baptist Church is set up on Girard Avenue, that is the end of Girard Avenue as a residence for whites."[48]

I noticed that the GPIA also relied on backstage racism to scare up outside funding. For instance, in early August of 1936, Stokes received an update on the fruits of a meeting with an executive at the Real Estate Trust Company, who in turn recommended contacts in the real estate departments of two local banks—Girard Trust and Fidelity Philadelphia—as well as members of the Bureau of Engineering and the Zoning Board of Adjustment in city hall.[49] These parties could be allies. Stokes also suggested that Higgins reach out to the FHA for funding to repair and convert the many large single-family homes throughout the parish into multiple units that would be more attractive to and affordable for smaller families, likely knowing that the agency offered tax exemptions to churches that bolstered segregation.

But it was the scuttlebutt around the "old Muhlenberg School" that really took my breath away when it came to the GPIA's backstage commitment to anti-Blackness. In May of 1937, Higgins wrote a letter to the Philadelphia school board urging them to vote against a proposal to reopen the school as a community center. "If this school is given over to the colored people for use as a community center, our white parishioners will be driven from this section," he pointed out to who he assumed was a group of whites. "For with colored people standing around the outside of the building every night, white people and especially white women, will fear to pass." Citing two recent assaults involving Black men and white women, Higgins predicted that should the center open, parishioners "living in that vicinity will be prevented from attending evening Church services."[50]

To ensure that his missive would be taken seriously, Higgins phoned a judge, A. L. Fitzpatrick, to see what might be done. He also called on a lawyer in the parish, Connie O'Brien, to lean on the school board.

"We are all sympathetic with the aspirations of the colored people to improve themselves," O'Brien wrote to a school board member on Higgins's behalf. "As a matter of fact it is my personal view that the colored man has been treated shamefully by his white brothers." However, O'Brien remained committed to the parish's efforts to "stem the tide of colored immigration."[51]

"Things of this sort are very annoying to all concerned," Higgins acknowledged in a note to thank O'Brien for his efforts. "But we are fighting for our lives to preserve this neighborhood and can't afford to leave any stone unturned."[52]

Things got much more annoying for Higgins. At some point before the school board vote, an outraged Fr. Clement Roach, CSSP, the Spiritan pastor of St. Peter Claver, the Black parish at 12th and Lombard, called Higgins. Not only had Higgins's maneuverings undermined Roach's efforts among Black Catholics in his parish, but they also had infuriated Dr. John P. Turner, the first Black member of Philadelphia's school board. Roach had a message from Turner for Higgins: retract his protest or Turner would go public with Higgins's letter to the school board in the Philadelphia papers and national Black press.[53]

It was clear to me that a panicked Higgins backpedaled once he realized the curtain had been pulled on his backstage racism. Using frontstage niceties, he attempted to assuage Turner through the same contacts he had used weeks earlier. "I made a very serious blunder," he wrote in a letter to a Philadelphia judge, Harry McDevitt, equating Turner's threats with "nothing short of blackmail." "I didn't know at the time that there was a colored man on the Board. Had I known so, I would never have written this letter." Higgins called upon his personal history of "laboring for [negroes] in the past" as evidence that he was not personally opposed to them, just opposed to them in "this particular location." Turner wasn't open to reason, Higgins complained. Going public, he feared, would "stir up such a campaign of publicity against me and my protest throughout the entire country as to make it appear that the Catholic Church is down on the negroes."[54]

BECOMING COVENANT-MINDED

I sensed from all of the capitalization and guilt trips in their announcements that the GPIA was frustrated with parishioners' lack of enthusiasm and running out of ideas. So early in the spring of 1937, just before the Muhlenberg school fiasco, the Jesuit force of nature of the GPIA, Fr. James Ignatius Maguire, SJ went on a fact-finding mission in Catholic parishes in Washington, DC, and Baltimore to learn "their methods of combatting the devaluation of properties through the influx of the negro into white residential sections."[55] Maguire returned with a strategy that took their efforts to the next level: covenants. The GPIA would canvas the blocks of the parish and convince all parishioners on those blocks to commit to each other that they would not rent or sell to Black people.

The word *covenant* struck me as weighty, particularly for Catholics. This was not simply a legal contract—although in 1926 the Supreme Court ruled that private agreements like covenants were indeed legal even if zoning based on race was unconstitutional. Rather, a covenant was more akin to a sacred vow to remain faithful to a relationship that brought about flourishing. The GPIA thought such a relationship among white parishioners was the last hope for defending the parish.

The GPIA rolled out the idea in successive parish calendars throughout 1937. The initial announcement in February explained that covenants are "binding on themselves and their heirs for period of 21 years—not to sell, rent, or permit the occupancy of their properties by persons of the color race," they explained.[56] Anticipating legal concerns, they further noted, "These pledges properly executed were sanctioned and upheld by both the lower court and the Supreme Court . . ."[57] And anticipating outward racial animus, they concluded, "While in no way detrimental to the colored race this has been effective in preventing a mixture of the races in neighborhoods and has been found to work to the mutual benefit of all concerned."[58] The GPIA also said covenants would protect Black buyers from being exploited by real estate speculators. "Surely," the initial announcement concluded, "our colored brethren are happier and more content in their own little neighborhoods."[59] The GPIA also couched covenants in the language of faith. "Let us progress on the **Golden Rule!**

No one wants his neighbor to do anything detrimental to his property; therefore, appeal to his sense of justice to do nothing detrimental to his **neighbor's** property."[60]

I wondered what Sophie and George made of the very clear fact that in the Gesu, Black people were not "neighbors." Reading over the finer points of the Gesu's racial covenant, I imagined yet another exchange in that front parlor on 823 N. 20th Street with Mrs. Bicking and Mrs. Conlan, who had become chairwomen of the Covenant Committee.

"This is a community stand," Mrs. Conlan said to Sophie. "It's a long pull and a hard pull, and we have to pull together.[61] Your signature does NOT bind you unless and until all your NEIGHBORS have joined with you."[62] The Gesu covenants would only have any value in staving off Black homebuyers if everybody signed.

From what I could tell by the tone of announcements in the parish calendars toward the end of 1939, the covenant idea was not catching on as the GPIA had hoped. By December, leadership tried a patriotic tack. "If the signers of the Declaration of Independence had withheld their signatures, each waiting for someone else to take the first step, where would we be today?" they asked of their fellow parishioners. "The question that confronts us today is a question of Independence!"[63]

"It's a matter of exercising our rights," Mrs. Bicking said to Sophie from the front step during their final pitch. "We have a right to preserve our homes and our neighborhood and to protect against deterioration . . . against any persons—whether owners or tenants—who by their living conditions is detrimental to the health and well-being of the immediate neighborhood."[64]

"As owners, you and George have a real investment to protect," Mrs. Conlan reminded her.[65] "Are we going to permit undesirable conditions to create in our neighborhood a force for depreciation of property values?"[66]

I like to imagine these ladies closing the deal with something along the lines of: "I think the question, Mrs. Yeager, is why *wouldn't* you sign?"

I came across another influence on my great-grandparents' answer in another cache of fliers and letters to Higgins. In August of 1939, Maguire decided to make an example out of James Gorman, a lifelong parishioner and homeowner on the 1300 block of 19th Street, who had rented his home to a Black family. Even though Gorman described his new tenants as "highly respectable and with indisputable references," Maguire intervened on moving day. He confronted Gorman's realtor to keep him from drawing up the lease and then went to Gorman's property where he attempted to keep the Black family from moving in. By Gorman's account, Maguire shouted: "You are not wanted. You destroy property. I will have you out of there in a wink." He eventually made good on his threat to have Gorman's property foreclosed upon. In a final letter to his pastor asking for assistance, Gorman forewarned, "If this course is not checked it will lead to serious trouble in the future as [Fr. Maguire] has to a great extent created race prejudice."[67] It was not long before Philadelphia's Black press agreed with Gorman. "One Father Maguire can do more to destroy good will between the races than hundreds of devout Catholics can create," a columnist from the *Philadelphia Tribune*, one of the city's leading Black newspapers, reported in February of 1941.[68]

I couldn't help but think that it was not just "good will" that Maguire and the GPIA were destroying with their efforts, but the very wills or desires of Gesu parishioners themselves. Returning to Grimes's ideas about anti-Blackness as a vice, the push to sign racial covenants was not merely the result of what white people were conditioned to do, but what they *wanted* to do because of the power and privilege over Black people that these covenants afforded them. The parish "acted as one, performing segregation in coordinated fashion with bishops, priests, and laity synchronizing themselves hierarchically."[69] To put it another way, in the Gesu my people learned what Grimes calls "the spatial logic" of anti-Blackness, or to associate homeownership with whiteness and with belonging. They learned that defending the racial purity of our neighborhoods and therefore our parishes was not just acceptable but expected, even demanded with threats of violence to those who did not comply. Cultivating this desire for power that came with belonging ensured that Sophie and George would lack moral courage when it came time for the tough choices like deciding upon potential renters, reporting on new Black arrivals on 20th Street, signing the Gesu covenant for 20th Street, or standing up to bullies like Maguire.

CATHOLIC ECUMENISM ANCHORED IN ANTI-BLACKNESS

For all of their talk about defending the parish against anti-Catholicism, I couldn't help but notice that from the outset the men on the GPIA sought coalitions with like-minded whites beyond the geographical and doctrinal boundaries of the parish in their campaign to maintain their "grand old neighborhood." At some point as early as the fall of 1936, Stokes shared with Higgins an idea proposed to him by Rev. Dr. Reese of neighboring St. Michael's Episcopal Church to buy up properties in the neighborhood before Black people could. There were not enough Episcopalians still living in the neighborhood, Reese had explained, so the fundraising would have to fall to the GPIA. Stokes was of the mind that other "financial institutions could be interested in this from the angle of investment."[70]

By 1940, a notorious "Committee of Ten" devised a plan to buy a Quaker school on the northwest corner of 17th Street and Girard Avenue that was to be sold and converted to a "clinic for colored people." Fr. Thomas Love wrote to Cardinal Dougherty in mid-October mapping out their strategy. Surely his Eminence knew that property values decreased by 50 percent or more when "acquired by colored people," Love pandered. And certainly the cardinal would agree no other section of the city had more to lose than Gesu's. Love explained that a "Mass Meeting" had been held in the hall of St. Matthew's Episcopal church where "Catholics and non-Catholics alike" adopted a resolution to collect through subscriptions enough money to buy the title of the property and hand it over to the Gesu School. They had pledges of more than $7,500 already in hand. Love offered for the Catholics on the Committee of Ten to meet with the cardinal or to offer any more information.[71]

Dougherty replied the very next day with what I can only describe as a frontstage "wanting to have it both ways" stance. On the one hand, he could appreciate the Jesuits' predicament. "It is needless to say that I should regret any injury to anyone's property, especially Church property," Dougherty wrote, tacitly approving of their motivations. On the other hand, he declined the request to meet not simply because the Committee of Ten's approach was wrong but rather because the optics might interfere with Dougherty's plans to "convert the Negroes of Philadelphia." Like whites today who reject the label of "racist" by naming their Black friends, Dougherty indicated his devotion to St. Peter Claver and his "intense admiration for Mother Katharine Drexel."[72] Even though he recognized the injustice inherent in denying Blacks from buying property, he did not use his unquestioned authority to shut down the Committee of Ten.

I was surprised to discover through coverage in the *Philadelphia Tribune* that the Jesuits moved forward without the cardinal's explicit blessing. In February 1941, the paper printed an exposé of the coordinated attempt to block the sale of the property, titled "Gesu Priests Advocate

Segregation."[73] A week later another article reported "evidence of the determined efforts" of Maguire "to set the white population of his parish against Negroes," including using his influence to prevent the sale of houses to Blacks and promising police reprisals for those who did so.[74] An unidentified and undated news clipping in the Gesu archive, which I presumed to be from late February of 1941, listed the 115 contributors to the campaign: Gesu Church with $2,000, Girard College with $1,000, Fr. Love with $500, and the Gesu Parish Improvement Society with $100. The notorious Committee of Ten identified in the column included two Jesuits (Love and Maguire), Reese of St. Matthews, Merle Odgers, the president of Girard College, one member of the Gesu vestry, two realtors from Girard Avenue, a public accountant, and two lay men.[75] That same month, the *Philadelphia Courier* ran its own exposé, highlighting the ability of Catholics to overcome their usual defensive postures toward other religious denominations when it came to racial segregation. "The group is finally prepared to strike out in the open, now that it finally has success in effecting a unity on an anti-Negro bias among heretofore scattered community segments of Catholics, Protestants, and Jews," the paper declared. "And has even enlisted city officials, high clergymen, church congregations, businessmen, realtors, politicians, and educators."[76]

Then an undated letter to the *Tribune's* editor, signed by Arthur Huff Fauset, the head of Philadelphia's chapter of the NAACP, and a realtor named Lenerte Roberts, suggested that the cardinal's silence on the issue reflected his willingness to support initiatives that bring Black Catholics into the Church but also his failure to address the structural causes of their marginalization within and outside of it. "Arc Negroes in Philadelphia to interpret the Cardinal's attitude as one which responds to situations where direct benefit is to accrue to the Catholic Church, but ignores the problems of Negros," the *Tribune* asked, "even going so far as to disdain the appeals of their leaders, where there is danger of running into conflict with other elements in the Catholic Church?"[77] A year earlier the Federated Colored Catholics of Philadelphia, as well as the St. Mary's Beneficial Society, an aid group of Black Catholics for Black Catholics, wrote to Dougherty asking for an explanation as to why "responsible and well-placed members within the Negro group," who had informed him of anti-Black activities in the Gesu, had gone unacknowledged.[78]

A month later, Fauset concluded in a later column that Dougherty's failure to respond "must be interpreted by Negroes as an unwillingness or inability on the part of the Catholic Church to deal forthrightly with realistic problems effecting the Negro race."[79]

ANNA MCGARRY AND CATHOLIC INTERRACIALISM

So where was Anna McGarry and her interracial justice movement in the midst of this ugly turn of events? I wondered this as I sat back in my chair in the former rectory that once housed many of the protagonists in this saga and tried to process the Committee of Ten business, while the sounds of gentrification droned on in the background. By the time of the Committee of Ten fiasco in 1941, McGarry had become the "Mother of the Philadelphia Interracial Apostolate." She had convinced Jesuit leadership at the Gesu to invite John LaFarge for a public lecture about white attitudes toward Black people. She had hosted an interracial forum in her home. She had collaborated with Fr. Edward Cunnie at St. Elizabeth's to start a Philadelphia chapter of the Catholic Interracial Council, and she worked with her daughter and her peers to establish chapters on six of the city's Catholic college campuses. I got the sense that Anna saw great potential for interracialism in the GPIA. For example, in August of 1937 she joined the executive committee and within a year was the head of the publicity committee. During this time, I noticed that the organization changed its name from "parish" association to the more inclusive and potentially ecumenical "parish and neighborhood" association. I also noticed a concentrated effort on securing city services that would benefit all residents, not simply white homeowners. She had played a leadership role in creating a Gesu credit union, which helped Black residents bypass roadblocks to government loans.[80]

My discoveries in McGarry's archival materials indicated that her phone at 844 Perkiomen Street was ringing off the hook in mid-February 1941. Her growing network of white and Black Catholics across the city were all buzzing with the news of how the Jesuits were "joining with the Protestants, Jews, and Girard College to prevent a community service to Negroes," namely the right to purchase property in the 47th Ward. "It is a sad commentary," one of Anna's Black Catholic acquaintances confided to her, "that these four groups who can find no common meeting ground on any other field can link hands in a concerted fight against one section of our people."[81]

Anna could not argue with them. I'm not sure how much she knew about the backstage segregationist machinations of the male leadership of the GPIA, since I noticed her name among initial contributors to fund the purchase of the Quaker school. But clearly hearing from Black people in her growing network galvanized her to intervene. In February of 1941 she wrote to Love encouraging him to see the difference between defending property values against devaluation and defending "against the 'colored people' as a group." She offered him an out. "I am convinced, however, that until a greater measure of interracial justice prevails, we are standing in our own light, morally, financially, and socially" she wrote, "for human beings cannot possibly be neglected as our Negro citizens are without causing results which affect us all."[82]

She included a clipping of a column she had been invited to write in the *Philadelphia Tribune*. She hoped it would help him understand that she was "endeavoring to bring the Church and our understanding of American ideals closer to the Negro." She also hoped to bring the issues "facing our Negro citizens to the attention of citizens who are not tinged with radical ideas."[83] In the column, Anna pointed out commonalities between the races when it came to housing. Both Black and white people, for example, exhibit "great variation in the standards of living" and struggle with conditions of poverty that give rise to the deterioration of homes. Both groups were negatively impacted by the "foolhardy" decisions to let homes deteriorate rather than integrate neighborhoods. She pivoted to the fact that Black families were "compelled to be herded together," a strategy with a chain reaction that to her mind affected Black people as well as white. Black people dealt with overcrowding, which deteriorated and devalued their properties, "to say nothing of wear and tear on human beings and detriment to little children's health and morals." Whites on the other hand were faced with the tax burden of the "extra costs" to provide necessary public services in these overcrowded neighborhoods: fire, police, public health, and social welfare. "It is contrary to common sense, even from the standpoint of maintaining neighborhood standing," she said, "to let properties fall away to deterioration."[84]

Anna's solution? Bring white Catholics "face to face with the fact that Negroes can be and are equal and many times superior in their personal culture." She reminded her readers, which she hoped would include Higgins, that "great minds in the Catholic Church have been directing the eye of Americans in general and of Catholics in particular to the NEED FOR MORE HUMANE ATTITUDES TOWARD NEGROES for years and right now it is essential that the rule of INTERRACIAL JUSTICE be applied to all concerned."[85]

A day later, Love penned a reply acknowledging receipt of her letters. He hadn't had a chance to read her clippings, but she could come by the rectory to pick them up at her earliest convenience.

The archival trail in the sixth floor of the old Gesu rectory went cold there, and announcements in parish calendars about the GPIA dwindled within months. Had public shaming forced the Jesuits to pack it in? Did the parishioners desert the GPIA army by relocating? Parish history books provided me some insight. By the time of the Gesu's one hundredth jubilee in 1963, the *Philadelphia Evening Bulletin* described the parish as being "surrounded by the decay of a once-fashionable neighborhood," a tenth of its original size and 65 percent African American.[86] The parish's centenary jubilee book noted that "overcrowding, poor education, and low income combined to make the once fashionable Gesu neighborhood a ghetto."[87] Another centenary story in the *Catholic Standard & Times* noted a shift "toward a missionary type ministry to serve Negros and Puerto Ricans who have moved into the neighborhood," which the parish itself described as "bringing help to people deeply in need and instilling in them a keen social awareness whereby they might one day overcome the problems of the ghetto."[88] There was no mention of the role of white Catholics in making that ghetto and all of its problems.

By 1968, only fifty-eight of the remaining families had been there for fifty years or longer. Anna McGarry was one of them. Bruised by her own battles with the GPIA and, as we'll see in the next chapter, with Philadelphia's hierarchy, she doubled down on efforts within the parish to maintain the dignity of the under-resourced parishioners who were contained there by federal housing regulations, zoning laws, and covenants that kept them from moving anywhere else. When she could no longer live independently, she sold her home to the parish in 1969 with hopes that the Jesuits would keep her tenants and continue to rent it to families in need. They sold it not long after. Anna spent five years in Ohio with Mary and her husband until her death in 1978. Fittingly, she was buried from the Gesu. The Archdiocese closed the parish in 1993.

Although late arrivals in the Gesu, the Yeagers stayed longer than most of their white neighbors. Georgia and Maurice left before they did, first renting a row home in the East Oak Lane section of the city shortly after they were married and then moving even further north into Elkins Park, the first suburb on its northern border. My grandparents bought their twin home in 1944 with FHA funding, then raised my dad and his older brother in it. Sophie and George drove out of the city for Sunday visits. A photo snapped on one of those occasions, presumably taken by Maurice, shows them clustered on the modest front lawn, a striped awning shading the front porch behind them, my dad in bibbed shorts and high white knee socks, shyly backed into Sophie. Thirty years later, after parents bought the twin home from Georgia (my grandfather died in 1964), Dad took a similar family picture on that same lawn. This time it's me and my sister shyly backing into Georgia.

When Sophie and George finally sold their home on 20th Street in 1956, they moved to a two-story Cape Cod style single home in Hatboro, one of Philadelphia's more northern suburbs. It is likely that housing costs in the rapidly developing inner ring suburbs remained beyond their reach, even with federal support for a mortgage. But eventually they departed the twelve-story Gesu and joined the nondescript St. John Bosco Parish, just three years old by the time they arrived, fulfilling Dougherty's master plan that white Catholics would populate the suburbs and that urban parishes like the one they left would remain "evangelization centers" for Black Catholics. Sophie and George's descendants never looked back.

ROUNDING THE GESU: RACIAL MERCY AND BECOMING POROUS

Making my penitential rounding of the Gesu spurred me to find the connection between what I discovered about the strategies that white Catholics used to block Black people from moving into the parish in the 1920s and 1930s and the strategies of gentrification that were pushing Black residents out of it eighty years later. It had to do with spatial dominance, or the ability not only to make race, but also to make and control space based on what sociologist Elijah Anderson calls the "social border of skin color."[89] Anderson notes that "in public, stereotypically, white skin color is most often associated with respectability, civility, and trust, and black skin color is associated with poverty, danger, and distrust."[90] In the Gesu then and now, white people exercised the power to decide who does and does not belong to a space, to deny the moral authority of those who do not belong, and to sanction practices used to defend the boundaries of such spaces. For white Catholics, this space-making power is an extension of the power to name God. If to be made in the image of God is to be made for relationship, then through their power to determine what Anderson calls *white space* and *black space*, white Catholics have the power to determine the borders and contours of that fundamental relationality.

In Gesu, for example, white Catholics decided that Black people did not belong in the 47th Ward and worked collectively, innovatively—with respectability, civility, and even ecumenism—to keep them out. Catholics denied the moral authority of Black people who named this exclusion as wrong, whether by refusing to see Black homebuyers, school board members, church leaders, and even the Black press as anything other than causes of danger, poverty, and mistrust. White Catholics threatened violence not only against Black people who arrived unwelcomed in the parish, but also against other white parishioners who sympathized with Black people or who named the GPIA's strategies as un-Christian and un-American. Today, after generations of ceding this formerly white space in the 47th Ward to black space, to use Anderson's term, whites are once again exercising the power to make space by reversing the economic conditions, political policies, and social practices that created the ghetto that the 47th Ward became and then working to "put [Black people] in their place" by dislocating them from these newly reclaimed white spaces.[91] In other words, if anti-Black forces that created ghettos in the neighborhoods surrounding the Gesu in the first half of the twentieth century can be manipulated by other anti-Black forces at the outset of the twenty-first century to make those ghettos disappear, then so, too, should the Black people who live in them.

Ultimately, both then and now, whites are driven not only by what we don't understand, an excuse we often banter about to explain our reactions to Black people in our spaces, but also more specifically by our own vulnerabilities about our social position, our integrity, our lovability that the simple presence of Black people in spaces where we don't expect to find them—never mind their advancement in those spaces—can provoke. Anderson suggests that "Black presence thus becomes a profound and threatening racial symbol that for many whites can personify their own travail, their own insecurity, and their own sense of inequality."[92] The fact that whites can be easily motivated to protect that space points to just how much racism has stunted our own capability for relationship—not only with others but also with our very selves. All of this shoring up and pushing out points to a radical insecurity on our part, which Anderson notes is a real source of danger for Black people.

Which of my patterns of behavior or habits come from living, working, and worshipping in a racially homogenous "racial habitat," to use Katie Grimes's expression?[93] Anderson's own walking tours through a variety of spaces in Philadelphia have helped me see my habits. I notice my discomfort when Black people show up in spaces that I don't anticipate—on the trails in the park near my house, in workshops that I help facilitate, in my classrooms. I get nervous, self-conscious, and even resentful at the changes I might need to make to accommodate them. I also expect that Black people—colleagues, students, co-facilitators, fellow parishioners—somehow try to prove themselves as different from the stereotypical Black people from "the ghetto" for me to feel safe or to take them seriously. I can also completely fail to see Black people—crossing streets or raising hands in classrooms or workshops—which suggests a persistent kind of imperviousness to Black presence that comes with living most of my life in white space. Lack of awareness of just how much space I take up—and the historic motivations for that behavior—makes me a liability for racial justice movements, not an asset.

Rounding the Gesu not only illuminated the roots of these behaviors in my family's history, but also their detrimental impact. Mindy Fullilove, a clinical psychiatrist and sociomedical scientist, suggests that perpetual spatial "sorting" in cities like Philadelphia is "both morally repugnant and morally dangerous" because it creates "a dysfunctional city, plagued by illness and paralyzed in the face of problems."[94] She says it's tempting to think that the "mad plagues" of sorted cities—poverty, disease, violence, environmental degradation—don't impact those at the top socioeconomic pyramids. But in fact they fracture us all, since spacial sorting shreds the very networks of relationship we need to solve these problems. If nothing else, COVID-19 has exposed us to that irrefutable truth.

Rounding the Gesu also points to the work white Catholics need to do to make our borders, whether personal or collective, porous. Racial mercy, that ability to enter into the chaos of another, helps us see that initial steps toward justice don't necessarily lie in moving into another's space to respond to pain or wrong there, but rather opening up our own spaces and allowing the presence of others who don't normally enter into them to create necessary dissonance or chaos in our whiteness. Racial mercy calls for sitting with that dissonance and acknowledging our vulnerability to punch holes in our borders and boundaries. It is the ability to remain porous rather than immediately reacting defensively. This porousness increases—not decreases—our capacity for relationships of mutuality, which are deeper than tolerance, and our ability for collaborating in communities that are deeply integrated and not just superficially diverse.

Racial mercy could be our contribution to what Anderson calls "cosmopolitan spaces" that exist between the hyper-segregated white and black spaces in cities like Philadelphia. These "islands of civility" or "settings of utter diversity" attract people simply because they provide a space for observing, encountering, and appreciating people who are different, all of which gives us a break from the way we've been socialized to see ourselves and others and a chance to create "new social patterns."[95] "Exposure to others' humanity generates empathy," explains Anderson. "Fears dissipate, and grounds for mutual appreciation appear."[96] To that end, racial mercy is a precondition for replacing what Fullilove calls the historical "divide and conquer" approach whites have been socialized into, with a more generative "mesh and prosper" stance.[97] I think racial mercy can make us conduits for the "flow" between peoples and communities that Fullilove calls for, rather than catalysts for the fracture that keeps us sorted.

In the end, as intense and ugly was it was, the GPIA fight didn't last long, because a solution literally opened up in the suburbs. But urban parishioners had been formed in those segregationist battles and brought their vices of anti-Blackness with them to ensure that their new parishes were white and would stay that way. I was headed to one of them next.

CHAPTER SEVEN

HOMESTEADING

St. Francis of Assisi

THIS CHAPTER UNSPOOLED ON MICROFILM. I logged hours scrolling past page after grainy page of newspaper reels looking for the silver bullet that would verify a sinking suspicion: that my maternal grandfather, William Gallagher, built a whites-only suburban subdivision just after World War II. If that were true, then he was a driver of one of the most significant developments of the twentieth century. "As surely as the Homestead Act of 1862 filled the prairies of the Far West, the G.I. Bill created and filled the suburbs," explains political scientist and historian Ira Katznelson. "It changed *where* and *how* Americans lived."[1] Suburban homesteading—government-supported land acquisition and residential development—had everything to do with race. To figure out if my grandfather had any part in it in Philadelphia, Richard Rothstein, author of *The Color of Law*, recommended that I examine the language in advertisements he likely placed in Philadelphia area newspapers to market his subdivision, Burnside Estates. Hence my microfilm hunt at the Montgomery County Historical Society.

Since I knew my grandfather bought the land in 1948 and sold the last house in 1953, I figured I would begin in one of the local suburban newspapers around 1950. On my first foray in the *Norristown Times Herald*—on my first reel of film in fact—a story from March 18, which had nothing to do with real estate, almost slid past me. But key words in the headline practically jumped off the screen, as if the story had been waiting for me to find it all along: *St. Patrick's Day . . . St. Francis Parish . . . Minstrel*

Time . . . I dialed the article back into view and zoomed in. It wasn't an ad for a segregated subdivision but rather a far more disturbing piece of evidence that confirmed my suspicion that the Gallaghers helped build the American *Catholic* dream of homeownership using familiar and evolving tools of anti-Blackness.

BIG BILL'S BIG PLANS

Everybody called my grandfather "Big Bill" Gallagher. Certainly it had something to do with his six-foot, two-hundred-fifty-pound physique and his even more imposing personality. But William Gallagher was also a man obsessed with "making it big" schemes. He kept after the unexplored angle, the untapped opportunity. It may have taken him a few extra years to graduate from Simon Gratz High School in Hunting Park in 1933, but his immediate successes afterward suggest that it wasn't just an undiagnosed case of dyslexia with a touch of ADHD that made school so difficult. It simply got in the way of his ambition.

Right out of Gratz he got a job selling dirt-moving machinery. Given the need for housing, there were lots of foundations to dig and building sites to grade. Sniffing out opportunity, Big Bill took out a loan, bought some equipment of his own, then hired an operator so he could subcontract directly to the builders. A few years later, when World War II disrupted the building boom, he opened the Philadelphia Mica Corporation at 10th and Tioga. Big Bill may have been classified 4-F due to chronic gout, but he did his part by hiring a cadre of blind men to sort mica, a hot commodity in the electrical industry. Thanks to a buddy who became blind as a kid, Big Bill knew that the visually impaired had the finger sensitivity for this kind of meticulous work.

He was running the mica gig and managing two other properties in Tioga when he married Catherine Hargadon, known as "Sis" by her six brothers, in St. Stephen's Church in 1941. Both families were parishioners. A mutual friend who worked for the real estate developer Albert M. Greenfield introduced them. Despite his connections in the neighborhood, Big Bill was looking for opportunities beyond Nicetown. Within a year of marrying Sis, he moved his clan—which included his mother-in-law, Belinda, and two adolescent brothers-in-law—to a pair of row homes on Pennfield Street in East Oak Lane. But even after three children in as many years, the first two only ten months apart, he grew restless on Pennfield Street too. Opportunity was in the air, and it blew from the north and west where open swaths of farmland just beckoned to be developed in time for newly returned GI's—many of them newlywed as well—to grow tired of doubling up in their in-laws' spare bedrooms or garage apartments. And if their relationships with their mothers-in-law were anything like his—Big Bill and Belinda referred to each other coolly as "Mr. Gallagher" and "Mrs. Hargadon"—then there were lots of motivated buyers out there.

I discovered just how accurate my grandfather's read on the situation was. The city's population had boomed with the Great Migration just as housing construction tanked due to the Great Depression and then the war effort. By 1946, 17 percent of Philadelphia's 90,000 homes were substandard, 65,000 families were doubled up, and the sale and vacancy rates hovered around 1 percent.[2] With the return of sixteen million GIs, the US government estimated the need for five million new homes.[3]

My grandfather took one of his closest buddies, Clarence McGowan, on tours of Philadelphia's rural counties looking for the ideal plot. To get the biggest bang for his buck, he needed a deal, something other land speculators would pass over. A thirty-seven-acre parcel in Jeffersonville, Montgomery County, with an encumbrance on the title was his ticket. Others couldn't be bothered to haggle with the Norristown Water Company, who owned the property and maintained underground pipes across one edge. Not Big Bill. The property was an ideal location—it was relatively flat, offered proximity to the steel mills in Conshohocken and some of the smaller industries in Plymouth Meeting. It was adjacent to Norristown, the county seat. Plus, it was situated in a respectable Catholic parish—St. Francis of Assisi, up and running for twenty-five years at that point, with a school and everything. He bought the parcel in April 1948 for $20,000.

The original owners of the property were the Halloways, likely sixth-generation descendants of some of the original settlers of Penn's Woods. Big Bill, a third-generation Irish American, was going to turn the three-story farmhouse on a knoll at the center of the property into the headquarters of a massive resettlement program through his LLC, Tractor Services. "The farm," as my mother's siblings still call it, also became the headquarters of the Gallagher family for the next eight years. Big Bill hired a small crew from Norristown, mostly vets, to clean up the farmhouse, more than a hundred and fifty years old at that point, and then build a crop of houses. It may have only been fifteen miles as the crow flies from Nicetown, but for Sis and the crew from the old neighborhood, Jeffersonville might as well have been Iowa. Big Bill didn't care. There was good money to be made.

CARDINAL DOUGHERTY'S LAND GRAB

The undeveloped land ringing Philadelphia had always been attractive to the city's elite, so I shouldn't have been surprised that Cardinal Joseph Dougherty had set his sights on it. Moreover, even before the onset of the Great Depression, many in his burgeoning flock were in need of housing. I *was* surprised, however, that he began buying suburban land as early as the mid-1920s, and by how much he leaned on one of the city's most successful real estate moguls, Albert M. Greenfield, to do so. They were an unlikely pair. Greenfield was a Russian Jew born in what is now Ukraine and Dougherty a second-generation Irish Catholic from the coal region of central Pennsylvania. And yet, as "overachieving empire builders," the combination of their respective skill sets and assets—Greenfield for real estate investment and casualty insurance, and Dougherty for autocratic control over a population bursting the seams of city neighborhoods—only increased their power and influence in a city whose Protestant economic and political elites had long sidelined them. Their thirty-three-year alliance grew the archdiocese under the leadership of its first cardinal: 105 new parishes, 75 churches, 146 schools, 7 nursing homes, 7 orphanages, and several massive cemeteries.[4] Most, if not all, were for white Catholics.

If the American Dream depended on homeownership, then Dougherty wanted to be sure his flock would have land on which to build. But he had to be on the down low about it. Dougherty and Greenfield went for Sunday drives, identifying desirable property well ahead of the market. They would discern next steps over Sunday dinner at one of Greenfield's homes or lunch in his Walnut Street office. If it was a go, Greenfield would often stand in as the buyer, especially as Dougherty's plans for suburban expansion become more widely known, and then sell the property to the archdiocese. If Dougherty did not have immediate plans for the development, he would lease the property back to the original owner until the time was right to plant a new parish or school. Then he would sell it at market rate to new parishioners through a low-interest diocesan loan, which they and their pastors would spend most of their lives trying to pay off through weekly and annual collections and fundraisers. American Catholic historian Charles Morris notes that with Greenfield as the "exclusive real estate agent for the Archdiocese" and his personal financial advisor, Dougherty developed "the strategy of a cash-rich, long-term player" in the real estate market. Paired with growth of Catholic institutions during Dougherty's reign, the archdiocese became "one of the state's biggest landowners." It was also practically debt-free, and at the time of Dougherty's death, real estate holdings were estimated in "the several hundred million range."[5]

According to Greenfield's biographer, Dan Rottenberg, it was a personal relationship that made it all work. Greenfield was said to have remarked, "If I weren't a Jew, I'd be a Catholic." Dougherty arranged for Greenfield to be given the title of Commander of the Order of Pius IX, and Greenfield contributed financially to the growth of Catholic infrastructure.[6] And yet I was struck by the fact that this Jew and Catholic, both targets of white supremacy during the '20s, did little to include Black people in their Catholic empire-building strategy.

That's not to say that I didn't come across Dougherty's plans for Black Catholics in his correspondences. The Great Migration expanded their number in Philadelphia to between 10,000 and 15,000 prior to World War II and increased it another 50 percent between 1940 and 1950. Dougherty needed to mine the 10 percent of Philadelphia's population that was Black for converts who could replace suburb-bound white Catholics. As early as 1924, he dispatched a scout to the Inter-Racial Committee of Philadelphia to gather intel about the Protestants' strategies. Fr. Vincent Dever reported an absence of Catholics among the largely Protestant efforts to shore up the welfare of Black families. "I could not but feel," Dever confessed to Dougherty in a letter, "that the result might be that colored people would feel that the non-Catholics were more interested in their welfare than the Catholics."[7] Dougherty also commissioned Dever to conduct demographic studies of neighborhoods in West Philadelphia where the archdiocese might build a new church specifically for Black Catholics, whose number was steadily rising and who were not welcome in existing parishes. According to Dever, Dougherty wasn't the only one with an eye for this "large and promising field for making converts" in West Philadelphia. Protestants were already engaged in "active propaganda."[8]

Dever therefore recommended that Dougherty build a separate parish for Blacks in West Philadelphia, since "at this stage of the inter-racial feeling non-Catholic colored people are more easily reached by separate Churches," an implicit nod to the anti-Black sentiment of Catholics in the surrounding territorial parishes.[9] He also recommended that Dougherty staff it with religious orders more familiar with ministering to Black Catholics, who would be financially responsible for the parish until it no longer served only Blacks. At that point it would revert back to diocesan control. In the meantime, in order to avoid perceptions of racial animus, Dever thought it best for Dougherty to announce that Black families had "the right to choose the local regular parish and school instead of the separate colored parish," knowing full well in this case that perception of such animus was indeed reality, since most Black Catholics were not welcomed in predominantly white parishes.[10] Morris notes that in order to officially integrate the archdiocese, Dougherty "would have had to declare war on white Catholics, and, grand gestures aside, he was not prepared to do that."[11] He was too busy laying groundwork for a master plan, which Catholic builders like my grandfather would execute.

GREENLINING PHILADELPHIA'S SUBURBS

Cardinal Dougherty certainly fertilized the soil for my grandfather's big idea by sprinkling the far reaches of the Philadelphia Archdiocese with dozens of little "country" parishes. From 1919 to 1951, he added 75 parishes to the archdiocese, half of which were located beyond the city limits.[12] But I couldn't help but think that he had also consulted the government's almanac to ensure optimal growing conditions for white Catholics. By the time Big Bill bought his parcel in Jeffersonville in 1948, government agencies had been racially segregating the private residential landscape across the country through significant forms of financial assistance for whites engaged in the housing market—whether as sellers or buyers. It wasn't just that Black people were contained in redlined areas that received little to no investment. Whites were shepherded into greenlined neighborhoods—and therefore parishes—into which those funds were funneled.

I had discovered in rounding the Gesu that from the end of World War I through the New Deal, the government favored segments of the white population when it came to housing within the city limits. But plans for developing swaths *beyond* the city began earlier than I had thought. Rothstein explains that in 1921, Secretary of Commerce Herbert Hoover organized an Advisory Committee on Zoning to assist all municipalities across the country in developing zoning ordinances to preclude racial integration while simultaneously encouraging "as many white families as possible to move from urban apartments to single-family suburban homes." In that same year, Hoover headed up Better Homes in America, a private organization that educated Americans on the benefits of homeownership, the rates of which in his estimation could be increased by avoiding "racial strife" and buying into "restricted residential districts" that prevented "incompatible ownership occupancy," code for racial integration.[13] Even as the Depression threatened the surge in homeownership for most middle-class whites, the Home Owners' Loan Corporation's residential appraisal maps, released the same year my grandfather graduated from high school, began directing federal New Deal funding for housing loans away from urban neighborhoods like Nicetown and toward suburban areas like Jeffersonville. Here, anti-Black appraisers deemed where the return on investment was most secure. The following year, the maps were coupled with a whites-only requirement for all loans backed by the Federal Housing Administration and later by the Servicemen's Readjustment Act of 1944, known as the GI Bill, administered by the Veteran's Administration. The VA adopted an identical mortgage-lending program just in time for the construction boom that added 13 million homes to the nation's housing stock between 1945 and 1954. Smaller-scale operators like my grandfather built the majority of these homes. Between 1950 and 1956, the Philadelphia metro area saw an increase of 225,000 dwelling units, with 82 percent in its seven surrounding counties, for an annual average of 27,600 suburban homes built a year.[14] There wasn't space for mass production in the city, and federal loans made it cheaper to own in the suburbs than to continue renting in the city.[15] In 1950, Philadelphia's population declined for the first time, and by 1960 the city itself accounted for less than 40 percent of metro population.[16]

I have good reason to believe that Big Bill likely received his $20,000 loan to buy the Jeffersonville parcel through an FHA-backed bank. I discovered that this was significant, since the FHA's *Underwriting Manual* did not just apply to individual buyers but to developers as well. According to Rothstein, "The FHA had its biggest impact on segregation, not in its discriminatory evaluation of individual mortgage applicants, but in its financing of entire subdivisions, in many cases entire suburbs, as racially exclusive white enclaves."[17] It is clear that my grandfather was a henchman of residential segregation, but I found myself wondering if he knew it at the time.

Big Bill got to work sometime in late 1948 or early 1949 with a primary focus on *what* to build if not necessarily to whom to sell. My mom's oldest brother, Big Bill's namesake, explained what he could remember of the operation. My grandfather assembled a construction crew akin to the old gang from the neighborhood: Pricey the foreman and Casey his number two, George Taylor who drove the heavy machinery, and a young guy from Norristown named Anthony DeLuca who became my grandfather's apprentice. This cast of characters became fixtures in the growing Gallagher family as single-family houses grew up around them. They drove bulldozers with the kids plunked on their laps, sometimes even driving them to St. Francis School. Meanwhile, Sis and Belinda worked ceaselessly to beat back the sea of mud on which the farmhouse seemed to float.

Big Bill first built thirty-five two-story houses with a basement, which he had ready to sell by 1950 for $4,999. But the blasting for the basements turned out to be too labor intensive. To improve his bottom line, he and Pricey drove out to the University of Illinois at Urbana–Champaign for a course on modern home manufacturing offered by their Small Homes Council. Big Bill came back with his preferred model: a two-bedroom, one-bath, 1,100-square-foot home with an unfinished attic. He knew it was risky to sell a house without a cellar to city buyers, but as the experts in Urbana predicted, with the right crew he could lay the foundation and have walls up within three days. The gamble paid off, since the Cape Cod model, similar to those William and Alfred Levitt were starting to build in an adjacent Bucks County subdivision, sold like hotcakes for $8,000 to $10,000. My grandfather named the subdivision Burnside Estates after the main entrance road, which ran east-west through Jeffersonville. It fit the characteristics of America's post-war suburbs: it was located on the periphery of the city, it featured low-density detached homes on lots that sat back from the street, its homes were architecturally similar and affordable.[18]

Once the houses were up, it came time to sell. Big Bill hired an aerial photographer to capture the network of gently curving streets that he named with post-war patriotism—Liberty, Constitution, Republic. Examining these photographs, I was struck by how what was once farmland appeared pocked with two hundred neat little houses with ample front and back yards. On the ground, Sis and Belinda staged a sample home. "Better get the papers ready," my uncle recalls Big Bill saying to Mr. Mc-Gowan, his buddy from Nicetown, who teamed up with him on the selling end of the venture. A car had just pulled up to the sample house with a young guy and his visibly pregnant wife, who was holding the hand of a toddler. "This guy doesn't want to buy a house; he *needs* to buy a house."

"Were they white?" I asked my uncle.

"I'm pretty sure they *all* were," he replied.

I was really worried about finding proof that my grandfather was part of a national movement to create entire suburban regions for white home-buyers. The absence of the FHA *Underwriting Manual* among his papers didn't necessarily bring me any relief. So it all rested on the language he used in his ads. If he indicated FHA or VA funding was available to potential buyers, then my grandfather was basically saying, "Whites only, thank you very much." And that's when I made the startling discovery about the evening of March 17, 1950, on my first reel of microfilm in the Montgomery County Historical Society.

MOM IN "MINSTREL TIME"

The St. Francis of Assisi Parish fundraiser was always held around St. Patrick's Day, but in 1950 the feast fell on a Friday, which increased the likelihood of a strong turnout on opening night, as well as the Saturday and Sunday afternoon and evening performances. The sixth annual event must have been a family affair for the Gallaghers that year, since two of the three Gallagher children at the time, Billy (my uncle) and Kathleen (my mom), were on the program. Sis and Belinda likely got all gussied up and Big Bill piled them all into the car, including three-year-old Mary Louise, for the quick drive to the school hall.

Folks at St. Francis were constantly raising money to support the parish and its school. At some point in the early 1920s, Cardinal Dougherty had purchased some farmland at the corner of Marshall and Buttonwood Streets in Jeffersonville for $22,000. While they waited for their church to be built, St. Francis parishioners gathered in a barn for a weekly Mass offered by the pastor of Norristown's substantial church, St. Patrick's. The Jeffersonville barn became the first iteration of the church in 1924 and the school opened three years later, with a convent for the Sisters of St.

Joseph on the upper floor. But new pastors bring new ambitions, and Fr. McGovern, who arrived at St. Francis just before the Gallaghers, wanted a new convent, rectory, *and* church. Fundraising efforts in the parish's twenty-fifth jubilee year of 1949 had them on track for the first two items on McGovern's wish list. But they had a long way to go to raise the funds for the new church. Everyone had to do their part—selling patron books, buying tickets for the annual shows, and offering up loose change at every turn.

For the minstrel fundraising event that year, the pupils may have been the draw, but a cast of adults were the real headliner: an "interlocutor," eight "end men," and a forty-member "chorus," more than half of whom were women. All of the faces were familiar, except perhaps for those belonging to the "end men," which were painted black. The many acts of "Minstrel Time," according to the *Times Herald* the next day, were "greeted with spontaneous laughter and enthusiastic applause."[19] The paper printed the name of everyone from the parish involved in the production, including Billy and Kathleen, as well as the three men on the "makeup committee."

That's how I discovered that my mom and oldest uncle were in a Catholic blackface minstrel show when they were in first and second grades in newly suburban Philadelphia: scanning the local paper for an ad that would prove my grandfather built a whites-only subdivision and instead finding Mom and Billy among the nearly one hundred St. Francis parishioners "Starring in St. Francis School Minstrel." As I stared in disbelief at the screen, I felt as though this piece of family history *wanted* to be uncovered. I hadn't even gone looking for it. I didn't know I should have been looking for it. As I turned the dial to sharpen the contrast, a host of questions came into focus along with the grainy images on the microfilm. Did Mom and Uncle Bill know what was going on? Did Sis and Big Bill know any of those blackened faces? Was this always a part of the parish's St. Patrick's Day celebration? Why St. Patrick's Day in the first place? What did my Irish-born great-grandmother Belinda make of it?

Digging into the scholarship on minstrelsy, I learned that for an Irish Catholic family like the Gallaghers, blackface minstrelsy was standard fare, even as late as the 1950s. That my family members were largely unaware of the Irish genealogy of this distinctively American form of entertainment only ensured its longevity beyond its high-water mark a century earlier.

Irish immigrants were targets of early minstrel parodies before this form of entertainment even reached America. In fact, Robert Nowatzki, a professor of English, notes that Irish immigrants were familiar with this theatrical form, since the English had parodied the Irish in the context of blackface minstrelsy, "suggest[ing] a proximity between the Irish and black people in the minds of English audiences as well as native-born white American audiences."[20] Also, Nowatzki explains that it is no coincidence that blackface minstrelsy rose to prominence in American culture as initial waves of Irish famine immigrants, like Maurice O'Connell back in chapter three, began flooding big cities. Irish were initially targeted by minstrel shows precisely because, like Black people, they were seen as "other" and economic, political, and cultural threats. However, antebellum Irish immigrants like the O'Connells of West Chester would have been surprised to encounter white Americans impersonating the Irish while in blackface. Seeing themselves parodied on minstrel stages signaled to Irish immigrants in the mid-nineteenth century that native whites had conflated them with Black people—that both groups were distinct from whites and more similar to each other in their very otherness.

Relatively quickly, the Irish used minstrelsy to transcend that ethnic otherness, while simultaneously creating a gap of racial otherness between themselves and Black Americans. Part of Irish assimilation involved a transition from watching their identities be performed by others to watching Irish both perform their own identities as well as those of Black people. In other words, the Irish assimilated precisely by ridiculing those who were not permitted to do so. In this way, "Irish-Americans helped to shape the meanings of blackness, whiteness, ethnicity, and American nationalism—all issues that dominated the minstrel stage during the mid-nineteenth century."[21] Performing in blackface on the minstrel stage allowed Irish immigrants to claim their Irish identity—Irish songs, reels, brogues, musical instruments—as fitting for America by also parodying, behind a temporarily blackened face, those whose actual Black skin ensured their permanent otherness.[22] According to Nowatzki, "by being able to wipe off the burnt cork from their pale faces, Irish-American minstrel performers were metaphorically wiping off their racial Otherness."[23]

The blackface minstrel show was a means for Irish immigrants to negotiate their tenuous relationship to three groups. They bridged the distance between themselves and native Protestant whites by doubling down on parodies of Black people. They increased the distance between themselves and Black Americans, particularly free Blacks, with whom they lived and worked in close proximity, through their power to appropriate and denigrate Black identity on stage. Finally, they created solidarity with other European immigrants in the process of assimilating to American culture via that very appropriation and denigration of Blackness.

I was struck by Nowatzki's conclusion that whether performing on the minstrel stage or spectating in the minstrel theater, Irish immigrants could be unapologetically Irish and confidently American. American cultural critics in the mid-nineteenth century claimed blackface minstrelsy as a distinctively American phenomenon in no small part because of the way Irish used it "to transform their image from ludicrous stage Irishmen into white Irish-Americans."[24] It follows that if minstrelsy was distinctively American, then so were the Irish performers who gradually stole the spotlight from Black counterparts also attempting to claim the power of the minstrelsy to their own advantage on stages in big cities. The minstrel stage was far more effective than mob violence against Black people when it came to the Irish winning the approval of white Americans, since violence reinforced native white stereotypes about the drunken, pugnacious Irishman. Labor historian David Roediger suggests it provided space to ease the strict behavioral codes of the industrial workplace, which placed new demands on a largely rural and agricultural immigrant group, and redirected stereotypes about their lack of sobriety and laboriousness onto Black people.[25] Either way, "because of the central role of Irish-Americans in minstrelsy, one could say that minstrelsy was as much an Irish-American invention as it was an American one."[26]

If that's the case, then blackface minstrelsy was also a Catholic phenomenon: Catholics gave it its staying power beyond the antebellum period by moving it from public theaters into urban parish halls—like St. Agatha's, the parish William and Mary O'Connell moved into after departing St. Charles Borromeo at the turn of the twentieth century and where I found traces of minstrelsy in the parish calendars. The impetus to make a parochial home for blackface minstrelsy reflected the tension at the heart of Irish involvement in minstrelsy in the first place: proximity to Black people. Irish proximity to Black workers in Philadelphia's industrializing economy and overcrowded neighborhoods in the nineteenth century morphed into Irish proximity to Black people migrating from the rural South into well-established city parishes in the twentieth century. If the parish was under siege by the threat of Black homeownership, then what better place than the stage of the parish hall to launch counterattacks via Irish ballads sung by blackened faces, a space that reminded Irish immigrants both of their own embattled entitlements to their homes and their parishes as well as of the otherness of Black people?

A generation later in suburban parish halls like that of St. Francis of Assisi in Jeffersonville, I got the sense that blackface minstrelsy eased any guilt that Sis and Bill Gallagher might have hauled with them to the suburbs as part of the Irish exodus from those urban parish strongholds. Blacking up in the new but familiar spaces of suburban parish halls reminded the descendants of Irish immigrants that they were more worthy and deserving of this bounty than their Black counterparts. It also soothed anxieties that came with abandoning the Irish parish enclaves that parents and grandparents had built and financed, because blackface minstrelsy was a tradition that kept Irish Catholics tethered to their Irish roots and heritage back in the racially segregated city parishes they had abandoned. What's more, minstrel shows served a similar pragmatic purpose. As they had in city parishes, shows like "Minstrel Time" in St. Francis parish on St. Patrick's Day in 1950 helped raise funds to pay off debt or bankroll the suburban pastor's latest development plans. The social and financial capital they generated bolstered the security of white Catholics and their parish territories.

I found the interplay between performance and space, two familiar dimensions of the Catholic sacramental imagination that shape individual and collective identity, to be a significant Catholic dimension of minstrelsy. Since we are a people with an active sacramental imagination—a belief that the Divine can be experienced or accessed in and through ordinary spaces, things, and actions—minstrelsy was more than a form of public entertainment for Catholics. It was a ritualized performance, with particular songs and sequences, arrangements of performers, and theatrical movements, that connected them to something bigger than themselves and encouraged them to become what they saw, what they received from the stage. As ritual, minstrelsy became an expression of tradition—a way of carrying or translating the content of the Catholic faith, both beliefs and practices, into new contexts or to new generations. The ritualized performances of blackface minstrelsy—first in urban parish halls and later in suburban ones—passed down to the next generation coming up in newly demarcated parish territories a set of consistently held beliefs: in Divinely ordained suburban manifest destiny, in clerically sanctioned

Black inferiority, in the naturally sanctioned givenness of racial segregation in housing. It also handed on a set of practices that shaped the collective ethos of suburban white Catholics: asserting claims to the good
life by denying them to others, defending parish territory against Black
incursions, building communities through bonds of exclusion, assuaging
guilt and anxiety by invoking a sense of moral and cultural superiority, and
refusing to be unsettled by the history in the rearview mirror.

Moreover, blackface minstrelsy was a Catholic phenomenon because
of the space in which these ritualized public performances took place.
Parish halls were different from public theaters. They were built with
funds raised by the people they contained, sometimes by the very hands
of the people in the folding chairs. In this way, parish halls were a kind of
Catholic public square that housed the various communal activities that
defined and sustained the life of a parish—meetings of the various fraternal organizations and societies, fundraising events, activities of the parish
school that was often located on the floors above, and youth sports. Con-
sequently, in the footprint of the urban and suburban parish complex, the
parish hall is the space that parishioners at least had more direct access
to if not equal control over. It is the space where the laity expressed its
agency, where the *sensus fidelium*, or the wisdom and will of the faithful,
developed and was exercised. As much as the church building, it is an
epicenter of the ethos of the parish.

And yet, the Catholic parish hall was not simply a community center.
It was a sacred space not only because it was located on parish property
but also because its stage was once the sanctuary in most parishes. As was
the case in the city parishes of their ancestors, suburban Catholics initially worshipped in parish halls as they waited for church buildings to be
completed. I found myself thinking that to perform blackface minstrelsy
on such a stage could not help but heighten a kind of Divine sanction
to the whole suburban white Catholic enterprise. It also reinforced lessons that Catholics so steeped in clerical culture had learned well by the
mid-twentieth century: those with access to sacred space and the rituals
performed in them are the ones granted power to determine access to
their spaces and rights for everyone else. In this way, blackface minstrelsy
in parish halls was ultimately about who had a right to join the Body of
Christ and the rights associated with that membership. In other words, if
theater historian Christian DuComb is correct in suggesting that "racial
impersonation served to mark and police the boundaries that organize

sociality among the axis of race, forcefully defining who and who cannot occupy what racial positions," then in the context of Catholic communities it took on an air of who could and could not be authentically Catholic.[27]

This question of access to Catholicism would have been particularly unsettling in the early twentieth century, as white Catholics interpreted ecclesial/archdiocesan evangelization efforts with Black Catholics in urban parishes as cultivating the kind of Black mobility to which blackface minstrelsy originally responded. Scholarship on minstrelsy confirms my gut sense that white Catholics carried this concern with them to the suburbs, where access to homeownership was a potential means for Black Catholics to integrate white territorial parishes and dismantle that ecclesial structure that kept them segregated in national parishes back in the city.

Rounding that scene in St. Francis's parish hall on St. Patrick's Day in 1950, I wondered if the blackface acts made the Gallaghers squirm a bit. After all, two Black people were part of their lives in their new home in Jeffersonville: Lillian Bagley, my grandmother's housekeeper who trekked out from the city every day, and Horace Davenport, my grandfather's lawyer, who made the whole homesteading venture possible in the first place. I had grown up hearing stories about Lillian, but Mr. Davenport was a name I had not heard until I started this research. My mom and her siblings were pretty blasé about the fact that their father's lawyer was Black, as if it wasn't a big deal in the midst of all of this suburban racial segregating. I, however, was gobsmacked. So I took a break from my microfilm search for the Burnside Estates ad and combed instead through the Montgomery County Historical Society's holdings on Horace Davenport, which offered a complicating perspective on my grandfather's relationship with him.

TWO HUNDRED WHITE HOMES AND ONE BLACK LAWYER

Horace Davenport wanted to be a lawyer as early as first grade. This was shortly after his maternal grandparents brought him with them sometime in the early 1920s on their migratory journey from Newberry, South Carolina, to Bridgeport, Pennsylvania, an industrial town adjacent to Norristown. Bridgeport was one of many long-standing, vibrant Black communities in Philadelphia's suburban counties, where small-scale manufacturing met transportation infrastructure like rivers, canals, and eventually rail-roads. A few years later, his parents and four siblings came North. His parents had two more children after they settled in Bridgeport.

Davenport's paternal grandparents remained on their farm in South Carolina, where he returned for two years as an adolescent and gained an appreciation for "hard work and education" from his grandfather, a man born into slavery who never learned to read or write.[28] As a teen-ager in Bridgeport, Davenport worked summer jobs in construction and delivered papers for the *Times Herald*. He graduated with honors from Norristown High in 1938, at which point a football scholarship took him South again. He played for Johnson C. Smith University, a historically Black college in Charlotte established just two years after the end of the Civil War and financially backed in 1924 by the Duke Endowment, which also funded Duke University. He was weeks away from graduation when World War II pulled him even further south—into the South Pacific with the Army Corps of Engineers, where he built and maintained airfields and saw combat at Iwo Jima and Guadalcanal.[29]

In 1944, he and more than a million other Black servicemen were honorably discharged. He married a woman from Washington, DC, and finished his undergraduate degree at Howard University in 1946. He returned North again for two graduate degrees from the University of Pennsylvania—one in economics at the Wharton School in 1947, and the other in law in 1950. Horace had hoped to practice insurance law, but he could not find companies willing to hire him. So he opened his own firm on Swede Street in Norristown, focusing on trusts and estates, zoning, and real estate law. I found myself thinking that the real estate side of things was likely lucrative, given that the GI Bill itself constituted 15 per-cent of the federal budget in 1948 and a significant portion of those funds, totaling $95 billion between 1944 and 1971, was earmarked for housing. The VA alone mortgaged 40 percent of newly constructed homes across the country.[30] But even though he was a veteran, I'm not sure if any of that social welfare went to Horace Davenport.

It's safe to assume that Big Bill would have been one of Davenport's earliest clients. But how that came to pass is far less certain. My uncle recalls a dispute with a neighbor about runoff as the catalyst. Perhaps Davenport came recommended through word of mouth by the informal network of Norristown's veterans that Big Bill tapped for much of his hiring. Maybe their commonalities allowed Big Bill to see past their racial

differences. Each had a "work ethic combined with country-bred com-
monsense" passed down from their respective paternal grandfathers—Big
Bill's grandfather had emigrated in the 1870s from British anti-Catholic
Ireland and Davenport's grandfather had survived anti-Black American
slavery and Jim Crow in South Carolina.[31] Maybe Davenport's billing
hours were a deal, just one of the many indignities due to his race the
Davenport family remembers him enduring.

Either way, Horace Davenport became my grandfather's lawyer for
the next twenty years. He was a regular at Burnside Estates and in the
farmhouse on Liberty Ave, walking property lines or reviewing paper-
work at the kitchen table or assessing property damage after a big fire in
the barn destroyed valuable lumber and machinery. All of my mother's
siblings remember Mr. Davenport in a matter-of-fact kind of way, like any
other of the many personalities that were a fixture of their childhood and
adolescent experiences. I think they were surprised by my surprise that a
Black lawyer was part of our family story in the 1950s and 1960s.

"My dad really didn't care what color you were," my Uncle Bill tried
to explain to me. "He would do business with anybody, because if they
were honest guys, then they were all going to make money."

Still, I find it striking that my grandfather worked just as closely with
Horace Davenport, a Black professional, in executing his big scheme to
raise houses in Jeffersonville as my grandmother worked with Lillian
Bagley, a Black housekeeper, to raise five children in the midst of that
operation. Maybe my surprise says more about the impact of residential
segregation on me than anything else. After all, according to Rothstein, increasing government restrictions on lending and zoning laws interrupted
a gradual process of integration that was unfolding around the country
in the wake of the Great Migration and both World Wars.[32] Big Bill experienced this himself as a graduate of Simon Gratz High School, where
he learned in integrated classrooms and played on an integrated football
team. Maybe it really was no big deal for him to hire a Black lawyer. The
social chasm the FHA created by racially segregating places like Nicetown
that were already integrating, or by preventing integration in places like
Jeffersonville or Norristown or Bridgeport, had not yet begun to widen.
The process of indoctrinating people into racially homogenous habitats
was only just underway.

Even though they both likely profited from Burnside Estates, I wonder how my grandfather squared the fact that he knew he would not have

been legally permitted to sell to Horace Davenport—a man as credentialed as any other professional in Jeffersonville—one of the homes the lawyer had helped him build. Nor could he have sold a home to Lillian Bagley, Sis's rock and source of sanity in the farmhouse. The only proof I have that my grandfather may been inclined to sell them homes was the fact that he paid into Lillian's social security, even though he wasn't required by law to do so since domestic work was not included in the New Deal act that created that social welfare benefit. If there were limits on Davenport's success, was theirs a partnership or just another form of exploitation? If Lillian couldn't be a neighbor, was she really an equal no matter how integral she was in the family dynamic? Did Belinda and Sis feel a bit uncomfortable, sitting among the laughing crowd at the St. Francis of Assisi minstrel show in 1950, as parishioners in blackface implicitly parodied their lawyer, the grandson of an enslaved American? Did they debrief the show in hushed tones, for fear that Lillian might overhear? I wonder if Billy and Kathleen had questions about what those adults were doing with all of that black stuff on their faces.

Even if my grandparents had turned to face some of those unsettling questions—and I have no real evidence that they did—the US Catholic bishops were of little help.

AN AURA OF REMOTENESS AND DIFFICULTY

In the mid-twentieth century, the American Catholic hierarchy, from cardinals to clerics, modeled for their white faithful three problematic stances for engaging with Black Catholics. I found a common denominator among them in one historian's description from the late 1960s of how the Philadelphia hierarchy viewed Black people: with "an aura of remoteness and difficulty."[33]

The first—a missionary stance that paired evangelization with charity—was by now very familiar to me. Pope Pius XII reinscribed it in his 1939 encyclical to mark the sesquicentennial of the Catholic hierarchy in America. "We confess that We feel a special paternal affection, which is certainly inspired of Heaven, for the Negro people dwelling among you," said the Pope. "For in the field of religion and education, we know that they need special care and comfort and are very deserving of it. We therefore invoke an abundance of heavenly blessing and We pray fruitful success for those whose generous zeal is devoted to their welfare."[34] I noticed that Black Americans were the only group the Pope named and that he specifically framed them in terms of their need and dependence. However, Pius XII failed to link threats to Black welfare to the social problems facing the well-being of all Americans or to apply the solutions from the Church's evolving social teachings to the causes of their suffering. In other words, the situation of Black people was difficult enough to warrant charity, but remote enough to remain beyond the Church's emerging principles of justice.

As was the case with papal statements on ending slavery a century earlier, the US bishops did not necessarily share the Pope's sense of urgency nor paternal affection for Black Americans. Since not instructed to do otherwise, the bishops continued to advocate for voluntary giving to the Collection for Negroes and Indians, which they initiated at their Third Plenary Council in 1884. For his part, Cardinal Dougherty chaired the bishops' Indian and Negro Mission Board for a number of years, which ensured Philadelphians' participation in the collections. He also visited monthly with Sr. Katharine Drexel—at her place, an "unwonted deferential gesture" according to historian Charles Morris—to discuss their shared affection for Black and Indian Catholics.[35] He supposedly integrated one of the archdiocese's orphanages by physically escorting a little Black girl named Florence into its chapel and dining hall and scolding the nuns who ran it.[36]

Yet like his brother bishops, Dougherty primarily saw the arrival of millions of Black people from the rural South into neighborhoods clearly mapped as Catholic territory as an opportunity for yet another burst of evangelization—a second harvest of Catholic souls in the already tilled soil of dwindling ethnic parishes, if you will. As was the case for European ethnic groups now moving out of city parishes in West, South, and North Philadelphia, evangelization for Black Catholics meant garnering respectability through what American Catholic historian Matthew Cressler calls a combination of religious beliefs and rituals as well as "social, sexual, and aesthetic norms" that involved becoming Catholic through "transformation of the self and the body."[37]

I found traces of Black people's assumed "unfitness" in the bishops' second stance toward Black people and Black Catholics: They were primarily a problem. They were a problem because in the eyes of Church officials, they arrived in Philadelphia as a largely unchurched populace. Moreover, the poverty of these new arrivals, especially those from the severely Jim

Crowed South, presented another problem. It was not enough to indoc-trinate these would-be Catholics. Their conversions were contingent upon a variety of social welfare services in employment, housing, and ed-ucation. Despite a vast institutional network of schools and hospitals, not to mention employment opportunities within them, the hierarchy in Phil-adelphia claimed to lack the capacity to deal with this dimension of the "Negro problem." So Dougherty handed over evangelization and care of Black Catholics to specialists—religious orders of nuns and priests either created specifically to minister to them or those with experience doing so. And he maintained the practice of separate but not-so-equal parish spaces for doing this evangelization work: the Holy Ghost Fathers at St. Peter Claver in South Philadelphia (1889), the Sisters of the Blessed Sacrament at Most Blessed Sacrament in Fairmount (1909), or the Vincentians at St. Catherine of Sienna in Germantown (1910).

Finally, the bishops continued to embody reluctant if not outright resistance to racial integration during this period. Historian William Os-borne's operative word in 1967 for the arrival of Black people into ethnic white parishes—primarily in North and West Philadelphia —was "pen-etration," hardly a neutral term. "For the past four decades," he wrote in 1967, "the pattern of Negro expansion has been attended by growing segregation. Negroes live with Negroes, except where there is transition process underway and the movement is from original penetration of non-whites to total segregation or nearly so." He described how Black people used national parishes like St. Peter Claver or St. Ignatius as "footholds" to "penetrate" surrounding parishes.[38]

Priests and pastors were not exactly proponents of integration in what they perceived as *their* territory. "It is a fact," Osborne reported, "that on numerous informal occasions some pastors and curates have made no se-cret of their distaste for racial change, expressing antipathy toward the en-try of Negroes into their areas," often to the shock of non-Catholic public servants and clergy.[39] In 1946, Dougherty ruled that if Black families so desired, they could become members of the parish in which they lived rather than travel to one of the six national "colored" parishes designated for them around the diocese. But that edict placed the onus on Black families to integrate predominantly white parishes, with their "attitudes of suspicion and prejudice" and "ill-conceived resentment" toward Black Catholics, rather than on the white pastors and parishioners who didn't want them there.[40]

Philadelphia Catholic schools, the primary social service provided by the American Church and the largest of any such network in the country, were just as segregated. "As in public schools, once Catholic school doors opened to African American students, the schools typically became either wholly African American or they remained almost exclusively Caucasian."[41] Dougherty had issued instructions in 1923 that Catholic children be able to enroll in the Catholic school where they lived, a practice that was not changed easily and took more than a decade to become official archdiocesan policy. This created more than a little confusion and trepidation for Black families. Should they send their children to their actual home parish or to their spiritual home in one of the city's Black national parishes? The answer only became clear as white families departed. "African American children gained unprecedented access to Catholic parochial schools only after white Catholics lost interest in them," says Katie Grimes.[42]

Given what I had learned about Dougherty and Greenfield's suburban real estate spree in the 1920s, it was difficult for me think that Dougherty wanted anything other than a racially segregated diocese. He and the FHA made it easier for white Catholic families to move away from the urban parishes that their ancestors had built and financed and to begin all over again rather than to remain and integrate. He made it easier to begin again with parish-making—the building campaigns and the financing and the debt collecting—than to stay and mend fractured parishes. He made it easier to segregate the gradually integrating spaces in the suburbs than to integrate segregated ones in the city. Grimes puts it this way: "rather than sharing parochial space with black people, white Catholics ceded it to them."[43] I got the sense that real estate developers knew this. While hunting for the Burnside Estates ad in Philadelphia's weekly *Catholic Standard & Times*, I noticed a familiar ad for another subdivision that I recognized from the *Philadelphia Evening Bulletin*. To attract the Catholic market to Westbrook Park in Clifton Heights, the Warner West Corporation tailored the ad for a Catholic readership by identifying "lovely St. Joseph's parish" as a primary amenity.[44]

So how did this stance impact my family out in Jeffersonville? I can't help but think that they learned that the difficulties facing the well-being of Black Catholics were neither structural nor the responsibility of the whole. If the hierarchy viewed Black people through an individualist lens rather than a social one, then what motivations did they have to ask *why* Black Catholics were less churched than white counterparts or *why* Black

Catholics had problems finding affordable housing or employment? If charity to "Negroes and Indians" in missions in some foreign territory, or even within the archdiocese itself, was more than sufficient, then what need was there to ask more challenging questions about the causes of their poverty? If the hierarchy further segregated them from their Black brothers and sisters within ecclesial institutions like parishes and schools, then why should they integrate? The main message my family received, according to Catholic ethicist Bryan Massingale, was that Black people "were a group in need of white sympathy and services," a "missioned to" group lacking a "sense of agency and initiative."[45]

What my family lacked in terms of guidance from the Church when it came to the "Negro problem," they received from the real estate industry.

BIG BILL AND THE *UNDERWRITING MANUAL*

I have two good reasons to assume that even if he were the most personally socially progressive of developers, Bill Gallagher segregated his thirty-seven-acre parcel of Montgomery County in the Archdiocese of Philadelphia.

First, like most developers in the post–World War II construction boom, my grandfather was a speculator. He gambled by building batches of houses he hoped people would buy. He rolled profits from initial sales into the second and third batches he cooked up. But those first homes, in addition to the $20,000 purchase of the land itself, required a significant outlay of cash, which sent him in search of a loan from a local bank. Any bank in turn would have applied to the FHA for insurance on that loan. FHA lending criteria from the 1930s through 1950s, although evolving, were clear when it came to who Big Bill's customer base could be if he wanted to make any money. Initially focused on ensuring that buyers of existing homes reflected the racial identity of the seller and the neighborhood, the FHA adapted its *Underwriting Manual* by 1938 to ensure racial homogeneity in homes that were under construction. To their minds, "the need for protection from adverse influences is greater in an undeveloped or partially developed area than in any other type of neighborhood."[46] Big Bill realized that in order to increase the "satisfaction, contentment, and comfort" of potential buyers, he would need to look for "persons with similar social attributes."[47] The manual put it to him plainly, as did the Veterans Administration, which adopted FHA lending policies: "Families enjoy social relationships with other families whose education, abilities, mode of living, and racial characteristics are similar to their own."[48]

It is likely that my grandfather "submitted drawings and specifications" for Burnside Estates to the FHA for approval, knowing that such an approval would make it possible for him to both negotiate low-interest loans for construction materials and to eliminate the need for further appraisal of each property at time of sale—one less step for the local bank—so long as he followed FHA and VA rules: "no loans will be given to colored developments" or for purchases where "compatibility among the neighborhood occupants was lacking."[49] In his course at the University of Illinois, my grandfather may have heard from builders around the country of cases where banks refused mortgages to qualified Black applicants or to real estate agents representing them. FHA regulations prohibited whites from even renting homes with mortgages backed by the FHA or VA to Black people.

Why risk it, he may have thought, on the long drive back. Even if he wanted to sell to Black families—and to be clear, I have no proof of that—my grandfather would not have been permitted to do so and turn a profit at the same time.

But Big Bill's reliance on FHA funding for Burnside Estates wasn't the only reason I suspected that he *intentionally* sold his houses only to white people. In the mid-twentieth century, white homeowners and developers took matters into their own hands and wrote restrictive covenants into their deeds, invoking the FHA *Underwriting Manual*, to protect against "the infiltration" of "inharmonious groups."[50] As was the case in the city neighborhoods they left behind, white suburban homeowners could convince neighbors to sign a covenant refusing to rent or sell their homes to Black tenants and buyers. Some covenants made homeownership contingent upon membership in homeowners' associations that barred Black membership. Since they were private agreements, covenants provided a work-around for two Supreme Court decisions that ruled state-sponsored housing segregation unconstitutional. In 1917, *Buchanan v. Warley* banned state-sanctioned racialized zoning. In 1948, just as Big Bill purchased his thirty-seven acres in Jeffersonville, *Shelley v. Kramer* made it illegal for state or federal judicial systems to enforce housing segregation, whether through the eviction of Black buyers or renters or by awarding damages to whites when Black people moved into the neighborhood. A variety of loopholes, however, protected the flow of federal money through the

FHA to white developers and mortgage seekers. For example, in an attempt to enforce the 1948 *Shelley* ruling, the US solicitor general said the FHA would not need to comply until 1950. According to Rothstein, "This delay could only have been designed to permit property owners to hurry, before the deadline, to record restrictions where they hadn't previously existed."[51]

I wondered if my grandfather was one of those builders who hurried, since he had bought the land for his subdivision in the same year as the *Shelley* ruling and may have feared that his profit margin would decrease should Black people be able to buy in Burnside Estates. Did my grandfather need Horace Davenport's expertise to interpret the various policies the FHA put into place in order to bypass the *Buchanan* and *Shelley* rulings for more than a decade? Did he take advantage of any of these loopholes in Burnside Estates?

To answer this question, Rothstein suggested I examine the deeds for Burnside Estate properties, so I launched yet another adventure into Montgomery County's microfilm archives, this time in the Office of Titles and Deeds at the courthouse in Norristown, the county seat. I started with the March 26, 1948, deed for my grandparents' original purchase of the thirty-seven-acre parcel for $20,000. I furtively scanned the grainy image for commonly used phrases such as "prohibition of occupancy except by the race for which they are intended" or "any other than those of the Caucasian race" or "cause of action for damages" against owners who sold or rented to anyone other than the Caucasian race.[52] There were restrictions with wording that echoed those being used to segregate housing developments, but in the case of my grandfather's deed, they did not include any mention of race. For example, I noticed a restriction on the "conformity and harmony" of their external design with existing structures, but none pertaining to racial conformity and harmony among residents. I found a requirement to create a committee of three (my grandparents and one of Big Bill's friends) to approve the design and location of the houses, but not the racial identity of who could inhabit them. There could be no "noxious or offensive trade or activity . . . which may be or become an annoyance or nuisance to the neighborhood," but this did not seem to extend to certain kinds of people.[53]

My relief was momentary, since I had yet to examine the deeds of individual properties my grandfather built. In November of 1948, seven months after buying the land, Big Bill sold 112 Liberty Avenue to George and Florence Krill of Conshohocken. There were no covenants on the deed at that initial sale, nor when the Krills sold the property to the Cantellos eight years later for $11,525. My grandfather sold 2016 Clearview to Ruth O'Hara in February of 1951 for $8,940. There were no restrictive covenants on that deed, nor on 30 Republic Ave, which he sold in early February 1953 for $8,900 to Paul and Johanne Roddenberry. I relaxed my shoulders a bit. But not for long. Only definitive proof—language like "FHA backed" or "VA funded" in a real estate advertisement—would answer the question. That ad may be out there on a microfilm reel I have yet to unspool.

But I do know that while Bill Gallagher sold a house to his sister and brother-in-law and another to his secretary, he neither sold nor rented a house to Horace Davenport, a man who helped him build Burnside Estates and his fortune—not through physical labor, as was the case in some subdivisions around the country, but with equally valuable intellectual heavy lifting given changing local ordinances and FHA lending policies. I'm not entirely sure what the Davenports' housing options were in the early 1950s, but Rothstein surmises that Mr. Davenport and his wife likely remained in an undervalued neighborhood, either as renters or homeowners.[54] When they did finally buy, it is likely that the appreciation of their home over three generations equated to about 20 percent of the wealth gained by the white families who bought into Burnside Estates. The wealth gap created by guaranteeing homeownership to whites ensured that suburban homeownership would be beyond the reach of Black people in Davenport's grandchildren and great-grandchildren's generations.

ROUNDING ST. FRANCIS: RACIAL MERCY AND REPARATIONS

Scrolling through endless loops of microfilm brought me face-to-face with the fact that in the Philadelphia metro area between 1946 and 1954, builders like my grandfather constructed 140,000 homes in 24 suburban Philadelphia parishes and less than 1 percent of them were sold to Black buyers.[55] Previously, I had assumed that guilt for that residential segregation lay largely with behemoths like the Levitts, who relied on federal funding to build 16,000 whites-only units in the Levittown planned community just outside of Philadelphia. In fact, segregation happened through smaller operators like my grandfather, whose FHA production advances and VA loans, and, oftentimes, racial covenants, ensured that their curvilinear subdivisions made crooked the path toward racially integrated housing. Burnside Estates in St. Francis of Assisi Parish was an outward expression of the inner anti-Blackness in the Church as well as the state. Cardinal Dougherty's plans for suburban Philadelphia and my grandfather's ability to cash in on the exodus of whites from urban parishes left me with the distinct impression that both of these Catholic men would have agreed with William's Levitt's comment: "We can solve a housing problem, or we can try to solve a racial problem. But we cannot combine the two."[56]

Racial mercy invites a willingness to enter into the chaos residential segregation has created in order to recognize that the federal and ecclesial policies of the mid-twentieth century have ensured that our housing problem is in fact a race problem, and that our race problem is in fact a housing problem. It was affirmative action—not merit or hard work or even luck—that made white accumulation of wealth through homeownership possible. Which also means that it is not for lack of merit or hard work or luck that Black Americans did not and do not share in this wealth. Long before we came to associate it with people of color, affirmative action was white, created by and for the exclusive benefit of white people. And affirmative action was Catholic, carried out by white Catholics, from bishops to bankers to builders. Racial mercy gives me the courage to sit with some of the most uncomfortable truths I've uncovered in this project because I can trace what Rothstein calls "an intergenerational trait" of the income and wealth gaps through my family line.[57] The anti-Blackness that drove residential segregation is the very foundation of my own financial well-being.

Thanks to Burnside Estates, my grandfather was a wealthy man for most of his life. Granted, his next big development scheme in Ocean City, New Jersey, didn't pan out as he had hoped. And his alcoholism eventually destroyed his business acumen and his relationships with my grandmother and his kids. But even so, the Gallaghers lived comfortably. My grandfather had the Jeffersonville crew build a Burnside Cape Cod model on the beach at 28th Street in Ocean City and another in Jenkintown, an inner-ring Philadelphia suburb. The entire household—Lillian included—split their time between these two homes through the '60s. Everyone but my mother went to college.

Whatever my grandfather failed to offer my mother in terms of emotional stability, she gained in terms of financial management and real estate savvy. She was able to turn a nest egg that she earned working for the Bell Telephone Company into the down payment on the first home she bought with my dad the year before I was born. They bought it from Georgia O'Connell (a widow nearly a decade at that point), whose own path to homeownership was paved by her whiteness. My parents took advantage of the quick appreciation of suburban real estate and poured equity from that property into a bigger detached home five years later, which they sold within ten years when the number of Black families in the neighborhood reached the real estate market's tipping point. Even though the impact of anti-Blackness depreciated the value of that second property, they were still able to buy their third home in the whiter Jenkintown Manor neighborhood, ironically just three blocks from the house my grandfather built in 1955. They also used their growing equity to purchase a handful of rental properties, the wealth of which I can only assume will come to me and my siblings upon their death.

In the meantime, my parents helped me with a down payment on my first home, which, like their first, is a side-by-side twin. But unlike them, I returned to the city. In fact, my generation is the first to do so since the 1940s. I bought my house from a Jewish woman whose grown mixed-race daughters were not in the financial position to do so themselves when she died. As I sat across from them at the closing table, I wondered what *their* paternal grandparents did during the homesteading period of the 1940s and 1950s, when affirmative action was white. I wondered how their current circumstances might have been different had their grandparents been given the same opportunity as mine by the US government to build wealth through homeownership. Grimes names the haunting feeling I sometimes get when I cross my threshold: "When Catholics incorporated themselves into their parish through homeownership, they also intensified their indoctrination into a system of white supremacy founded upon antiblackness."[58]

In 1973, the year I was born, the US Commission on Civil Rights concluded that the "housing industry, aided and abetted by Government, must bear the primary responsibility for the legacy of segregated housing . . . Government and private industry came together to create a system of residential segregation."[59] By that point, my family was three generations into living in whites-only spaces, sanctioned as such by the government and blessed by our Catholic Church. Osborne's conclusion about the Church's inability to deal with the social inequalities of racism rings as true today as it did when he wrote it in 1967: "The formulation of a long-term, well-informed and coherent approach to social problems is still a thing of the future for all but a handful of dioceses."[60]

Reparations are another way of thinking about a long-term, well-informed, and coherent approach to any number of the social problems created by racism. Racial mercy helps us to hear with our hearts the stories and histories of *de jure* and even *de magistra* segregation, by which I mean segregation that was legally sanctioned and ecclesiastically blessed. It helps us recognize that affirmative redress, or attempts to make right these structural inequalities, is what is required of those who have benefited from them. Massingale defines *affirmative redress* as "healing the psychic wounds, material harms, and economic disadvantages inflicted by racial injustice and its resulting social chasms."[61] More than seeking forgiveness or converting hearts, affirmative redress involves systemic and structural change. If our government and our Church—at their respective national, state, and local levels—worked in tandem to create and enforce policies and practices that segregated metro areas like Philadelphia, then they are also capable of working together to repair some of that damage by enacting policies and practices that reintegrate these neighborhoods. "Catholics cannot merely change the way we inhabit space," says Katie Grimes. "We also must change the character of the space we inhabit."[62]

What might affirmative redress in the church look like? Grimes suggests that the archdiocese could sponsor a truth and reconciliation commission that could facilitate listening sessions across the diocese and integrate rituals of healing and penitence to begin to cleanse and bind wounds. We could begin to tell a more honest history about the diocese as a whole and the individual parishes it comprises, and incorporate that history into curricula across the diminished but resilient Catholic school system. We could cultivate virtues of integration through liturgies and rituals so that such openness becomes part of the *sensus fidelium*, or the wisdom of the people that gets practiced in our various walks of life—as lawyers and cops, nurses and teachers, builders and real estate agents.

As we turn to face this history, we can bring a structural and forward-looking orientation. Grimes suggests privileging existing Black parishes in our ongoing mergers and closures, perhaps moving the center of ecclesial focus and initiatives back into city neighborhoods, ideally before they gentrify. Diocesan officials might look at shuttered parish real estate—whether in inner-ring suburbs or the inner core—as an opportunity for innovation in mixed-income housing, particularly in rapidly gentrifying neighborhoods. Parishes could partner with innovative nonprofits like Habitat for Humanity to make necessary repairs to aging housing stock in order to allow lower-income families to continue to build the intergenerational wealth that comes with homeownership, or they could organize with housing rights activists to advocate for tax abatements for Black residents and developers, or they could reject exclusionary zoning. Rothstein suggests that the archdiocese consider closing the wealth gap created by residential segregation by offering scholarships to Catholic schools from the primary to the university level to students who live in once redlined areas.

Given the resistance white people often have around the whole idea of reparations, racial mercy is a way of "remembering forward," which peace builder John Paul Lederach describes in a poem as "keeping our frail filaments soft and supple."[63] In other words, to enter into the chaos of racism, we not only need to remember the past and tell the truth about it, but we also need to do so in a way that keeps us from getting our backs up when people recommend what this history means for their futures. Racial mercy helps us to remain open enough to engage in a give and take with others who have thought deeply about this structural repair and whose very futures are at stake.

CHAPTER EIGHT

DOUBTING

Catholic Higher Education

DURING THE FALL OF 2016, I taught an undergraduate course called "The Beloved Community?: Theology and Racism in America." I had only ever offered this course at La Salle University, one of six Catholic universities in the US founded by the Brothers of the Christian Schools, aka The Christian Brothers. The campus is located in the northwest corner of Philadelphia. Black students make up 19 percent of our student body, which is 10 percent higher than the national average for Catholic colleges and universities. More than half of the students enrolled in my course were people of color, a rare composition for Catholic university classrooms.

Given mounting tensions around the country and campus, I didn't want us to walk away with just an intellectual understanding of what racism is. I wanted us to experience in our bodies, in our spirits, what being part of a beloved community *feels* like. So we collectively entered into a covenant to orient us in our engagements with ideas and each other. We publicly committed to each other to speak our truths, be present with our minds and bodies, provide room for growth, and accept non-closure.[1] Then we went seeking after the beloved community for three hours each Wednesday afternoon in the midst of a country tearing itself apart with racial fear and resentment.

We were making steady progress, until our class session the day after the election. The energy in the classroom was a mixture of "I can't believe it" disbelief and "I told you so" suspicion. It wasn't until our next class that Raheem (I've changed his name for anonymity) brought us back to the promise of the beloved community. Raheem, a tall, lean Black student an easy sly smile (especially when he strolled in a bit late) cut through all of the confusion, defensiveness, anger, and mistrust with a simple plea: "When it comes to racism, I just wish people would believe me."

The emotion in his voice was palpable. Students of color signaled their agreement with nods and finger snaps. The white people in the room, particularly those who identified as Catholic, including me, fidgeted. Maybe we were taking a minute to honor the covenant, to absorb Raheem's point and be present to his truth. But I suspect many of us were also using that silence to formulate our "Okay, but what about" retorts. Okay, but what about my family's experience of discrimination? Okay, but what about the Black neighbors around the campus who hate white students? Okay, but what about the Black kids who only sit with other Black kids in the food court? Okay, but what about Black on Black crime? Okay, but, but, but . . .

I still find myself wondering what makes Raheem's request—even as a thought experiment—so difficult to accept. Why the resistance? What makes classrooms such easy spaces for whites to doubt if not dismiss questions and appeals to the truth from Black students and colleagues?

Craig Wilder offered me some answers in *Ebony and Ivy*, a groundbreaking study of the interplay between slavery and higher education in America.[2] Wilder reveals how the wealth generated by slavery made American higher education possible on both sides of the Mason–Dixon Line. In return, American colleges spread ideas about racial superiority and inferiority that justified the acquisition of land from Indigenous people and bolstered the slave economy. He does not think it a coincidence that higher education in the United States expanded along with the slave trade. "The academy never stood apart from American slavery," claims Wilder. "In fact, it stood beside church and state as the third pillar of a civilization built on bondage."[3]

The College of Philadelphia, better known today as the University of Pennsylvania, provides a compelling example. Benjamin Franklin formally established the school in 1755 when he himself was still a slave owner. Franklin, who in Wilder's estimation was "taken with the possibility of purifying North America," saw education as critical for civilizing "tawny" Germany and Scotch Irish immigrant arrivals to Pennsylvania.[4] "The belief in the biological supremacy of white nations allowed him to flatten the cultural barriers between European peoples and bridge the religious or denominational divisions that had been the organizing basis of the colonies."[5] The University of Pennsylvania was also home to the nation's first medical school, and its graduates soon populated others, most of which became the epicenters of a politicized scientific racism sponsored by "slave owners, planters, land speculators, and Atlantic merchants" that sought to prove the inferiority of Black people.[6] In short, Wilder concludes universities were not so much in search of the truth as they were interested in redefining it.

No wonder we resist Raheem's truth, since it calls into question frameworks of meaning on which American higher education is built.

And yet, as much as some of this history might explain white disbelief in college classrooms about racism, Raheem did not ask classmates at the University of Pennsylvania or any of the city's other secular institutions to believe him. He asked members of a *Catholic* college community, of which, as I write this, there are ten in the Philadelphia metropolitan area. So I find myself asking, what makes *Catholic* college and university classrooms such difficult spaces for Black students to make simple requests of their white peers and professors when it comes to racism? What distinct contribution did white Catholics make in the interplay between slavery and education—especially given the role of education in the missionary histories of the religious orders who founded American Catholic colleges and institutions, many relying on enslaved people to do so?

My discoveries in rounding different parts of the city over the course of the eighteenth and nineteenth centuries offered some insights. For example, the fact that the Augustinians and Jesuits first planted the seeds of Catholic higher education in Philadelphia during the antebellum period—Villanova in 1842 and Saint Joseph's College in 1851—ensured that anti-Blackness was implicitly embedded in their response to the anti-Catholicism that motivated these foundings in the first place. Then, after the Civil War, the growth of Philadelphia's three Catholic colleges—most notably La Salle College, founded by the Christian Brothers in 1863—suggests a readiness to answer the clarion call of Reconstruction not in terms of rebuilding the nation through Black people's economic and political participation, but rather in terms of binding the white wounds and shoring up white economic and political strongholds at the expense of those of Black people and their freedom. Later, Cardinal Dougherty's edict in the 1920s that Catholic parents could only send their children to Catholic colleges (segregated by sex) ensured the growth of Catholic higher education precisely during a period of racial segregation of parishes and subsequently parish schools across the archdiocese. The religious orders of women who opened six colleges for women over the following three decades felt no compulsion to integrate, nor did their male predecessors, since there were more than enough white students to keep their operations humming. Like their secular counterparts, Philadelphia's Catholic post-secondary schools began to integrate in measurable ways in the wake of Brown v. the Board of Education in the latter half of the twentieth century, but anchoring the recruitment and retention of students of color in their Catholic identities and respective missions remains a challenge in the first two decades of the twenty-first.

But what about my own grasping for the right words in response to Raheem that afternoon, my own *Okay, but* skepticism? Clearly, something about my own experiences within Catholic colleges and universities in Philadelphia inclined me to doubt him. I decided to round three distinct moments of my own history in Catholic higher education in Philadelphia to determine why I doubt Black people when they tell me that racism is real.

SAINT JOSEPH'S UNIVERSITY: FORGETTING

In April of 2016, the *New York Times* ran an exposé about how Georgetown University escaped economic ruin in 1838 by selling 272 enslaved people, including dozens of children, to three plantation owners in Louisiana.[7] Historian Thomas Murphy, a SJ Jesuit himself, notes that these people served on six Jesuit-owned plantations in Maryland, encompassing more than eleven thousand acres in total.[8] The story detailed how the Jesuits worked with a broker to ensure that the enslaved people, known now as the GU272, would be sold to Catholic owners so that they would be separated neither from their faith nor their families. The sale netted about $3.3 million in today's terms. Even though they promised their superiors in Rome that no funds would be used to prop up the college, Jesuit leadership in the Maryland Province used the down payment to settle college debts.

The *Times* also recounted the agony of those who were sold. Some pleaded with their Jesuit masters to be spared the inevitable separation from their kin and the hardship of forced labor in the Deep South. Some had to be "dragged by force" onto ships named *Katherine* or *Margaret* bound for the port of New Orleans while others ran away upon hearing the news of the sale. Some Jesuits had expressed regret at the time of the sale, and the following year, in 1839, the Pope banned Catholics from engaging in the slave trade. The article's embedded links took readers to Jesuit archival material from a decade later describing the enslaved people's new lives in Louisiana from the perspective of their former owners—hard labor, family separation, and physical distance from Catholic churches.

When a colleague sent me the link to the story, I suddenly remembered that I already knew about this ugly history. In fact, I had carried it with me for more than two decades.

In the fall of 1994, my history professor at Saint Joseph's University threw down the gauntlet just days before the topic of my senior thesis in American history was due. "There's a diary of a Jesuit Brother in the Georgetown archives, Miss O'Connell," Randall Miller told me during office hours. It belonged to Brother Joseph Mobberly, SJ an overseer from 1806 to 1820 at St. Inigoes, a two-thousand-acre Jesuit plantation at the southern tip of the longest peninsula in the Chesapeake Bay. It was established in 1638, just four years after the first Jesuits arrived in Maryland on a pair of ships, the *Ark* and the *Dove*, among other English Catholics and with two "Molato" servants and one "black" servant among those indentured to them.[9] By the time Mobberly began keeping his log, enslaved people far outnumbered whites at St. Inigoes.

"Somebody other than the Jesuits should take a look at that diary," Dr. Miller dared. So down to Georgetown I went.

Scrolling through the *Times* story, snippets of my 1994 encounter with Mobberly's diary came back to me. I remember how tricky it was to take notes with gloved hands and a golf pencil. I remember how my eyes gradually grew accustomed to the slant of his handwriting and how I sketched Mobberly's map of St. Inigoes on one of my pages of loose-leaf paper.

As I reached the end of the 2016 *Times* story, which closed with heart-wrenching comments from the handful of descendants that genealogists with the Georgetown Memory Project had located at that point, I had a sickening feeling. How could I have forgotten that I knew a piece of their ancestors' story? How could I have forgotten, especially given my intervening years immersed in subjects that connected me to that history: my dissertation on unjust suffering, my scholarship on theology and critical race theory, my undergraduate and graduate social justice courses? How could I have forgotten that I had drawn so close to such an ugly story of Catholic anti-Blackness? More to the point, *why?*

To remember exactly what I had forgotten, I made my way to my own archive, which my mother had curated in plastic bins in the closet of my old bedroom. Digging through academic memorabilia, this time without white gloves, I eventually found it. The paper had not yet yellowed, but a giant rusted paperclip lent it an air of historical gravitas: "St. Inigoes—A Jesuit Plantation." My mother had even managed to save my fifty-eight pages of handwritten notes. Paging through them I was startled to remember that I had used Mobberly's diary and other historical accounts that Jesuits had written to describe the decades that immediately preceded the sale of the GU272.[10] I hunched over my notes, fascinated by what had fascinated me more than twenty years ago.

I was immediately haunted by things I had forgotten: Mobberly's conclusion, however uncomfortable, that a firm hand made for a more compliant workforce; the exchanges within the Jesuit network of enslaved Black labor and goods; marriages and the challenges he faced in keeping family units together, especially since St. Inigoes had so few men. My notes were filled with names of enslaved people who had lived and worked in St. Inigoes in those decades—Aunt Lucy, Mathias, Jacob, Enoches, Nelly, Charles, John, Old Jack, Sarah the midwife, Granny Sucky the cook. I caught tidbits of their days through Mobberly's eyes: their crowded log huts; the garden plots where they supplemented their diets and income with sweet potatoes, cabbage, and chickens; and their oyster harvesting on Sundays despite mandates against working on the Sabbath.

My twenty-something self noticed that Mobberly had been preoccupied with whether or not owning slaves made the farm more efficient. Rising costs in maintaining enslaved people in food, clothing, and medicine tethered the Jesuits to farming large plots of tobacco and corn, which depleted the soil and required more labor than they had on hand. "Having dutifully considered all things, I then thought as I do now, that the farm would do much better without them," he wrote.[11] I also noted that Mobberly seemed untroubled by whether it was even moral for the Jesuits to own people in the first place. "Slavery is good, is necessary," he said in answer to the question as to whether it was lawful to own people at all. "It may be absolved with confidence that at least two fifths of the human family are deficient in point of intellect and know not how to manage for and take care of themselves."[12]

Nevertheless, he found himself in a conundrum: "I sincerely regret that slaves were ever introduced into the United States, but as we have them, we know not how to get rid of them."[13] Although he was no longer overseer in 1838, I read Mobberly's foretelling of the sale of 91 people from St. Inigoes and 163 others from five other plantations around the province. "Some [owners] contract great debts [in owning Black people] and in the end are compelled to sell their land or slaves to discharge them," he wrote at some point toward the end of his tenure at St. Inigoes. "They perhaps will sell their blacks and send them to Georgia or the Carolinas . . . To be separated, wife from husband, children from their parents. Is this Christianity?"[14]

Is this Christianity?

I lingered over my own transcript of Mobberly's diary and noticed that I had not highlighted that sentence as I prepared to write my thesis. I cross-checked my final paper. His question didn't appear there either. Like Mobberly and any other white Catholics who drew close to this slave-owning and slave-selling history over the ensuing generations, I too had dodged an uncomfortable truth that called into question the integrity of the Jesuit tradition Mobberly and I shared. I knew that 10 enslaved people from St. Inigoes had been sold in the decade leading up to the sale of the 272. I knew that the overseer at St. Inigoes, one of Mobberly's successors, had encouraged enslaved people there to run away. I knew that 91 people were shipped down the Chesapeake on boats bound for the Port of New Orleans. I knew the Jesuits wanted buyers with plantations big enough to employ family units to avoid separation. I knew they wanted their enslaved people to have access to a priest. I knew they wanted future owners to care for young and old out of charity. I knew that half of those sold in 1838 were too old or young to work. I *knew. I* knew.

Perhaps most importantly, I knew as a college senior at a Jesuit institution in Mobberly's own Maryland province that this story had something to do with me. It wasn't until the last paragraph of my twenty-two-page tome that I wrote the only sentence to earn an exclamation point from my beloved Dr. Miller: "Theoretically," I posited, "St. Joseph's College, [founded] in 1851, was established in part as a result of the sale of the Jesuits' previous efforts on plantations such as St. Inigoes in St. Mary's County, Maryland."[15] Full stop.

Like Mobberly, I doubted the unsettling answer enslaved people offered to the question of whether or not the practices of slave owning were consistent with Christianity, since after drawing close to the radical

suffering that white Catholics inflicted on Black Catholics and then making an unsettling connection between that history and my present circumstances, I promptly averted my eyes, my attention, my burgeoning
vocation. I submitted my paper for the history department's academic
journal, received departmental honors at commencement, then archived
my exposure to all that unsettling knowledge in my bedroom closet and
moved on. It would take the voices of the descendants of the GU272
nearly a quarter of a century later to remember that I ever knew about the
enslaved people of St. Inigoes and that I had doubted the significance of
their story to my Catholic heritage, to my Jesuit education.

As I try to explain my amnesia, I keep turning to the curriculum of
Catholic higher education, since that was the context in which I encountered that truth about Jesuit slave owning, as well as the context in which I
continued to forget about it for two decades. Part of my willful forgetting
stems from the connection between education and hierarchy in the Catholic tradition. Historically, education was part of the missionary impulse of
the Church, particularly when it came to subduing and exploiting Indigenous and enslaved peoples. In fact, Wilder notes that the success of a variety of Catholic religious orders in Latin and South America hinged upon
building schools along with military, religious, and economic infrastructure.[16] Theologian Willie James Jennings notes that missionaries practiced
a pedagogical imperialism that reinforced their permanent position as in-
structor, evaluator, and arbiter of a truth already fully revealed. In rejecting the possibility that they, too, could be students or that truth could be
further revealed in unfamiliar contexts, Catholic missionaries ensured that
only certain ways of knowing were viable, only certain things were worth
knowing, and only certain people were worthy of teaching. To Jennings's
mind, this preference for an evaluative stance—to judge the worthiness of
others—impaired the "imaginative capacity of Christianity."[17]

If that imaginative capacity was gone by Mobberly's time—evidenced
by his lack of curiosity about the lived experience of the Black people in
his St. Inigoes "family" or his inability to empathize with their subjugated position despite his ability to name it as such—then it was certainly
gone by mine. Where in my own Jesuit-inspired curriculum could I have
turned to further investigate the questions my encounter with Mobberly's diary raised? If the Church had long assumed that there was little to
learn from people who came from places and cultures other than Europe,

then I could hardly have expected to find centers of sustained intellectual inquiry about such things on my Catholic campus, much less people of color leading them. Without such spaces of inquiry or guides, it was easy to sidestep troubling questions by doubting the significance if not the veracity of their source. What did it matter, really, that the Jesuits owned people and sold them to save their most prestigious college?

Jennings says that such a compromised imaginative capacity dislocated me from the physical space in which I learned—Jesuit institutions in the mid-Atlantic—and concealed my own participation in the history of those spaces. In other words, I operated with a "spacial obliviousness" that kept me from seeing or experiencing the power dynamics of race that define so many boundaries within communities, that deny relations and connectivity among people in spaces.[18] It concealed historical processes from me, particularly the historical processes that give rise to compromises required when people fail to live up to and out of their truest values. This silence increases the likelihood that these historical processes will repeat themselves. People who intentionally forget know that what is forgotten will never be fully remembered. So when we in future generations do attempt to remember, we don't even realize how much we've forgotten. It is no wonder I struggled with Raheem's request in 2016 that I believe him. My missionary sensibility had been hindering my imaginative capacity for empathy for thirty years.

If I look even deeper for the cause of my doubt about the significance of what I encountered in that Georgetown archive, I encounter the Catholic character of my undergraduate degree. One might think, with its three required courses in theology, that it would have at least afforded me the tools to answer Mobberly's seemingly rhetorical question, "Is this Christianity?' But Jeannine Hill Fletcher explains that such an encounter with this history or ideas about racism in those courses would have been unlikely, since the primary function of the academic discipline of theology was to create "symbolic capital" that helped give meaning to the world and the people in it according to a divinely ordered hierarchical and racialized pattern or scale. "It was in the academic spaces of theological training," she says, "that ideas of Christian supremacy were manufactured as knowledge, to be put to the project of conquest, colonization, and conversion as they made their way from lecture hall to pulpit to legislative assemblies."[19] To her mind, the words that Christian theologians used literally created worlds that were weighted differently, both materially and economically, depending on one's racial identity. It's tempting to think that these words and worlds are historical artifacts at this point. But Hill Fletcher suggests Christian theology still weights the world. "When White theologians say nothing to disrupt this exploitative relationship [between White Christians and their efforts to create White superiority], their theological production protects White interests."[20] So Raheem's request that I believe him when he says racism is real would require shifting more than just the weight of our classroom.

Finally, one of my graduate school professors, Jim Keenan, SJ, recently helped me understand that the institutional Church's public stances on other ethical issues lead many of us to falsely assume that the Church itself is ethical. It was Mobberly's pastoral responsibilities for the physical and spiritual well-being of enslaved people that compelled Philadelphia's Bishop Kenrick to write a moral manual shortly after St. Inigoes's Black Catholics were sold. His manual brought respectability and even divine sanction to Catholic slaveholders precisely because it was a teaching issued by the Catholic hierarchy. Keenan suggests that this assumption of respectability is also extended to Catholic universities: "As it once was with the church, the university is still today presumed to be ethical because it teaches ethics."[21] Our public claims in Catholic higher education about being rooted in the Catholic intellectual tradition lead us to believe that we function ethically when in fact we fail to do so if our curriculum reinforces the Eurocentrism of that intellectual tradition as well as our institutional structures and cultures. We are unaccustomed to standing in the critical gaze of those who expose our false assumptions with their lived experiences of our hypocrisy. In the end, we doubt students like Raheem, who suggest that our failure to believe what they are saying about their suffering provides evidence of our very participation in it.

Rounding my undergraduate experience in Catholic higher education points to the role of curiosity in racial mercy. To enter into the chaos of racism, we need to be curious about this mess—its origins, its impact on other people, its impact on us—rather than skeptical observers who primarily demand proof. Racial mercy can help us create spaces of curiosity in our curricula—through courses, classroom covenants, brave conversations, sustained personal and collective reflection—that draw us into the liberating truths of our respective stories of being messed with by racism.

LA SALLE UNIVERSITY: GATEKEEPING

While looking for something else entirely in Cardinal Dennis Dougherty's papers in the Philadelphia archdiocesan archives, I stumbled upon a letter to him that helped me put a finger on another source of doubt when it came to believing students like Raheem. In January of 1938, Ethel L. Lee wrote Cardinal Dougherty on behalf of the Philadelphia chapter of the Federated Colored Catholics (FCC) to inform him about the infeasibility of his expectation that Black Catholic families send their children to Catholic schools if institutions like La Salle University refused to enroll them. Perhaps hoping to get Dougherty's Irish up, Lee enclosed a copy of a similar letter that the FCC had sent a month earlier to La Salle's president that highlighted how La Salle's policy, as well as their refusal to engage with the FCC, contradicted the "influence" Dougherty himself had exerted "on behalf of the underprivileged Negro."[22] Were the Christian Brothers doubting the cardinal's authority?

The FCC itself had roots in higher education. Dr. Thomas Wyatt Turner, a professor of biology at Howard and later at Cornell, founded it from his living room in the heart of St. Augustine Parish in Washington, DC, to address racial disparities in social welfare after World War I as well as reports about racial discrimination at Catholic University. A national coalition by 1924, members called on the US bishops, and even the Vatican, to respond to concerns about the "spiritual and temporal" welfare of Black Catholics. According to historian Cyprian Davis, the FCC built solidarity among Black Catholics, advanced their access to Catholic education, raised their status within the Church, and prepared them for broader civic engagement.[23] Unlike their white counterparts who privatized their faith through insular parish devotionalism, the FCC "emphasized the social implications of Catholicism."[24] They drew sharp contrasts between Church teaching and the prejudiced practices of white Catholics as well as racist ecclesial policies. They named racism as sinful and therefore the responsibility of Catholics to address. They doubted whether those who refused to do so were true Catholics.

In a 1931 letter to the US bishops, Dougherty the most prominent among them, the FCC called these "good shepherds" to task for the fact that their high school, college, university, and seminary flocks were missing a good number of sheep "not because they [were] lost but because the gate of the fold was closed against them."[25] To the FCC's mind, the bishops' solution—support for the historically Black Xavier University in

Louisiana, founded in 1925 by Philadelphia's Mother Katharine Drexel—
was insufficient, as some families did not wish to send their sons to New
Orleans, especially when cities like Philadelphia had so many institutions
with closed gates. Philadelphia's chapter of the FCC did something similar their letter to La Salle's president, Br. Edwin Anselm, FSC. They refuted any doubts that the Christian Brothers may have had in keeping two
Black students out: they were Catholic, had graduated from the Brothers'
own West Catholic High School, and were able to pay—one through a
scholarship named for Dougherty himself and the other with cash. FCC
concluded they were denied because they were Black.[26]

In her letter on behalf of the Philadelphia FCC, Ethel Lee indicated
that La Salle's decision was contrary to the "principles on which [their]
noble order was founded" and to "tenets of Christian social justice."
Moreover, she predicted that it would also "prolong racial misunder-
standing" at a time "when there is so much effort being exerted to improve racial relations through the practice of Catholic action." Lee made
the group's intentions clear: Ambrose was to ensure that his name would
be added to "that of other Catholic colleges in this vicinity who actually
put into practice the theories propounded by Holy Mother Church, emphasized by Our Holy Father, and stressed by His Eminence Cardinal
Dougherty."[27] Lee invoked the Holy Trinity, so to speak. Not hearing
from Anselm by mid January, Lee played upon one of the Cardinal's own
fears in the FCC's letter to him: "This disbarring of Negroes from Catholic Colleges is furnishing the Communists with additional propaganda to
lure the Negro from the Catholic Church."[28]

The letter struck me as the political maneuver of a group with a
strong sense of self and purpose. This made sense when I learned that in
1932, the Philadelphia chapter made a decision to remain aligned with
Turner's primarily Black and lay-led movement and his unapologetic insistence on Black equity. To that end, the FCC in Philadelphia embodied
a Catholic expression of Black activism. They did not adopt a position
of "active waiting," couched in a "cordial tone," nor did they practice a
"politics of civility and racial uplift."[29] Their no-nonsense tone made even
more sense when I learned a bit about the Philadelphia chapter. Ethel
Lee, secretary, was one of twelve children and herself a descendent of
enslaved people owned and sold by the Jesuits in Maryland. Her father
was a prominent Catholic Philadelphian and two of her sisters entered
the Oblates of Providence, the first successful Black order of religious

women. The Philadelphia chapter expected a particular kind of response from Ambrose and threatened to invoke their power and respectability via their connection to the person at the top in Philadelphia should Ambrose not comply.

Their letter campaign worked. Although I was surprised that neither Dougherty's nor Anselm's papers included a response, the minutes from La Salle's Community Council in February 1938 indicate that Br. Anselm raised "the question about admitting Negroes." Those attending considered the issue "important" in light of the likelihood of similar cases and the possibility of the whole situation "reaching the ears of His Eminence." The Council agreed that a "favorable attitude should be adopted," assuming "the Catholic Negro meets all of the College's entrance requirements."[30] La Salle's lackluster commitment to integration over the coming decades, however, suggests that changes in attitude rooted in fear of reprisal from the cardinal were not effective motivators for changing policies and procedures around college admissions. Although La Salle enrolled its first Black student in 1938, the first Black student didn't graduate until 1946; Black students remained tokens until the late 1990s when they began to represent a steady segment of the undergraduate student body.

La Salle was but one institution across the matrix of higher education in Philadelphia with similar inanimate commitments. In his 1967 history of race relations in the Catholic Church, William Osborne notes that although the Catholic education infrastructure in Philadelphia was "unrivaled," a 1960 survey indicated that of the 11,000 students enrolled in the ten colleges and two junior colleges at the time, only five enrolled 125 Black students in total.[31] The year before I encountered Raheem in my classroom, Black students on average comprised 11.2 percent of Philadelphia's Catholic colleges and universities, dramatically lower than their 44 percent representation among college-aged Philadelphians.[32] As of the fall of 2018, that figure is 9 percent in the 260 Catholic colleges and universities across the country, compared with 12 percent at public institutions and 13 percent at other private nonprofit institutions.[33]

So how did this piece of history contribute to my doubts about Raheem's experiences with racism in 2016, which he shared in a classroom in the iconic building the FCC wanted to access almost seventy years earlier? I suspect it has to do with the fact that doubts about Black students—their abilities, their resilience, their financial capabilities—continue to allow whites to keep the gates of higher education closed to them. Our closed gates create self-fulfilling prophecies about Black achievement and economic success, which we rely on to justify their continued exclusion from our campuses. They also keep our white students contained in cocoons of comfort and lend our institutional mission statements an air of hypocrisy.

As proof that doubts about Black students linger, a groundbreaking 2013 report from the Center on Education and the Workforce at Georgetown University indicates that while many more students of color pass through the gates of more colleges today, far too few of them are admitted to elite institutions, including Catholic ones. Rather, students of color are more likely to be tracked into "crowded and underfunded colleges" where they do not "fully develop," in part because there are fewer resources to dedicate to their success.[34] This is true in Philadelphia, where at our most elite institutions, including the one at which I am currently employed, Black students comprised only 7.9 percent of the student body in 2015.[35] Gerald Beyer, a colleague from my cohort in graduate school at Boston College and himself a native Philadelphian who now teaches at Villanova University, notes that elite Catholic institutions with higher endowments—Notre Dame, Georgetown, Boston College—tend to enroll fewer Pell grant recipients or students coming from families making less than $40,000 a year.[36] Georgetown's Center spells out what that means: white graduates from the nation's top 468 institutions accrue more than $2 million in higher earnings over the course of a lifetime, as well as access to jobs and careers that "bring personal and social empowerment," all of which contributes to the "systemic reproduction of white privilege across the generations." In other words, American colleges and universities, including its Catholic ones, "amplify" racial disparities in education at elementary and secondary levels to such an extent that higher education itself is a "dual system of racially separate and unequal institutions."[37]

So how do doubts about Black students' fitness for college in general—but particularly at elite institutions or those like mine hoping to become more selective—harm them? Funneled into under-resourced institutions at higher rates than their white counterparts, Black students drop out at higher rates.[38] Unlike their white peers, Black students dedicate a significant amount of financial, intellectual, and emotional resources navigating what some call the "hidden curriculum" of our predominantly white institutions: the intricacies of financial aid (88 percent receive grants, compared with 76 percent of white students, and 71 percent take out loans, compared with 56 percent of white students); balancing part- or even full-time employment with school; acclimating to predominantly white institutional cultures or breaking into predominantly white professional networks for internships and job opportunities.[39] As they manage all of this, it should come as no surprise that as of 2017 only 38 percent of Black undergraduates "persist" to graduation, compared with more than 62 percent of white undergraduates. Moreover, Black students accrue more debt whether they complete their degrees or not. More than half of Black students who took out loans reported defaulting on them, compared with 23 percent of white student borrowers.[40] And even with a degree in hand, twenty years after enrolling, the median white borrower will have paid off 94 percent of their college debt, while a Black borrower will still owe 95 percent.[41] That's due in part to the fact that even with a bachelor's degree, Black graduates earn less than white students and the employment rates of white students are two-thirds higher on average.[42] So no matter how you cut it, college is more of a financial risk than a sure investment for Black students.

Moreover, Catholic colleges and universities are gatekeepers of generational economic mobility, both upward and downward. Catholic higher education, so heavily skewed to white students at its elite institutions in particular, has only further shored up white privilege, power, and our sense of entitlement to higher education—all of which are obstacles to solidarity with those who have been shut out. Many white students at Catholic colleges unknowingly begin their climb toward success already near the top of the educational ladder, standing on the shoulders of generations of government and ecclesial support for Catholic higher education. This echoes my story in Catholic education in Philadelphia. My immigrant great-grandparents belonged to a Catholic parish that ensured a spot for their children in Philadelphia's Catholic primary and secondary schools; my high school–educated grandparents achieved the goal of a college education for their sons in Philadelphia's Catholic universities, whose mission focused on educating the sons of immigrants; my father created an admissions legacy for me and my siblings at his increasingly elite alma mater of Villanova University, even if we instead attended its storied rival, Saint Joseph's; my siblings and I coupled his advanced degree–level earnings with merit-based aid that our private Catholic secondary educations helped us secure, which in turn ensured we would graduate without debt; my brother can now dedicate more of his own debt-free, advance-degree earnings to college savings for my double legacy niece and nephews when they head to college a decade from now.

These statistics not only make me doubt the viability of Catholic higher education as opening the gates to social mobility beyond college for our Black students, but they also make me doubt whether we in fact contribute to the common good as so many of us claim. Moreover, our historical failure to address the racism embedded in our admissions policies and procedures makes me doubt whether our institutions can be effective epicenters for social change. Dr. Turner, founder of the FCC and himself a college educator, recognized as much toward the end of his life: "With evidence of the worst type of discrimination existing widely in churches there has been little opportunity for the development of a spirit of brotherhood among Catholics of different groups." He went on to say that "none of these organizations have developed a truly fundamental unity of white and colored in its group nor have they concerned themselves with the serious problems with which colored Catholics are faced in Catholic institutions."[43]

Rounding my experience as an educator in a Catholic institution, I find racial mercy summoning me to be vigilant for the places where I exercise gatekeeping power when it comes to accessing the benefits of a college education. I can investigate ways in which I allow the system of Catholic higher education to continue to function precisely as it was designed to function: as a catalyst for increased social mobility primarily for white students. In addition to paying attention to how I design my courses or the dynamics I create in my classrooms, I can look for places where my institution serves white students better than Black, Latin American, and Asian students and name the dangerous impacts of that disparity. I can be vigilant for how messaging about excellence or rigor might be signaling an institutional desire for a more elite, and therefore a more white, student body and academic culture. Since systems are human creations, I can also be alert to make or take advantage of opportunities to collaborate with colleagues and students of color in redesigning the system of Catholic higher education so that it might function as a driver of racial equity.

ROSEMONT COLLEGE: ACKNOWLEDGING

That 2016 *New York Times* story about the Jesuits' 1838 sale of 272 Black people was one of many about American colleges and universities who, compelled by Black students, faculty, and alumni, faced ugly histories that might otherwise have remained unremembered. All around the country, pockets of people who insisted that these histories—their histories—mattered challenged higher education leadership to redress, repair, reconcile. Colleges and universities removed statues of Confederate leaders. They renamed buildings commemorating slave-owning patriarchs or white supremacists. They funded institutes for the study of slavery or African American culture. They appointed chief diversity officers. The idea of reparations became less far-fetched. In fact, impatient with university leadership, undergraduate students at Georgetown passed a referendum to donate $27.20 each from their student fees to a fund to support the estimated 10,642 descendants of the 272 people the Jesuits sold in 1838.[44] In March of 2021, the Jesuits of the United States and descendants of the people they once owned created the Descendants Truth & Reconciliation Foundation, which vowed to raise $100 million to be distributed among racial justice initiatives, as well as scholarships and social welfare support for descendants.

In 2016, I found myself serving in another capacity at a Catholic institution of higher education in Philadelphia, this time as a trustee of Rosemont College. The Sisters of the Holy Child Jesus opened Rosemont in 1921 on the Philadelphia Main Line estate of Joseph Sinnott, a whiskey distiller. For most of its history it was a women's institution. Unlike many of my fellow trustees, I was short on treasure. I got a chance to make good on my offer of my talents as a theologian and department chair, however, when the college president, an alumna herself, asked me to serve on a commission to examine an aspect of the college's history, hidden in plain sight but recently uncovered by an undergraduate history class: Cornelia Connelly, the Philadelphia-born founder of the Society of the Holy Child Jesus, the religious order that founded Rosemont, at one time had four enslaved Black people as members of her household: Abraham, Jenny, and a mother and daughter named Mary Phoebe and Sarah (known as Sally) Grayson. I soon learned that for us to believe students like Raheem requires that I call into doubt the integrity of holy people and storied institutions that are deeply ingrained in my own identity as a Catholic and my vocation as an educator.

Our charge was to compile what we could glean from the historical records available to us and to make recommendations for ways in which the college community might acknowledge and respond to this history. Our information about these four Black people came from four main sources: scant mentions by some of Cornelia's biographers; evidence in her papers in the SHCJ archives in Oxford, England; baptismal records and records of sale kept by the Jesuits; and personal research conducted by descendants of Phoebe and Sally Grayson, who ended up being the most traceable of the Connellys enslaved people.[45] Cornelia Peacock Connelly was born in 1809 into a well-heeled Philadelphia family with ties to a sugar plantation in Jamaica. She married an Episcopal priest, Pierce Connelly, in 1831 and immediately moved to Natchez, Mississippi, where Pierce became pastor of Trinity Episcopal Church and ministered to some of the state's largest and wealthiest plantation owners. In 1832 one parishioner, Dr. Newton Mercer, who himself had Philadelphia connections by way of a medical degree from the University of Pennsylvania, gave the Connellys Sally from among his more than one thousand enslaved people on the occasion of the baptism of the Connellys' first child, whom they named for their Natchez benefactor.[46] Best estimates place Sally in her mid-teens at the time. It's not entirely certain if Phoebe was part of Mercer's gift or her age at the time of the transaction.

Phoebe and Sally worked for the Connellys until December of 1835, when they departed for Europe so Pierce could convert to Catholicism in Rome. At this point the Connellys likely returned them to Mercer, although there is no archival evidence to suggest their whereabouts during this period. Cornelia converted to Catholicism before they departed on their two-year Italian sojourn, during which time they had a private audience with Pope Gregory XVI in 1837, a year before he publicly condemned the transatlantic slave trade. An economic downturn that same year forced the Connellys return to Natchez.

Within months of their arrival in the spring of 1838, the Jesuits offered Pierce a position as an English teacher at their just-opened St. Charles College in Grand Coteau, Louisiana.[47] The Sisters of the Sacred Heart, who ran an adjoining primary and secondary school, welcomed Cornelia as a music teacher.[48] Mercer returned Phoebe and Sally to the Connelly household. Unlike in Natchez, where Catholics were scarce, in Grand Coteau Pierce and Cornelia were not only embedded in a thriving Catholic community through their positions at two prestigious Catholic institutions, but they also collaborated with two Catholic religious orders—the Jesuits and the Society of the Sacred Heart—who relied on enslaved labor to run these institutions. The nuns had opened their school in 1821 on land donated by a wealthy slave-owning Catholic family. An undetermined number of enslaved people became part of the congregation's assets when they were given as dowries by wealthy families whose daughters entered the convent. The Jesuits had arrived just before the Connellys in 1838 by way of St. Louis and brought with them enslaved people from their missions in Maryland to help build the order's first college in the Southern states. Researchers are still trying to parse possible connections between the 1838 sale of enslaved people coordinated by Jesuits at Georgetown to Catholic slave owners in Louisiana and the opening of St. Charles Borromeo in that same year. Either way, these two congregations of vowed religious "shared enslaved persons between the schools and the [sisters'] property."[49] This slave-owning Catholic ecosystem surely impacted the Connellys, whose commitment to Catholicism ripened through their engagement with these priests and nuns in Grand Coteau.

The enslaved members of the Connellys' household also mingled with their Catholic counterparts at Sacred Heart and St. Charles Borromeo. It is likely that Sally's marriage to Ignatius (Nace) Gough, a member of the one of the families owned by the Jesuits in Maryland, compelled her baptism in 1839, since it was Jesuit practice to insist that their enslaved couples receive the sacrament of matrimony and baptism would have been a sacramental prerequisite for Sally.[50] Cornelia Connelly served as godmother to Sally, who had come into her family on the occasion of her own son's baptism nearly a decade earlier. A year later, Cornelia stood as godmother to James Henry, the first of Sally and Nace's three children. In 1840, not long after the Connellys' youngest child succumbed in Cornelia's arms to an agonizing death due to severe burns, Pierce informed Cornelia that he was called to the Catholic priesthood. Once again they prepared for a departure for Rome, this time permanently, in order to receive a Deed of Separation that would dissolve their marriage so that Pierce could join a seminary there. In May of 1842, Pierce sold Sally and her children George (from a prior relationship), James Henry, and Marie to Joseph Stoller, SJ, president of St. Charles College, for $1,500. There is no record that he took money for Phoebe, presumably because of her advanced age.[51] Abraham and Jenny were also part of the Connelly's liquidation, although the details of their initial acquisitions and respective sales is less clear.[52]

Pierce entered a seminary in Rome while Cornelia and their two surviving children took up residence in a convent run by the same order she had served in Grand Coteau. In 1846, Cornelia accepted an invitation from Bishop Nicholas Wiseman in England to found a religious congregation; later, she opened a school in Derby with three companions, who eventually became the first members of the Society of the Holy Child Jesus. Before she died in 1879, Mother Cornelia commissioned six of her sisters to missionary work in the United States—in her native Pennsylvania no less—where they established the first schools in what would become a vibrant collection of institutions across the country from the elementary through college level.[53]

As for the entire Grayson-Gough family, in the eyes of white Catholics they remained little more than property in the years after the Connellys departed Grand Coteau to formalize their religious vocations in Europe. At some point between 1852 and 1859, the Jesuits sold Nace, Sally, and their children to Dr. Henry Jackson Millard in Grand Coteau. They had six more children, only three of whom lived to adulthood. Nace died at thirty-nine in 1861, but Sally lived to see freedom, to work as a domestic, and then to be cared for by her grandchildren until her own death at some point between 1902 and 1904.[54]

With some of these facts in hand (and others included here that have emerged since), we on the Rosemont College commission faced a conundrum. What connection did the *college* have to this history? After all, Cornelia herself did not found the college; members of her community did so more than thirty years after her death. Also, Cornelia did not own Phoebe and Sally when she founded the Society of the Holy Child Jesus in England in 1846. Nor did we have proof that she had access to the proceeds of their sale or used them to found the order. Also, Cornelia may have dispatched her first delegation of Sisters to America in 1863, but they came to Pennsylvania and set up schools without relying on the labor of enslaved people. Rosemont itself opened sixty years after the Emancipation Proclamation, so unlike other American colleges and universities wrestling with these questions, no enslaved people labored on any of Rosemont's iconic buildings, none of which were named for people with ties to white supremacy. None of our earliest families were slave owners, nor did the capital invested in the college have its origins on the backs of enslaved labor. In short, what wrongdoing did the commission have to acknowledge? And without direct complicity in slavery, what recommendations could we possibly make?

We also faced a dilemma trying to situate slave owning in Cornelia's own story. For example, the few of Cornelia's biographers or memory keepers who mentioned Phoebe and Sally insisted that Cornelia and Pierce didn't actively purchase Phoebe and Sally upon their arrival in Natchez.

They were gifts. Moreover, as a woman of the mid-nineteenth century and wife to a domineering man, how much agency did Cornelia really have? Through the legal practice of "coverture" in which a wife's legal and economic rights were "covered" or usurped by those of her husband, Phoebe, Sally, and Sally's children technically belonged to Pierce.[55] Even if we were able to trace the financial benefits that the Grayson-Gough family unit brought to the Connellys, especially from their sale to the Jesuits, Cornelia would have been invisible in the records. The rupture in her life story between her married life in the Deep South and her vowed one in England could be a result of cutting herself off from her former life in order to give herself completely to her new vocation, an expectation of the time; or the fact that her earliest biographers were either European or American historians unfamiliar with the dynamics of the antebellum South that shaped her life; or her desire to distance herself from a peculiar institution she did not relish being associated with in the first place.

The temptation to use these facts to distance ourselves from this history was very real. We considered that responding to this story was more the responsibility of the Society of the Holy Child Jesus than that of the Rosemont College community. The Society had already done some significant research in that regard—members had even met with some of Phoebe and Sally's descendants during a visit to Grand Coteau in 1929.[56] But they currently seemed uncertain about how to relate to this history for some of the same reasons we were.

The commission moved forward without sure footing. We offered predictable recommendations make this dimension of the Cornelian legacy more publicly accessible, create spaces to explore slavery and its afterlife in the curriculum and programming, host a memorial service for descendants, develop appropriate rituals of remembrance. We did our institutional due diligence: we acknowledged and we recommended. We presented our final report, which we called a living document to ensure that the work would continue, and the few descendants of Phoebe and Sally that the Sisters knew of were invited to join, via videoconference, the campus meeting where we shared the findings. One of them, Erin Brown, a descendant of Sally's second son, came to campus for a dinner with the members of the commission a month later. There was a write-up and group photo in the college magazine.[57] The outgoing college president delegated recommendations to appropriate departments across a campus in the midst of a COVID-19 lockdown. Done and done.

But the whole process left me unsettled. I was disturbed by the thought that we moved too quickly and glossed over this history with the secret hope that we could relegate it once again to the past. That we could be one of the "good" Catholic institutions who acknowledged the past and made some recommendations for the future, without really understanding the implications of this part of Cornelia's story for either. I worried about an unresolved impulse to disassociate ourselves from Cornelia—whether from that particular period of her history or in this particular moment in Rosemont's history. I worried that implied a choice to disassociate also from descendants, also on a journey to find their family in Catholic spaces, as well as the people who are Black like them in the Rosemont campus community. I worried that a new administration, the first without any alumni, would not feel the same compulsion to wrestle with the implications of this history in an ongoing way, although an inaugural vice president for diversity and belonging is a promising indicator otherwise.

Racial mercy in this context helps me take seriously a pearl of wisdom from the GU272 group descendants: *nothing about us without us.*[58] Certainly it's easier to tell truths and make amends when we're not doing so in the presence of or in relationship with the people we have harmed. Racial mercy increases our capacity for the kind of discomfort that comes with looking back at a shared history from across a racial chasm that history created. A small group of us from the commission started working alongside Erin, placing her desires for our collaborative work front and center. Primarily, she hopes that her family members will become more than names on slips of paper that recorded transactions, whether sacramental or financial. They are people with deep reserves of faith and stories that need to be shared. The presence of Catholicism in her family's histories is not uncomplicated, since it is Catholic recordkeeping that provides archival access to her ancestors and Catholicism itself that keeps her tethered to them.

Working with Erin has helped us shift our focus away from the white figures whose exoneration or absolution we often seek in doing this memory work and onto the fascinating lives of the people who likely made their vocations and institutions possible. It is through Phoebe's and Sally's eyes that we can begin to be more honest with ourselves about Cornelia and her institutional legacy, which undoubtedly includes Rosemont. With them as our guides, we can also be more honest about the oppressive dimensions of Catholicism that have held us all back, especially our propensity to whitewash our history and rely on hagiographical accounts of holy and yet human people. And it is through dimensions of Phoebe and Sally's faith, which survives through the generations despite little support from the institutional Church, that we can find the spiritual resources we need to move toward each other in creating Catholic campus cultures of belonging.

UNDOING

AS A THEOLOGIAN always on the hunt for the next epiphany—unexpected moments where I encounter some kind of mind-blowing truth about my tradition—four years of rounding the parishes connected to my family's history in Philadelphia certainly kept me in a steady "no way!" state of mind. But these epiphanic moments were different. For one, I didn't have to look too hard to find them. Clearly, anti-Blackness was unapologetically part of business as usual given how thoroughly it was woven into so much of the historical record of my family's parishes. Moreover, these were not exactly truths to get excited about. I experienced no joy in sharing them and worried about how they would be received, whether by members of my family or members of the Catholic institutions to which I belong and am deeply committed.

I didn't want to believe these epiphanies, especially as proof of their veracity relentlessly unfolded around the country as I worked away on this book: white Catholics' fervor for Trump through two presidential elections; the continued police killings of hundreds of unarmed Black people; National Guard presence at the corner of my campus during protests in the summer of 2020; the contentious appointments of two white Catholics to the Supreme Court; the Department of Education's threats to ban curricula informed by critical race theory; COVID-19's racial disparities in everything from testing and mortality rates to unemployment and mental health; and finally the insurrection at the Capitol by white Christian nationalists on the actual Feast of the Epiphany in 2021. As I scoured boxes of yellowed archival materials and scrolled through my

Twitter feed, I felt perhaps the most significant epiphany of all: the past and the present colliding.

Tugging, even as gently as I did, on the threads of anti-Blackness in my family's Catholic story unraveled, parish by parish and generation by generation, the entire garment of the Catholic tradition in which I am wrapped. Given the suffering—the social death even—that our anti-Blackness created and sustained, my Catholic identity no longer felt like a mantle but rather a shroud.

And yet, encountering these truths has been the most liberating work of my life. Equipped with an awareness of how we wove anti-Blackness into the fabric of my Catholic identity—in no small part with the help of the Catholic institutions that formed the people who formed the people who formed me—I find myself freer to move toward others in the work of creating a whole new cloth. I can now put my finger on the knots, at least five of them, that have been holding me—holding us white Catholics—back. Remaining vigilant about these knots, like fingering the beads of a rosary, can keep me alert for ways I'm either an obstacle to or a conduit for racial justice as a white Catholic woman.

For example, I'm now aware of the knot of apathy and separation that has entangled me and my people in Black suffering, given our proximity to both slavery and its unfolding afterlife. To be in such proximity to injustice and do nothing has diminished our emotional capability for empathy. We have learned to accept certain kinds of suffering as normal, as unavoidable, and certainly as other peoples' problems. Our proximity to pain has also been the driver of my family's desire to put as much distance as possible between ourselves and Black people as soon as we could. We expended tremendous energies separating ourselves not only from Black people but also from movements of change to which we also had proximity at different points in history. Undoing this knot requires working to convert that proximity to actual closeness that might rekindle my ability to genuinely connect with others. This isn't just happening to Black people; it is happening to people who I know, I collaborate with, I care about, I love.

Second, I want to keep undoing the knot of my white Catholic missionary sensibility, which was the primary way that my people dealt with our proximity to the pain of racial inequality and still shapes the way I see and engage with Black people. Here is the pattern I saw again and again in the white parishes my family members belonged to: Black people are defined by their need and deficiencies; they are different from the white norm and a liability to it. When it comes to our engagements with Black people, I found a similar pattern: Black people either need special resources to be developed and administered by white Catholics specifically for and to them, or Black people need to be integrated or welcomed into our white Catholic communities—whether parish, school, or university—on our terms, to mitigate the negative impact they might have on our white Catholic enterprises.

Undoing this missionary knot might be the most significant work any of us could take up. I can begin by practicing the fundamental first step of Catholic anti-racism: rejecting the idea that Black people require our charity and the notion that our charity is a sufficient response to racial inequity. For example, I can continually call myself out when I operate out of my well-programmed assumption that my primary responsibility as a good white Catholic is to meet the material and spiritual needs arising from the unjust social order my ancestors helped create. Instead, I can examine the way my do-gooding maintains the alignment of the economic, political, and ecclesial powers that sustain so much of my own white Catholic comfort and stability. Once I begin to build that kind of mental and moral muscle, I can orient myself toward becoming a co-conspirator with Black people and other people of color in changing oppressive structures and systems.

Related to my missionary sensibility is my knot of self-preservation through which my people convinced ourselves that ours is a tradition and enterprise that is under threat and must be preserved at all costs. Granted, anti-Catholicism was a real dynamic for some of my ancestors. But I now question long-suffering claims to being a despised and targeted group, particularly when white Catholics moved from an embattled minority to a cultural majority who leverage unprecedented amounts of social and political capital. Cries of anti-Catholicism provided cover for anti-Black behavior that had adverse effects on white Catholics in the long run as well. Insisting on our value by denying the value of others or conforming to white Catholic uniformity ultimately bankrupted us morally and culturally. We felt insecure, but not because we didn't belong—rather because the conditions we set for belonging were hypocritical. Since that hypocrisy was and still is obvious to others, we get tangled up in the knot of performing our patriotism and our goodness. Whether marching under a giant flag on the way to a war to end slavery—but not to secure meaning-ful freedom for Black people—or in a Klan-inspired march down Broad Street at the sesquicentennial, my people paraded the complementarity of our Catholicity and Americanness at a variety of points by proving that we, too, could be anti-Black. Out of fear of being labeled racists, we also performed our moral goodness—perhaps to assuage our own doubts about it—through that missionary impulse to meet needs but never ask why need exists, to feel absolved from wrongdoing that we never con-fessed, or to be seen as standing on the right side of a history we don't fully know. We can loosen these knots by contributing to emerging efforts on the part of Black, Latin American, Indigenous, and Asian Catholics to mainstream latent traditions of multiculturalism and inclusion in Ameri-can Catholicism. We can replace superficial performances with meaning-ful strategies for creating communities of belonging.

Finally, I've learned that many of our knots ironically come from our ability to create spaces without them. My own experience suggests that our American Catholic communities are operating precisely as they were designed to. The all-white Catholic existence to which I am accustomed is actually my inheritance given the efforts, even sacrifices, of previous gen-erations to create and maintain homogenous Catholic spaces. Given my success in the predominantly white Catholic institutions with which I am affiliated, I am the embodiment of a century-old dream in my family. But I find myself asking to what end, particularly as I witness the aftermath of this voluntary segregation or preference for comfort over courage. My parish and school, St. James, closed five years ago, my current university stands on the brink, my colleagues and students of color experience real pain on a daily basis.

Too many of our parishes, schools, university classrooms and curric-ula, and boardrooms are echo chambers of sameness and amnesia. The cognitive dissonance, lack of constructive conflict, disruptive memories, and disquieting truth talk only make white Catholics—and the Catho-lic institutions that we run—more fragile. Instead, we need knots that connect different people, knots of true belonging to each other that can bolster white Catholic courage for racial justice and in turn build multi-cultural communities that can withstand the forces of white supremacy that intend to separate us. To begin to tie those multicultural knots, how-ever, white Catholics need to undo those knots that keep us comfortable.

So I'm going to keep on rounding because becoming undone is an iterative journey. I'll invoke the prayer for pilgrims offered by the late Irish poet John O'Donohue as I go:

> May you travel in an awakened way,
> Gathered wisely into your inner ground;
> That you might not waste the invitations
> Which wait along the way to transform you.[1]

—PENTECOST, 2021

ACKNOWLEDGMENTS

I HAVE MANY TO THANK for gifting me with not just the insights but, more importantly, the courage to write this book.

I am grateful to colleagues at La Salle University whose embodiment of the Christian Brothers' charism of "together and by association" nourished me in my writing process. Maggie McGuinness and Jack Downey graciously oriented me in the trending discourses in American Catholic history. Catherine Holochwost and Candace Roberston-James helped me harness the creative dimensions of teaching in our shared course about La Salle's northwest Philadelphia neighborhood of Belfield, which made writing about particular places of my family's past much more fun. A number of colleagues kept me informed about the growing edges of anti-racist teaching, learning, and activism: Rochelle Peterson-Ansari, Rosemary Barbera, Laura Frank, Chip Gallagher, Rhonda Hazell, Tara Carr-Lemke, Luisa Ossa, Anthony Paul Smith, Karen Reardon, Laura Roy, Cherylyn Rush, Sara Shuman, and Caitlin Taylor. Christen Rexing's 6:30 a.m. daily Zoom parallel writing sessions in the spring of 2020 helped me meet deadlines in the midst of pandemic swirl. I learned so much from students in two semesters of Theology and Racism who were willing to wade into troubled waters at turbulent times to emerge with new perspectives and commitments. I also want to thank students in two first-year seminars, Catholic Philadelphia Then and Now, who without a doubt were the first audience for my ideas. Thanks also to senior academic administrators, who granted me a research leave in the midst of considerable financial challenges, and Adriane Adams, our department administrator, who helped me manage my department chair responsibilities in the midst of the research and writing process.

I am grateful to colleagues in the Lasallian world beyond my institution, who taught me how to integrate commitments to anti-racism into ways of being Catholic and human, particularly leaders of the newly formed Lasallian Colleges and Universities in Association for Justice and the Lasallian Education Council's Ad Hoc Committee on Advocacy, especially: Kenenna Amuzie; Katie Bauser; Jim Burke; Christian Comacho; Grace Crumbaugh; Keith Donovan; Maryann Donohue-Lynch; Jacqueline Martin; Karin McClelland; Abbey Michels; Ernest Miller, FSC; Maggie Noughton; Dylan Perry, FSC; Jennifer Pigza; and Conor Reidy.

I want to thank communities of teaching and learning who have opened up space for me to think through questions of this book and the unsettling answers I unearthed. Former colleagues at the Dorothy Day Center for Service and Justice at Fordham University, particularly Jeannine Hill Fletcher, accompanied me in a series of trainings with the People's Institute for Survival and Beyond, whose framework for anti-racism informs so much of this project. I am grateful to the Rosemont College Commission on the Legacy of Slavery for what I learned about the interpersonal and intentional *how* of acknowledgment and redress—particularly Roseanne McDougall, SHCJ; Elena Sisti; Emily Siegel; and Erin Brown—and who allow me to be part of a continuing process of unearthing and learning from the legacy of Cornelia Connelly where Catholics and slavery are concerned. The Ignatian Solidarity Network regularly offered me opportunities to share insights from my research, and its members offered edifying feedback. An assemblage of writers in a workshop on Writing the Spiritual Life, sponsored by the Collegeville Institute and under the masterful facilitation of Lauren Winner, opened me up to the world of spiritual writing and introduced me to the fundamentals of creative nonfiction. I am grateful to Lauren for teaching me how to be a more effective companion to my readers as I revised my first draft. Thank you to the creative community at Beacon Press, particularly my fantastic editor, Amy Caldwell, who helped me conjure even bigger dreams for this book, and the editorial team of Katie Robinson and Raquel Pidal who helped me better articulate them.

I could not have completed this book without the guidance and responsiveness of several archivists. Shawn Weldon got me set me up with my first cart of boxes at the Catholic Historical Research Center of the Archdiocese of Philadelphia and Patrick Schenk took it from there, seeing me through to the tedious process of editing my endnotes. Katie Carey, the university archivist at La Salle University, not only helped me track down gems in our own collection but also has been a generous partner in recreating for my students the kind of deep learning experiences in archives that planted the seed for this book when I was an undergraduate. Judy Ng, Dan Oh, Pamela Powell, and Jasmin Smith helped me get a handle on the antebellum reality of my family in the Chester County Historical Society, and Phil Runkel oriented me to Anna McGarry's papers in Marquette University's extensive Catholic social justice collection. Bill Conners, my sixth grade teacher in St. James Elementary School, continued to model for me the excitement of learning by cluing me in to materials related to the Gesu Parish, housed in the Villiger Archives at Saint Joseph's Prep where he now teaches. I thank Leo Vacarro at Villiger as well. Chris Dixon and Leslie Carey assisted at my alma mater, Saint Joseph's University. Randall Miller, while not an archivist, is responsible for my undergraduate encounter with the Mobberly diary in the Georgetown University archive twenty-five years ago that haunted me enough to dare to write this book. I appreciate the wisdom he continues to impart.

Several communities of faith continually grounded me in God while I wrote this book. I am blessed to be part of a parish community willing to stay in the struggle to become anti-racist, and so I am grateful to the members of St. Vincent de Paul who commit so much of themselves to building an intentionally inclusive Catholic Community, especially our pastor, Fr. Sylvester Peterka, and members of the Reconciliation and Unity Ministry, including Sharon Browning, Doug Copeland, Maceo Hood, Mary Laver, Chris Bolden-Newsome, and Wiley Redding. My co-conspirators in radical justice, Tia Pratt and Sharon Browning, helped me claim my expertise as we dreamed up workshops that we might—and eventually did—offer to communities of faith seeking to become anti-racist. For fourteen months (and counting) of the COVID-19 pandemic, members of the virtual "House Church" I helped to convene provided weekly sustenance and witness to the power of intentional communities who persevere with candor, joy, laughter, and dancing: Molly and Dave Harty; Frank and Suellen Monaghan; Rick and Judy Rodes; Jenn, Jeff, Maggie, and Callie Swetland; Kerry Thompson and Kenli; Tina Wahl, Liz Wilkey, and a handful of family members I'll name shortly.

I am lucky to have good friends who are also teachers of so many things connected to writing books and doing justice. I'm grateful to Donna Freitas for her mentorship in finding the right publisher and my voice in very initial drafts. Natalia Imperatori-Lee and Brenna Moore offered their expertise on feminist ecclesiology and twentieth century Catholic history, respectively, and solidarity in our professional and personal lives, irreverently, as they unfolded these past four years. Kristin Heyer was my loyal accountability partner for my healthy strivings where anti-racism and living with intention are concerned. Kerry Thompson regularly reminded me of my hopes for this book once out of my head and in the world. Dear friends from Philadelphia, all working with a variety of communities to build a more robust common good with people who are currently marginalized from it, affirmed my inclinations here, especially Kristin Gavin, Sally Poliwoda, Linda Hawkins, Jennifer Swetland, and Ken Houston.

Finally, I am grateful to members of my family for both trusting me in telling this story and enduring me as I tried to do so. My mother, Kathleen, and three of her siblings—Bill, Mary Louise, and Patrick Gallagher—dug through closets and memory banks to provide insights into the Gallagher and Hargadon families. I am grateful to them for being so willing to share stories that were usually heartwarming but often heartbreaking too. I thank my mom for reading early drafts and, more importantly, for instilling in me a sense of family as a verb. I thank my dad, George, whose ability to retain particular details about his maternal grandparents helped me commune with them as I wrote. I know I get my sense of wonder from him too, and I needed that in good measure for this project. Thanks, too, to my brother, Thomas, my sister-in-law, Christine, and their four children, Seamus, Brendan, Beatrice, and Thomas. All kids deserve a better future where racism is concerned and so these four in particular kept me motivated. I'm lucky to have a kindred spirit in my sister, Corinne. I thank her for constantly showing me how integrity starts whenever we try to begin again. And my husband, Dan, whom I was lucky enough to marry halfway through this project, made it part of his own journey. I am grateful for the ways his sociological practicality balances my theological loftiness. My knots are no match for his love, confidence in me, and easy way of being.

NOTES

INTRODUCTION: MATTERING

1. Let me offer a brief explanation on the method of capitalization I will use
in this book. I capitalize *Black* because this term refers to both people of a racial
category—imposed on them by members of another racial group—and to a distinct
American culture that enslaved Africans and their descendants created after being
severed from their native cultures during the Middle Passage. I acknowledge the
rationales for also capitalizing *white*: doing so raises white people's consciousness
of our racial identity, reminds us of our historical ability to eventually transcend
ethnic identities to become white, and makes more visible our collective power
to design racial categories, designate people to them, and distribute privileges
and resources accordingly. However, I will not capitalize that term in this book.
Since I intend all of my words here to heighten my white readers' awareness of the
evolution of our racial identity in ways that will help us take stock in our power and
privileges and redirect us as partners in racial equity work, I do not need to rely
on capitalizing *white* to accomplish that task. I especially don't want to capitalize
that term if doing so re-centers white readers in our whiteness or is experienced by
Black people as an equivocation of their experiences with the processes of racialization in the US or an affront to their efforts to claim their dignity and value in the
midst of ongoing debates about that very thing, especially in Catholic circles. I am
grateful to colleagues Dr. Tia Noelle Pratt, Dr. Laurie Cassidy, and Dr. Jeannine
Hill Fletcher for sharing their different perspectives about this complicated and
critical discourse. For a helpful summary in support of capitalizing the term *white*,
see Nell Irvin Painter's opinion piece, "Why 'White' Should Be Capitalized, Too,"

Washington Post, June 22, 2020, https://www.washingtonpost.com/opinions/2020
/07/22/why-white-should-be-capitalized/; for an opinion piece against capitalizing
white, see Julie Craven, "Capitalizing *White* Won't Fix the Media's Racism Problem," Slate, August 5, 2020, https://slate.com/news-and-politics/2020/08
/capitalizing-white.html.

2. Anna Orso, "One Year Later: A Timeline of Controversy and Progress Since
the Starbucks Arrests Seen 'Round the World," *Philadelphia Inquirer*, April 12,
2019, https://www.inquirer.com/news/starbucks-incident-philadelphia-racial-bias
-one-year-anniversary-stutter-dilworth-park-homeless-tables-20190412.html.

3. Christopher Koettl et al., "How the Philadelphia Police Tear-Gassed a
Group of Trapped Protestors," *New York Times*, June 25, 2020, https://www.nytimes
.com/video/us/100000007174941/philadelphia-tear-gas-george-floyd-protests
.html.

4. Don Gonyea, "Majority of White Americans Say They Believe Whites Face
Discrimination," National Public Radio, October 24, 2017, https://www.npr.org
/2017/10/24/559604836/majority-of-white-americans-think-theyre-discriminated
-against.

5. Traci Blackmon, "Plenary Panel on Racism," World Meeting of Popular
Movements, US Regional Meeting, Fresno, CA, February 17, 2017.

6. W. E. B. Du Bois, *The Souls of Black Folk* ([Place of publication not identi-
fied]: G&D Media, 2019), 9.

7. Lauren Camera, "Segregation Reinforced by School Districts," *USA Today*,
July 25, 2019, https://www.usnews.com/news/education-news/articles/2019-07-25
/racial-and-economic-segregation-reinforced-by-school-district-boundaries.

8. City Council of Philadelphia, "Philadelphia Poverty Action Plan: Report
of the Special Committee on Poverty Reduction and Prevention," March 3, 2020,
https://phlcouncil.com/council-announces-poverty-action-plan/; Pew Charitable
Trusts, "The State of Philadelphians Living in Poverty, 2019," April 11, 2019,
https://www.pewtrusts.org/en/research-and-analysis/fact-sheets/2019/04/the-state
-of-philadelphians-living-in-poverty-2019#:~:text=Poverty%20is%20one%20of
%20Philadelphia%26rsquo,nation%E2%80%99s%2010%20largest%20cities
.&text=And%20nearly%20half%20of%20all,below%20the%20federal%20
poverty%20line.

9. Mike Shields et al., "Income Inequality among Philadelphia's Workforce: An
Update," Economy League of Greater Philadelphia, August 5, 2020, https://econo-
myleague.org/providing-insight/leadingindicators/2020/08/05/incomeinequality
update2020.

10. Shields et al., "Income Inequality among Philadelphia's Workforce: An
Update."

11. Pew Charitable Trusts, "The State of Philadelphians Living in Poverty,
2019."

12. Holly Otterbein, "Philly is the 4th Most Segregated Big City in the Country," *Philadelphia Magazine*, September 22, 2015, phillymag.com/citified/2015/09
/22/philadelphia-segregated-big-city/. Otterbein cites Nate Silver, "The Most
Diverse Cities Are Often the Most Segregated," FiveThirtyEight, May 1, 2015,
https://fivethirtyeight.com/features/the-most-diverse-cities-are-often-the-most
-segregated/.

13. Mike Shields et al., "The Color of Inequality 3: Structural Racism and
Public Education," Economy League of Greater Philadelphia, June 17, 2020,
https://economyleague.org/providing-insight/colorofinequalitypart3.

14. Mark Dent, "The Share of Black Students at Philly Colleges Is Steadily Shrinking," *BillyPenn*, December 3, 2015, https://billypenn.com/2015/12/03/the -share-of-black-students-at-philly-colleges-is-steadily-shrinking/; Don Sapatkin, "Study of Philly Neighborhoods Finds Big Disparities in Health-Care Access by Race," *Philadelphia Inquirer*, August 8, 2016, https://www.inquirer.com/philly /health/20160809_Study_of_Phila__neighborhoods_finds_big_disparities_in _health-care_access_by_race.html.

15. Philadelphia Department of Public Health, "Close to Home: The Health of Philadelphia's Neighborhoods," Summer 2019, https://www.phila.gov/media /20190801133844/Neighborhood-Rankings_7_31_19.pdf.

16. Philadelphia Department of Public Health, "Covid-19 Impact by Age and Race/Ethnicity in Philadelphia," August 2020, https://www.phila.gov/media /20200918100441/CHARTv5e7_revise.pdf.

17. Pew Charitable Trusts, "Philadelphia 2021: The State of the City," April 13, 2021, https://www.pewtrusts.org/en/research-and-analysis/reports/2021/04/ philadelphia-2021-state-of-the-city.

18. Patrick Kerkstra, "36,000 Black Men Are 'Missing' from Philadelphia," *Philadelphia Magazine*, April 21, 2015, https://www.phillymag.com/citified/2015/04 /21/black-men-missing-philadelphia/.

19. Pew Charitable Trusts, "Philadelphia's Poor: Who They Are, Where They Live and How that Has Changed," November 2017, 1, https://www.pewtrusts.org /-/media/assets/2017/11/pri_philadelphias_poor.pdf.

20. George Yancy, "Dear White America," *New York Times*, December 24, 2015, https://opinionator.blogs.nytimes.com/2015/12/24/dear-white-america/.

21. Bryan Massingale, "The Magis and Justice," keynote address at the Ignatian Family Teach-In for Justice, Washington, DC, November 7, 2017, https:// ignatiansolidarity.net/iftj-17-video/.

22. James Baldwin, *The Price of the Ticket: Collected Nonfiction 1948–1985* (New York: St. Martin's Press, 1985), xix.

23. Joe R. Feagin, *The White Racial Frame: Centuries of Racial Framing and Counter-Framing* (New York: Routledge, 2010), 95.

24. James F. Keenan, SJ, *The Works of Mercy: The Heart of Catholicism* (Lanham, MD: Rowman & Littlefied Publishers, 2007), xvii.

25. Martin Luther King Jr., "Montgomery Bus Boycott." Speech at the First Montgomery Improvement Association Mass Meeting, Montgomery, AL, December 5, 1955, https://www.digitalhistory.uh.edu/disp_textbook.cfm?smtid=3&psid =3625.

26. For more on this spiritual practice, see Michael P. Carroll, *Irish Pilgrimage: Holy Wells and Popular Catholic Devotion* (Baltimore, MD: Johns Hopkins University Press, 1999); for the interplay of space, movement, and memory in the Irish experience, I turned to Rebecca Solnit, *A Book of Migrations* (New York: Verso, 1997); for Celtic spiritual practices, including that of pilgrimage, see Christine Valters Paintner, *The Soul's Slow Ripening: 12 Celtic Practices for Seeking the Sacred* (Notre Dame, IN: Sourin Books, 2018).

27. Blackmon, "Plenary Panel on Racism."

CHAPTER 1: WITNESSING

1. "Excerpts from Commission's Report on Bombing," *New York Times* Archives, March 7, 1986, https://www.nytimes.com/1986/03/07/us/excerpts-from -commission-s-report-on-bombing.html.

2. For more on the history of MOVE, see Hizkias Assefa and Paul Wahrhaftig, *The MOVE Crisis in Philadelphia: Extremist Groups and Conflict Resolution* (Pittsburgh, PA: University of Pittsburgh Press, 1990); Michael Boyette and Randi Boyette, *Let it Burn: MOVE, the Philadelphia Police Department, and the Confrontation that Changed a City* (San Diego: Quadrant Books, 1989); Jason Osder, dir., *Let the Fire Burn*, (2013, Zeitgeist Films). For first-person accounts, see Lindsey Norwood, "The Day Philadelphia Bombed its Own People," *Vox*, August 15, 2019, https://www.vox.com/the-highlight/2019/8/8/20747198/philadelphia-bombing-1985-move; Joseph L. Puckett, "MOVE on Osage Avenue: 1982–1985," West Philadelphia Collaborative History, https://collaborativehistory.gse.upenn.edu/stories/move-osage-avenue.

3. Clark DeLeon, "The MOVE Raid and a City Changed Forever," *Day to Day*, National Public Radio, May 5, 2005, https://www.npr.org/templates/story/story.php?storyId=4651110.

4. Francis X. Clines, "15 Years and Millions Later, Bombing Plagues Philadelphia," *New York Times*, April 13, 2000, https://www.nytimes.com/2000/08/13/us/15-years-and-millions-later-bombing-plagues-philadelphia.html.

5. For a historical overview and critical assessment of the US Catholic Bishops' social teaching on racism, see Bryan Massingale's *Racial Justice in the Catholic Church* (Maryknoll, NY: Orbis Books, 2010), 43–82; and Olga M. Segura, Birth of a Movement: Black Lives Matter and the Catholic Church (Maryknoll, NY: Orbis Books, 2021), 43–49 and 67–81.

6. Nate Tunner-Williams, "The Catholic Side of the MOVE Bombing," *Black Catholic Messenger*, May 12, 2021, https://www.blackcatholicmessenger.com/the-catholic-side-of-the-move-bombing/.

7. Richard Kent Evan, *MOVE: An American Religion* (New York: Oxford University Press, 2020), 89–122.

8. Kent, *MOVE: An American Religion*, 111–115; Sally A. Downey, "Charles V. Devlin, 81, Cleric and Mediator," *Philadelphia Inquirer*, February 20, 2020.

9. Carol Anderson spells out facets of white rage in different historical periods of American history, in *White Rage: The Unspoken Truth of Our Racial Divide* (New York: Bloomsbury, 2016).

10. Eddie Glaude, *Democracy in Black: How Race Still Enslaves the American Soul* (New York: Broadway Books, 2016), 29–50.

11. Ta-Nehisi Coates, *Between the World and Me* (New York: Spiegel & Grau, 2015), 10–11.

12. Solnit, *A Book of Migrations*, 49.

13. For more on the history of federal and municipal housing segregation, see Richard Rothstein, *The Color of Law: A Forgotten History of How Our Government Segregated America* (New York: Liveright Publishing, 2017).

14. Ibram X. Kendi, *Stamped from the Beginning: The Definitive History of Racist Ideas in America* (New York: Nation Books, 2016), 3. Kendi explains that he pulled the phrase "stamped from the beginning" from an address Senator Jefferson Davis delivered to the Senate in April 1860 rejecting a bill to fund Black education in Washington, DC.

15. Katie Walker Grimes, *Christ Divided: Anti-Blackness as Corporate Vice* (Minneapolis: Fortress Press, 2017), 101.

16. Coleman Andrews, "These Are the 56 People Who Signed the Declaration of Independence," *USA Today*, July 3, 2019, https://www.usatoday.com/story/money/2019/07/03/july-4th-the-56-people-who-signed-the-declaration-of-independence/39636971/; Madeline Hooke Rice, *American Catholic Opinion in the Slavery*

Controversy (Gloucester, MA: Peter Smith, 1964), 132; and "Charles Carroll of Car-ollton," Charles Carroll House of Annapolis (website), https://charlescarrollhouse .org/the-carrolls/personal-biography-2.

17. Associated Press, "Statue of First Catholic Supreme Court Justice Re-moved Because He Wrote Dred Scott Decision," *Crux*, August, 18 2017, https:// cruxnow.com/church-in-the-usa/2017/08/statue-first-catholic-supreme-court-jus-tice-removed-wrote-dred-scott-decision/; and Menachem Wecker, "At New Smithsonian African-American History and Culture Museum, Catholic Stories Emerge," *National Catholic Reporter*, February 17, 2017, https://www.ncron-line.org/news/media/new-smithsonian-african-american-history-and-culture-museum-catholic-stories-emerge.

18. Feagin, *The White Racial Frame*, 26.

19. Equal Justice Initiative, "Lynching in America: Confronting the Legacy of Racial Terror (Third Edition)," 2017, https://eji.org/reports/lynching-in-america /?gclid=CjoKCQiApsiBBhCKARIsAN8o_4iIMzHjVoQCpxCw6iaAZXBXI-uQkCTfoFOzSh9oeAomTGmURPC2_sDEaAqlwEALw_wcB; Michelle Alexan-der, *The New Jim Crow: Mass Incarceration in the Age of Colorblindness* (New York: The New Press, 2010); 20–58; "Correctional Facilities Industry in the US – Market Research Report," IBIS World, November 24, 2020, https://www.ibisworld.com /united-states/market-research-reports/correctional -facilities-industry/#:~:text=poll%20Average%20industry%20growth%202015 %E2%80%932020%3A%200.8%25&text=Over%20the%20five%20years%20to ,0.8%25%20to%20reach%20%245.1%20billion.

20. Pew Research Center, "How the faithful voted: A preliminary 2016 analysis," November 9, 2016, https://www.pewresearch.org/fact-tank/2016/11/09/how-the -faithful-voted-a-preliminary-2016-analysis/; and Frank Newport, "Religious Group Voting and the 2020 Election," *Gallup*, November 13, 2020, https://news.gallup.com /opinion/polling-matters/324410/religious-group-voting-2020-election.aspx.

21. Katherine Burton, *The Golden Door: The Life of St. Katharine Drexel* (Kansas City, MO: Angelus Press, 2014), 232–233.

22. Barbara Applebaum, *Being White and Being Good: White Complicity, White Responsibility, and Social Justice Pedagogy* (New York: Lexington Books, 2011), 27–51.

23. John Gramlich, "The Gap Between the Number of Blacks and Whites in Prison Is Shrinking," Pew Research Center, April 30, 2019, https://www. pewresearch.org/fact-tank/2019/04/30/shrinking-gap-between-number-o f-blacks-and-whites-in-prison/.

24. Massingale, "The Magis and Justice."

25. Santiago Slabodsky, "It's the Theology, Stupid! Coloniality, Anti-Blackness, and the Bounds of Humanity," in *Anti-Blackness and Christian Ethics*, Vincent W. Lloyd and Andrew Prevot, eds. (Maryknoll, NY: Orbis Books, 2017): 19–40.

26. Joseph Barndt, *Becoming an Anti-Racist Church: Journeying Toward Wholeness* (Minneapolis: Fortress Press, 2011), 94.

27. Barndt, *Becoming an Anti-Racist Church*, 95.

28. Barndt, *Becoming an Anti-Racist Church*, 105–111.

29. Barndt, *Becoming an Anti-Racist Church*, 108.

30. Barndt, *Becoming an Anti-Racist Church*, 110.

31. W. E. B. Du Bois, *Black Reconstruction in America: 1860–1880* (New York: The Free Press, 1998), 700; Martin Luther King Jr., "Our God Is Marching On," speech at the State Capitol, Selma, AL, March 25, 1965, https://www.historynet .com/famous-letters-and-speeches-of-martin-luther-king-jr.

32. Pope Francis, *The Church of Mercy* (Chicago: Loyola Press: 2014), 19.

33. Keenan, SJ, *The Works of Mercy*, xvii.

34. Pope Francis, *The Name of God Is Mercy*, Oonagh Stransky, trans. (New York: Random House, 2016), 9–12.

CHAPTER 2: ALIGNING

1. "Andrew Little," *West Chester Daily Local News*, June 14, 1886, County Clippings by Surname, Little, CCHS.

2. "Lancaster County Once Boasted Nearly 500 of These Silent Stone Sentinels. Today Fewer than 20 Percent Remains. Unlock the Mystery of these Ancient Masonry Guardians," Uncharted Lancaster, March 20, 2019, https://uncharted lancaster.com/2019/03/30/lancaster-county-once-boastd-nearly-500-of-these-silent -stone-sentinels-today-fewer-than-20-percent-remains-unlock-the-mystery-of -these-ancient-masonry-guardians/.

3. "John Carroll," *American Republican*, June 10, 1873, County Clippings by Surname, Carroll, CCHS; and "Emily Carroll," *West Chester Daily Local News*, January 18, 1911, County Clippings by Surname, Carroll, CCHS.

4. "Personal Property," *The Jeffersonian*, November 11, 1871, County Clippings by Surname, Little, CCHS.

5. Lucy Maddox, *The Parker Sisters: A Border Kidnapping* (Philadelphia: Temple University Press, 2016), 16.

6. Maddox, *The Parker Sisters*, xiv. For early and somewhat hagiographical accounts of the treatment of refugees from the South in Chester County during the antebellum period, see R. C. Smedley, *The History of the Underground Railroad in Chester County and the Neighboring Counties of Pennsylvania* (Lancaster,PA: Office of The Journal, 1883).

7. Histories of Chester County and southeastern Pennsylvania during this period include Maddox's *The Parker Sisters*; Richard Newman and James Mueller, eds., *Antislavery and Abolition in Philadelphia: Emancipation and the Long Struggle for Racial Justice in the City of Brotherly Love* (Baton Rouge, LA: Louisiana State University Press, 2011); and William C. Kashatus, *Just Over the Line: Chester County and the Underground* Railroad (University Park, PA: Penn State University Press, 2001). Chester County population figures are from Kashatus, *Just Over the Line*, 25.

8. *The Jeffersonian*, May 16, 1848, County Clippings by Subject, Black History, CCHS.

9. Julie Winch, "Self-Help and Self-Determination: Black Philadelphians and the Dimensions of Freedom," in *Antislavery and Abolition in Philadelphia*, 66–89: 69.

10. Kashatus, *Just Over the Line*, 3.

11. "County Convention," *American Republican*, February 14, 1837, County Clippings by Subject, Black History, CCHS.

12. "Localities . . . The Nigga Meetin'," *The Jeffersonian*, October 27, 1854, County Clippings by Subject, Black History, CCHS.

13. Kevin Starr, *Continental Ambitions: Roman Catholics in North America: The Colonial Experience* (San Francisco: Ignatius Press, 2016), 517.

14. Maddox, *The Parker Sisters*, 51.

15. Maddox, *The Parker Sisters*, 45.

16. Maddox, *The Parker Sisters*, 4.

17. Kelly Brown Douglas, *Stand Your Ground: Black Bodies and the Justice of God* (Maryknoll, NY: Orbis Books, 2015), 54.

18. James Jones, "The Borough's Hotel History," Digital Commons @West Chester University, http://digitalcommons.wcupa.edu/hist_wchest/45.

19. Maddox, *The Parker Sisters*, 6.

20. "An Underground Railroad Heading South," *Village Record*, March 27, 1860, County Clippings by Subject, Black History, CCHS.

21. See Kashatus, *Just Over the Line*, 28–31; Maddox, *The Parker Sisters*, 63–74.

22. Michael Omi and Howard Winant, *Racial Formation in the United States* (New York: Routledge, 2016), 3.

23. Omi and Winant, *Racial Formation in the United States*, 124–127.

24. Omi and Winant, *Racial Formation in the United States*, 13.

25. Feagin, *The White Racial Frame*, 10.

26. Feagin, *The White Racial Frame*, 11.

27. Maddox, *The Parker Sisters*, 104; quoting Walter Johnson, *Soul by Soul: Inside the Antebellum Slave Market* (Cambridge, MA: Harvard University Press, 1999), 129.

28. *American Republican*, October 17, 1843, County Clippings by Subject, Black History, CCHS.

29. Gary Nash, "Race and Citizenship in the Early Republic," in *Antislavery and Abolition in Philadelphia*, 109, citing Patrick Rael, *Black Identity and Black Protest in the Antebellum North* (Chapel Hill: University of North Carolina Press, 2002), 73.

30. Omi and Winant, *Racial Formation in the United States*, 111.

31. Kashatus, *Just Over the Line*, 30.

32. Maddox, *The Parker Sisters*, 25.

33. Edward E. Baptist, *The Half Has Never Been Told: Slavery and the Making of American Capitalism* (New York: Basic Books, 2014), 9.

34. Kendi, *Stamped from the Beginning*, 12.

35. Baptist, *The Half Has Never Been Told*, 157–158.

36. Feagin, *The White Racial Frame*, *33*; and Kendi, *Stamped from the Beginning*, 189–190; see also Baptist, *The Half Has Never Been Told*, 332–342.

37. Kashatus, *Just Over the Line*, 28.

38. Noel Ignatiev, *How the Irish Became White* (New York: Routledge, 1995), 8–38.

39. Omi and Winnant, *Racial Formation in the United States*, 127.

40. Three published histories of St. Agnes inform this chapter. One marked its centenary: William Barrett, *Historical Sketch of St. Agnes' Church, West Chester, PA* (Philadelphia: Bradley Brothers, 1894); the second its sesquicentennial: William B. Schuyler, *The Pioneer Catholic Church of Chester County: Saint Agnes, West Chester, Pennsylvania 1793–1943* (Philadelphia: The Peter Reilly Company, 1944), 131–132; the third its bicentennial: Alfred D. Roberts, *St. Agnes, West Chester: 200 Years of Catholic Faith: 1793–1993* (self-published, 1993).

41. Kashatus, *Just Over the Line*, 27; see also Ira Berlin, "Slavery, Freedom, and Philadelphia's Struggle for Brotherly Love," in *Antislavery and Abolition in Philadelphia: Emancipation and the Long Struggle for Racial Justice in the City of Brotherly Love*, Richard Newman and James Mueller, eds. (Baton Rouge, LA: Louisiana State University Press, 2011), 19–141; History.Com Editors, "The Fugitive Slave Act of 1793," History, https://www.history.com/topics/black-history/fugitive-slave-acts#section_2.

42. Matthew Desmond, "In Order to Understand the Brutality of American Capitalism, You Have to Start on the Plantation," *New York Times Magazine*, August 14, 2019, https://www.nytimes.com/interactive/2019/08/14/magazine/slavery-capitalism.html.

43. For an overview of Jesuit history in Maryland and Delaware as it pertains to Christ's Church, see Barrett, *Historical Sketch of St. Agnes' Church*, 1–14. For a sense of the interplay between the Jesuit missions with Christ's Church, as well as the roles of

some of its founding members, see Joseph Wilcox, "Biography of Rev. Patrick Kenny, AD 1763–1840," *Records of the American Catholic Historical Society* 7 no. 1 (March 1896): 27–79, at 28–34. For the economic impact of Jesuit slave-owning in that region from the colonial through antebellum periods, see Thomas Murphy, SJ, *Jesuit Slaveholding in Maryland, 1717–1838* (New York: Routledge, 2001), 33–61.

44. Barrett, *Historical Sketch of St. Agnes' Church*, 5.

45. Jeannine Hill Fletcher, *The Sin of White Supremacy: Christianity, Racism, and Religious Diversity in America* (Maryknoll, NY: Orbis Books, 2017), 48.

46. Joseph S. Rossi, SJ, "Jesuits, Slaves and Scholars at 'Old Bohemia,' 1704–1756, as Found in the *Woodstock Letters*," *U.S. Catholic Historian* 26, no. 2 (Spring 2008): 1–15.

47. Murphy, *Jesuit Slaveholding in Maryland*, 45; see also his assessment of the ships' manifests on page 17. For the earliest record of Jesuit slave owning, see "Deed of Gift between William Hunter, SJ and Thomas Jameson, January 30, 1717," Georgetown Slavery Archive, http://slaveryarchive.georgetown.edu/items/show/403.

48. Hill Fletcher unpacks the relationship to this notion and religio-racial projects in *The Sin of White Supremacy*, 45–48; for Perkinson's argument, see James W. Perkinson, "Reversing the Gaze: Constructing European Race Discourse as Modern Witchcraft Practice," *Journal of the American Academy of Religion* 72, no. 3 (2004): 603–629.

49. See the first chapter of Hill Fletcher's *The Sin of White Supremacy*, "How Christian Supremacy Gave Rise to White Supremacy," 1–44.

50. Slabodsky, "It's the Theology, Stupid!," 20.

51. Slabodsky, "It's the Theology, Stupid!," 24–25.

52. Barrett, *Historical Sketch of St. Agnes' Church*, 5.

53. Roberts, *St. Agnes, West Chester: 200 Years of Catholic Faith*, 21.

54. Willie James Jennings, "Disfigurations of Christian Identity: Performing Identity as Theological Method," in *Lived Theology: New Perspectives on Method, Style, and Pedagogy*, Charles Marsh and Peter Slade, eds. (New York: Oxford University Press, 2016), 67–85, at 68.

55. Jennings, "Disfigurations of Christian Identity," 73.

56. "Extracts from the Diary of Rev. Patrick Kenny, March 25, 1805 – November 11, 1813," ed. Martin I. J. Griffin, *Records of the American Catholic Historical Society* 7, no. 1 (1896): 94–137, at 110–111.

57. "Extracts from the Diary of Rev. Patrick Kenny, March 25, 1805–November 11, 1813," 96.

58. "Extracts from the Diary of Rev. Patrick Kenny, March 25, 1805–November 11, 1813," 114.

59. Joseph Wilcox, "Extracts from the Diary of Rev. Patrick Kenny, from September 3, 1821 to October 11 1825," *Records of the American Catholic Historical Society* 9 no. 3 (September 1898): 305–342, at 342.

60. Joseph Wilcox, "Extracts from the Diary of Rev. Patrick Kenny, June 23, 1827 to February 1829," *Records of the American Catholic Historical Society* 9 no. 2 (June 1898): 223–246, at 251–252.

61. Wilcox, "Extracts from the Diary of Rev. Patrick Kenny, from September 3, 1821 to October 11 1825," 431.

62. Barrett, *Historical Sketch of St. Agnes' Church*, 15.

63. Barrett, *Historical Sketch of St. Agnes' Church*, 15.

64. Schuyler, *The Pioneer Catholic Church of Chester County*, 131.

65. Schuyler, *The Pioneer Catholic Church of Chester County*, 132.

66. Schuyler, *The Pioneer Catholic Church of Chester County*, 132.

67. For a history of the participation of Christian communities in the Underground Railroad, see William Switala, *Underground Railroad in Pennsylvania* (Mechanicsburg, PA: Stackpole Books, 2008), 165–175; for an overview of participation of white and Black citizens of Chester County and West Chester Borough, see Kashatus, *Just Over the Line*, 49–67.

68. Wilcox, "Biography of Rev. Patrick Kenny, AD 1763–1840," 29.

69. Switala, *Underground Railroad in Pennsylvania*, 201.

70. Schuyler, *The Pioneer Catholic Church of Chester County*, 60.

71. "Old St. Agnes Church—A Century of Roman Catholicism in West Chester," *West Chester Daily Local News*, January, 16, 1893, County Clippings by Subject, Churches, CCHS.

72. Hill Fletcher, *The Sin of White Supremacy*, 81.

73. Valters Paintner, *The Soul's Slow Ripening*, 3.

74. Orlando Patterson, *Slavery and Social Death: A Comparative Study* (Cambridge, MA: Harvard University Press, 1982).

75. Grimes, *Christ Divided*, 6.

76. Grimes, *Christ Divided*, 6.

77. Grimes, *Christ Divided*, 8.

78. Grimes, *Christ Divided*, 6.

79. Hill Fletcher, *The Sin of White Supremacy*, 65.

80. Feagin, *The White Racial Frame*, 17.

81. Feagin, *The White Racial Frame*, 198.

CHAPTER 3: GRAFTING

1. Much of what I know about my father's paternal ancestors I gleaned from a distant cousin's research, now on file with the Chester County Historical Society: Joseph V. O'Connell, "The O'Connell Family: Being Primarily a History of the Descendants of Maurice O'Connell and Margaret Donovan, His Wife," 1979, Manuscripts & Genealogy, CCHS. In a genealogical supplement completed in 2000, Joseph O'Connell posits three different points of entry for Maurice based on the historical record: Maine in 1942, and either New York or Philadelphia in the second half of 1850. For the sake of conjecture, I have chosen the earliest date. Either way, his application for citizenship places him in West Chester in 1854 and at a time when naturalization laws would have required at least 5 years of residency.

2. Carroll, *Irish Pilgrimage*, 155.

3. Carroll, *Irish Pilgrimage*, 10.

4. "Grafting for the Beginner," Move to the Country, https://movetothe country.org/2015/12/30/grafting-for-the-beginner/#:~:text=The%20scion%20(the %20top%20part,still%20visible%20after%20the%20graft.

5. Richard Ned Lebow, *White Britain and Black Ireland: The Influence of Stereotypes on Colonial Policy* (Ann Arbor: University of Michigan Press, 1976). The Catholic experience in Ireland strikes me as similar to those of what Isabel Wilkerson names as "subordinate," "bottom," or "disfavored" castes in her book *Caste: The Origins of Our Discontents* (New York: Random House, 2020).

6. William Penn, *My Irish Journal, 1669–1670* (Cork: Eighteenth Century Irish Society, University College, Cork, 2013, 2017), https://celt.ucc.ie//published /E660001-002.html.

7. Jonathan Bardon, *A History of Ireland in 250 Episodes* (Dublin: Gill & Macmillan, 2008), 352. See also Jay P. Dolan, *The Irish Americans: A History*, first edition (New York: Bloomsbury Press, 2010), 4–9.

8. Terrence McDonough and Eamonn Slater, "Colonialism, Feudalism and the Mode of Production in Nineteenth-Century Ireland," in *Was Ireland a Colony?: Economics, Politics and Culture in Nineteenth Century Ireland*, Terrence McDonough, ed. (Dublin: Irish Academic Press, 2005), 30.

9. Dolan, *The Irish Americans*, 77.

10. Dolan, *The Irish Americans*, 46.

11. Angela F. Murphy, *American Slavery, Irish Freedom: Abolition, Immigrant Citizenship, and the Transatlantic Movement for Irish Repeal* (Baton Rouge: LSU Press, 2010), Kindle, 29.

12. Murphy, *American Slavery, Irish Freedom*, 32.

13. Murphy, *American Slavery, Irish Freedom*, 50.

14. Murphy, *American Slavery, Irish Freedom*, 50, emphasis mine.

15. Lebow, *White Britain and Black Ireland*, 95.

16. Tom Chaffin, "Frederick Douglass's Irish Liberty," *New York Times*, February 25, 2011, https://opinionator.blogs.nytimes.com/2011/02/25/frederick-douglasss-irish-liberty/.

17. Tom Chaffin, *Giant's Causeway: Frederick Douglass's Irish Odyssey and the Making of an American Visionary* (Charlottesville: University of Virginia Press, 2014), 3.

18. Tom Chaffin, "Frederick Douglass's Irish Odyssey," *Irish Times*, February 15, 2015, https://www.irishtimes.com/culture/books/frederick-douglass-s-irish-odyssey-1.2084550.

19. Colum McCann, *Transatlantic* (New York: Random House, 2014), 64.

20. Chaffin, *Giant's Causeway*, 62.

21. Frederick Douglass, *Life and Times of Frederick Douglass* (Boston: De Wolfe & Fiske, 1892; revised edition, independently published, 2019), 199.

22. Chaffin, *Giant's Causeway*, 63.

23. For the historical grounding and theological significance of this myth, see Kelly Brown Douglass, *Stand Your Ground*, 3–131. For historical comparison between Catholic Irish and African experiences, see Theodore W. Allen, *The Invention of the White Race: Volume I: Racial Oppression and Social Control* (New York: Verso, 2012), 84.

24. Allen, *The Invention of the White Race*, 46–47 and 81–90.

25. Kendi, *Stamped from the Beginning*, 49.

26. Steve Garner, *Racism in the Irish Experience* (London: Pluto Press, 2004), 124.

27. Frederick Douglass, "The Slavery Party," speech to the American Anti-Slavery Society, May 13, 1853, https://courses.lumenlearning.com/introliterature/chapter/my-bondage-and-my-freedom-by-frederick-douglass/.

28. Ignatiev, *How the Irish Became White*, 191.

29. Chaffin, *Giant's Causeway*, 86.

30. Maura Farrelly, *Anti-Catholicism in America: 1620–1860* (New York: Cambridge University Press, 2018), 134–157.

31. W. Jason Wallace, *Catholics, Slaveholders, and the Dilemma of American Revolution* (South Bend, IN: University of Notre Dame, 2010), 67.

32. Ignatiev, *How the Irish Became White*, 189.

33. Murphy, *American Slavery, Irish Freedom*, 9–10.

34. John Quinn, "The Rise and Fall of Repeal: Slavery and Irish Nationalism in Antebellum Philadelphia," *Pennsylvania Magazine of History and Biography* 130, no. 1 (January 2006): 45–78, at 53.

35. Quinn, "The Rise and Fall of Repeal: Slavery and Irish Nationalism in Antebellum Philadelphia," 46.

36. Murphy, *American Slavery, Irish Freedom*, 88–89.

37. Quinn, "The Rise and Fall of Repeal: Slavery and Irish Nationalism in Antebellum Philadelphia," 57–58.

38. Ignatiev, *How the Irish Became White*, 29.

39. Garner, *Racism in the Irish Experience*, 98.

40. Garner, *Racism in the Irish Experience*, 100.

41. Garner, *Racism in the Irish Experience*, 111.

42. Ignatiev, *How the Irish Became White*, 145.

43. Quinn, "The Rise and Fall of Repeal: Slavery and Irish Nationalism in Antebellum Philadelphia," 61.

44. John O'Shea, *The Two Kenricks: Most Rev. Francis Patrick, Archbishop of Baltimore, Most Rev. Peter Richard, Archbishop of St. Louis* (Philadelphia: J. J. McVey, 1904). See also, Dale Light, "The Reformation of Philadelphia Catholicism, 1830–1860," *Pennsylvania Magazine of History and Biography* 112, no. 3 (July 1988), 375–405.

45. Francis Patrick Kenrick, *Diary and Visitation Record of the Rt Rev. Francis Patrick Kenrick: Administrator and Bishop of Philadelphia 1830–1851, Later, Archbishop of Baltimore: Translated and Edited* (London: Forgotten Books, 2017).

46. Charles Morris, *American Catholic: The Saints and Sinners Who Built America's Most Powerful Church* (New York: Random House, 1997), 79.

47. Pope Gregory XVI, *In Supremo Apostolatus*, December 3, 1839, https://www.papalencyclicals.net/greg16/g16sup.htm.

48. Desmond, "In Order to Understand the Brutality of American Capitalism . . .".

49. Hooke Rice, *American Catholic Opinion in the Slavery Controversy*.

50. Morris, *American Catholic*, 79.

51. Rev. Joseph D. Brokhage, *Francis Patrick Kenrick's Opinion on Slavery: A Dissertation* (Washington, DC: Catholic University of America Press, 1955), 43.

52. Kenneth J. Zanca, *American Catholics and Slavery: 1789–1866: An Anthology of Primary Documents* (Lanham, MD: University Press of America, 1994), 199.

53. Brokhage, *Francis Patrick Kenrick's Opinion on Slavery*.

54. Brokhage, *Francis Patrick Kenrick's Opinion on Slavery*, 3.

55. Brokhage, *Francis Patrick Kenrick's Opinion on Slavery*, 81, 78, 71, 86.

56. Brokhage, *Francis Patrick Kenrick's Opinion on Slavery*, 119.

57. Brokhage, *Francis Patrick Kenrick's Opinion on Slavery*, 80.

58. Brokhage, *Francis Patrick Kenrick's Opinion on Slavery*, 80.

59. Brokhage, *Francis Patrick Kenrick's Opinion on Slavery*, 88.

60. Brokhage, *Francis Patrick Kenrick's Opinion on Slavery*, 183.

61. Brokhage, *Francis Patrick Kenrick's Opinion on Slavery*, 188–190.

62. Brokhage, *Francis Patrick Kenrick's Opinion on Slavery*, 194.

63. Brokhage, *Francis Patrick Kenrick's Opinion on Slavery*, 186.

64. Brokhage, *Francis Patrick Kenrick's Opinion on Slavery*, 237, 199.

65. Brokhage, *Francis Patrick Kenrick's Opinion on Slavery*, 187.

66. Brokhage, *Francis Patrick Kenrick's Opinion on Slavery*, 187.

67. Brokhage, *Francis Patrick Kenrick's Opinion on Slavery*, 162.

68. Brokhage, *Francis Patrick Kenrick's Opinion on Slavery*, 130–135.

69. Brokhage, *Francis Patrick Kenrick's Opinion on Slavery*, 121.

70. Nicholas M. Creary, "The Demands of Humanity and Religion: The U.S. Catholic Church, Colonization, and the Mission to Liberia, 1842–44," *Catholic Historical Review* 100, no. 1 (Winter 2014): 27–51 at 28.

71. Schuyler, *The Pioneer Catholic Church of Chester County*, 144–145.

72. Roberts, *St. Agnes, West Chester*, 23.

73. Randall M. Miller, "Catholic Religion, Irish Ethnicity, and the Civil War," in *Religion and the America Civil War*, Randall M. Miller, Harry Stout, and Charles Reagan Wilson, eds. (New York: Oxford University Press, 1998), 261–296, at 263–64.

74. Miller, "Catholic Religion, Irish Ethnicity, and the Civil War," 283.

75. Roberts, *St. Agnes, West Chester*, 27.

76. Roberts, *St. Agnes, West Chester*, 23.

77. Miller, "Catholic Religion, Irish Ethnicity, and the Civil War," 283.

78. Roberts, *St. Agnes, West Chester*, 23.

79. Pamela Powell, "Frederick Douglass and Horticultural Hall," Chester County Historical Society, http://www.chestercohistorical.org/frederick-douglass-and-horticultural-hall.

80. Miller, "Catholic Religion, Irish Ethnicity, and the Civil War," 263.

81. Powell, "Frederick Douglass in Horticultural Hall."

82. Robert Bussel, "'The Most Indispensable Man in His Community': African-American Entrepreneurs in West Chester, Pennsylvania, 1865–1925," *Pennsylvania History* 64, no. 3 (Summer 1998): 324–349 at 326.

83. Pamela Powell, "History's People: During Visit to Chester County, Douglass Advocates War to Destroy Slavery," *Daily Local News*, March 23, 2021, https://www.dailylocal.com/lifestyle/historys-people-during-visit-to-chester-county-douglass-advocates-war-to-destroy-slavery/article_ead33920-b553-57e9-a4f3-d1cfb755e504.html.

84. Barndt, *Becoming an Anti-Racist Church*, 104–105.

85. Barndt, *Becoming an Anti-Racist Church*, 108.

86. Barndt, *Becoming an Anti-Racist Church*, 109.

87. Barndt, *Becoming an Anti-Racist Church*, 108.

88. Barndt, *Becoming an Anti-Racist Church*, 105.

89. Yancy, "Dear White America."

90. John R. McKivigan, *The Frederick Douglass Papers, Series Three, Correspondences Volume 1: 1842–1852* (New Haven: Yale University Press, 2009), 94.

91. Brokhage, *Francis Patrick Kenrick's Opinion on Slavery*, 123.

92. Massingale, *Racial Justice and the Catholic Church*, 111.

CHAPTER 4: MANUFACTURING

1. See the collection of articles in "The 1619 Project," *New York Times Magazine*, August 14, 2019, https://www.nytimes.com/interactive/2019/08/14/magazine/1619-america-slavery.html.

2. Anderson, *White Rage*, 8.

3. Anderson, *White Rage*, 7.

4. Desmond, "In Order to Understand the Brutality of American Capitalism . . .".

5. Heather Cox Richardson, *The Death of Reconstruction: Race, Labor, and Politics in the Post-Civil War North 1865–1901* (Cambridge, MA: Harvard University Press, 2001), xiii.

6. For more on Hepburn and two other prominent Black entrepreneurs in West Chester, see Bussel, "'The Most Indispensable Man in His Community.'"

7. Francis A. Walker, *The Statistics of the Population of the United States, Ninth Census (1870), Volume 1* (Washington: Government Printing Office, 1872), https://www.census.gov/library/publications/1872/dec/1870a.html.

8. Bussel, "'The Most Indispensable Man in His Community,'" 326.

9. Edward Blum, *Reforging the White Republic: Race, Religion, and American Nationalism 1865–1989* (Baton Rouge: Louisiana State University Press, 2005), 6.

10. Abraham Lincoln, "Second Inaugural Address," speech at presidential inauguration, Washington, DC, March 4, 1865, https://www.nps.gov/linc/learn/historyculture/lincoln-second-inaugural.htm.

11. Frederick Douglass, "Reconstruction," *The Atlantic Monthly*, December 1866, https://www.theatlantic.com/magazine/archive/1866/12/reconstruction/304561/.

12. William A. Osborne, *The Segregated Covenant: Race Relations and American Catholics* (New York: Herder & Herder, 1967), 22.

13. Miller, "Catholic Religion, Irish Ethnicity, and the Civil War," 263.

14. Peter Guilday, *The National Pastorals of the American Hierarchy, 1792–1919* (Washington, DC, National Catholic Welfare Council, 1923), 197.

15. Peter Guilday, *A History of the Councils of Baltimore: 1791–1884* (New York: The Macmillan Company, 1932), 195.

16. Guilday, *A History of the Councils of Baltimore*, 192, quoting John Lancaster Spalding, *The Life of the Most Rev. M.J. Spalding, D.D., Archbishop of Baltimore* (New York: 1878), 298–300.

17. Douglass, "Reconstruction," *The Atlantic Monthly*.

18. Blum, *Reforging the White Republic*, 87–119.

19. US Catholic Bishops, "The Pastoral Letter of 1866," in *The National Pastorals of the American Hierarchy 1792–1919*, Peter Guilday, ed. (Westminster, MD: The Newman Press, 1954), 220–221.

20. US Catholic Bishops, "The Pastoral Letter of 1866," 219.

21. US Catholic Bishops, "The Pastoral Letter of 1866," 221.

22. US Catholic Bishops, "The Pastoral Letter of 1866," 221.

23. Guilday, *A History of the Councils of Baltimore*, 192; and US Catholic Bishops, "The Pastoral Letter of 1866," 221.

24. US Catholic Bishops, "The Pastoral Letter of 1866," 223.

25. Richardson, *The Death of Reconstruction*, 26.

26. Richardson, *The Death of Reconstruction*, 6–40.

27. Michael Katz and Thomas Sugrue, "Introduction: The Context of *The Philadelphia Negro*" in *W. E. B. Du Bois, Race and the City:* The Philadelphia Negro *and its Legacy*, Michael Katz and Thomas Sugrue, eds. (Philadelphia: The University of Pennsylvania Press, 1998), 2.

28. Dennis Clark, *The Irish in Philadelphia: Ten Generations of Urban Experience* (Philadelphia: Temple University Press, 1973), 84.

29. Tera W. Hunter, "The 'Brotherly Love' for Which This City Is Proverbial Should Extend to All: The Everyday Lives of Working-Class Women in Philadelphia and Atlanta in the 1890s," in *W. E. B. Du Bois, Race and the City*, 128.

30. Richardson, *The Death of Reconstruction*, xiii.

31. Bobby J. Burke, "St. Charles Borromeo Parish South Philadelphia: 1868–1993," *Records of the American Catholic Historical Society of Philadelphia* 104 (1993): 91–121, 97.

32. Clark, *The Irish in Philadelphia*, 77–84.

33. "Topics Tersely Touched," *West Chester Daily Local News*, June 7, 1904, Clippings by Subject, Black History, CCHS.

34. Ignatiev, *How the Irish Became White*, 200.

35. Elijah Anderson, "Introduction to the 1996 Edition of *The Philadelphia Negro*," in *The Philadelphia Negro: A Social Study*, W. E. B. Du Bois (Philadelphia: University of Pennsylvania Press, 1996), xiv-xv.

36. Du Bois, *The Philadelphia Negro*, 39.

37. Du Bois, *The Philadelphia Negro*, 5.

38. Du Bois, *Black Reconstruction in America*, 30.

39. Jacqueline Jones, "'Lifework' and its Limits: The Problem of Labor in *The Philadelphia Negro*," in *W. E. B. Du Bois, Race and the City*, 103–125 at 103.

40. Du Bois, *The Philadelphia Negro*, 98.

41. Du Bois, *The Philadelphia Negro*, 128.

42. Du Bois, *The Philadelphia Negro*, 146.

43. Katz and Sugrue, "The Context of *The Philadelphia Negro*," in *W. E. B. Du Bois, Race and the City*, 1–37 at 4.

44. Du Bois, *The Philadelphia Negro*, 98.

45. Du Bois, *The Philadelphia Negro*, 325.

46. W. E. B. Du Bois, "The Study of the Negro Problems," *Annals of the American Academy of Political and Social Science* 11 (January, 1989): 1–23, 7.

47. Du Bois, *The Philadelphia Negro*, 394.

48. Du Bois, *Black Reconstruction*, 700.

49. Du Bois, *Black Reconstruction*, 700.

50. Du Bois, *Black Reconstruction*, 701.

51. Du Bois, *Black Reconstruction*, 700.

52. Du Bois, *Black Reconstruction*, 701.

53. David Roediger, *The Wages of Whiteness: Race and the Making of the American Working Class*, second edition (New York: Verso, 2007), 60.

54. John T. McGreevy explores aspects of this power in *Parish Boundaries: The Catholic Encounter with Race in the Twentieth Century Urban North* (Chicago: University of Chicago Press, 1996). For more on Archbishop James Wood, see James F. Connelly, ed. *The History of the Archdiocese of Philadelphia* (Wynnewood, PA: The Archdiocese of Philadelphia, 1976), 253–260.

55. US Catholic Bishops, "The Pastoral Letter of 1884," in *The National Pastorals of the American Hierarchy 1792–1919*, Peter Guilday, ed. (Westminster, MD: The Newman Press, 1954), 226–264, at 234–235.

56. US Catholic Bishops, "The Pastoral Letter of 1884," 234.

57. US Catholic Bishops, "The Pastoral Letter of 1884," 263, 225.

58. Burke, "St. Charles Borromeo Parish South Philadelphia 1868–1993," 96.

59. *Silver Jubilee Book of St. Charles Borromeo Parish 1876–1901*, Parish History Collection 27, CHRC of AoP.

60. Burke, "St. Charles Borromeo Parish South Philadelphia 1868–1993," 98.

61. Michèle Lamont and Virag Molnár, "The Study of Boundaries in the Social Sciences," *Annual Review of Sociology* 28 (2002), 167–195 at 168.

62. Sociologist Robert Putnam explores the concept of "social capital" in American society in *Bowling Alone: The Collapse and Revival of American Community* (New York: Simon & Schuster, 2001). To draw comparisons to the types of social capital I refer to Tristan Claridge, "Functions of Social Capital—Bonding, Bridging, Linking," *Social Capital Research*, January 20, 2018, https://www.social capitalresearch.com/wp-content/uploads/2018/11/Functions-of-Social-Capital.pdf

63. Burke, "St. Charles Borromeo Parish South Philadelphia 1868–1993," 100.

64. Burke, "St. Charles Borromeo Parish South Philadelphia 1868–1993," 100.

65. Du Bois, *The Philadelphia Negro*, 219.

66. Stephanie Morris, "St. Peter Claver Church and School, Philadelphia, PA: A Collaborative Effort," *American Catholic Studies* 128, no. 1 (2017): 101–113, at 101.

67. Morris, "St. Peter Claver Church and School," 101–113, note 2. Ms. Drexel went by Catherine Drexel as a laywoman and then Katharine once she took her religious vows.

68. Morris, "St. Peter Claver Church and School."

69. Burke, "St. Charles Borromeo Parish South Philadelphia 1868–1993," 106–107.

70. Blum, *Reforging the White Republic*, 15.

71. William J. Barber III, *The Third Reconstruction: How a Moral Movement Is Overcoming the Politics of Division and Fear* (Boston: Beacon Press, 2016), xiii. Barber unpacks this idea in the ninth chapter of this memoir, 111–126.

72. Massingale, "The Magis and Justice."

73. Massingale, *Racial Justice and the Catholic Church*, 97.

74. Robin DiAngelo, *White Fragility: Why It's So Hard for White People to Talk about Racism* (Boston: Beacon Press, 2018), 94.

CHAPTER 5: MANEUVERING

1. For more background on this mural and others like it in Philadelphia, see Maureen O'Connell, *If These Walls Could Talk: Community Muralism and the Beauty of Justice* (Collegeville, MN: The Liturgical Press, 2012), 135–144.

2. "Nicetown–Tioga," Wikiwand, https://www.wikiwand.com/en/Nicetown %E2%80%93Tioga; for more history since the mid-twentieth century, see Elizabeth Greenspan, "Nicetown," *Places Journal*, June 2019, https://placesjournal.org /article/nicetown-inequality-in-philadelphia/.

3. St. Stephen's Parish Calendars, 1905–1909; 1910–1918; 1929, Parish Calendar Collection 27, CHRC of AoP.

4. McGreevy describes a variety of aspects of the "dense social networks" of the urban American parish in the first half of the twentieth century in *Parish Boundaries*, 1–28. I also find that Robert Orsi's description of a "domus centered society" in his study of Italian Catholics in East Harlem speaks to some of the elements of my great-grandparents' experience in North Philadelphia during the same time period. See *The Madonna of 115th Street: Faith and Community in Italian Harlem, 1880–1950*, third edition (New Haven: CT, Yale University Press, 2010), 75–106.

5. Marcus Anthony Hunter, *Black Citymakers: How the Philadelphia Negro Changed Urban America* (New York: Oxford University Press, 2013), 84.

6. Hunter, *Black Citymakers*, 80; for description of discrimination newly arrived Black Philadelphians faced, see 69–113.

7. J. A. Emerick, "The Colored Mission of Our Lady of the Blessed Sacrament," *The Woodstock Letters* 42, no. 2 (1913): 176–188 at 187.

8. Loïc Wacquant, *Urban Ghettos: A Comparative Sociology of Advanced Marginality* (Malden, MA: Polity Press, 2008), 51–91.

9. St. Stephen's Parish Calendar, September 1909, 10, Parish Calendar Collection 27, CHRC of AoP.

10. John F. Watson, *Annals of Philadelphia* (Philadelphia: E. I. Carey & A. Hart, 1830), 394.

11. Watson, *Annals of Philadelphia*, 395.

12. Watson, *Annals of Philadelphia*, 395.

13. St. Stephen's Parish Calendar, May 1929, 7, Parish Calendar Collection 27, CHRC of AoP.

14. Michael I. Griffin, "Dr. John Michael Browne, the Alleged Priest of Colonial Philadelphia—Dr. Thaddeus Murphy, His Brother-in-Law, Also a Reputed

Priest," *Records of the American Catholic Historical Society* 16, no. 3 (September 1905): 296–313; and no. 4 (December 1905), 391–415.

15. Griffin, "Dr. John Michael Browne . . . ," no. 3, 299.

16. Grimes, *Christ Divided*, 192.

17. Griffin, "Dr. John Michael Browne . . . ," no. 3, 309.

18. Griffin, "Dr. John Michael Browne . . . ," no 4, 409.

19. Osborne, *The Segregated Covenant*, 155.

20. St. Stephen's Parish Calendars, February 1908, 13, Parish Calendar Collection 27, CHRC of AoP.

21. St. Stephen's Parish Calendars, February 1908, 13, Parish Calendar Collection 27, CHRC of AoP.

22. Dennis Clark, *The Irish Relations: Trials of an Immigrant Tradition* (Rutherford, NJ: Fairleigh Dickinson University Press, 1982), 64.

23. Dolan, *The Irish Americans*, 95.

24. St. Stephen's Parish Calendars, 1910–1918 and 1929, Parish Calendar Collection 27, CHRC of AoP.

25. McGreevy, *Parish Boundaries*, 13–15.

26. Dolan, *The Irish Americans*, 115.

27. Morris, *American Catholic*, 194.

28. Dolan, *The Irish Americans*, 237.

29. McGreevy, *Parish Boundaries*, 195.

30. Letter from Thomas Nolan to Joseph Dougherty, June, 18, 1926, 80.7579, Dougherty Correspondence, CHRC of AoP.

31. KKK flier, June 1926, 80.7579, Dougherty Correspondence, CHRC of AoP.

32. Morris, *American Catholic*, 177.

33. Copy of letter to membership by Paul Winter, December 24, 1924, 80.8468, Dougherty Correspondence, CHRC of AoP.

34. Thomas H. Keels, *Sesqui!: Greed, Graft, and the Forgotten World's Fair of 1926* (Philadelphia: Temple University Press, 2017), 176.

35. Morris, *American Catholic*, 170.

36. Keels, *Sesqui!*, 180.

37. Letter from Joseph Dougherty to Thomas Nolan, June 27, 1926, 80.7579, Dougherty Correspondence, CHRC of AoP.

38. Keels, *Sesqui!*, 136.

39. Keels, *Sesqui!*, 204.

40. Kendi explains this concept in *Stamped from the Beginning*, 92–103, and offers examples throughout his study.

41. See Keels's entire chapter on this subject, "The Philadelphia Negro at the Sesqui," in *Sesqui!*, 205–229.

42. Bruce J. Evensen, "'Saving the City's Reputation': Philadelphia's Struggle over Self-Identity, Sabbath-Breaking and Boxing in America's Sesquicentennial Year," *Pennsylvania History: A Journal of Mid-Atlantic Studies* 60, no. 1 (January 1993): 6–24, at 20.

43. Evensen, "'Saving the City's Reputation,'" 20.

44. Letter from Rosa White, M. Gertrude Palmer, and Clara Baptist-Jones to Joseph Dougherty, April 15, 1926, 80.4879, Dougherty Correspondence, CHRC of AoP.

45. Letter from Rosa White, M. Gertrude Palmer, and Clara Baptist-Jones to Joseph Dougherty, April 15, 1926.

46. Letter from Joseph Dougherty to Rosa White, M. Gertrude Palmer, and Clara Baptist-Jones, April 17, 1926, 80.8133, Dougherty Correspondence, CHRC of AoP.

47. Keels, *Sesqui!*, 216.

48. Keels, *Sesqui!*, 172; he illuminates the eugenic undercurrent of the Sesqui in 167–185.

49. Kendi, *Stamped from the Beginning*, 302.

50. Keels, *Sesqui!*, 169.

51. McGreevy, *Parish Boundaries*, 33.

52. "80,000 Men March in 2 Divisions," *Catholic Standard & Times*, October 9, 1926, SB 23, Folder 287, CHRC of AoP.

53. "80,000 Men March in 2 Divisions," *Catholic Standard & Times*.

54. Letter from Joseph Dougherty to Evelyn and Mildred McCormick, October 4, 1926, 80.7030, Dougherty Correspondence, CHRC of AoP.

55. "1,000 Prostrated by Scorching Sun at Stadium Mass," *Philadelphia Inquirer*, October 4, 1926, SB 23, Folder 283, CHRC of AoP.

56. "80,000 Men March in 2 Divisions," *Catholic Standard & Times*.

57. "300,000 Heads Bow at Stadium for High Mass," *Philadelphia Public Ledger*, October 4, 1926," SB 23, Folder 277, CHRC of AoP.

58. Henry Hart, "Multitude Observes Jubilee of Freedom at Mass in Stadium," *Philadelphia Record*, October 4, 1926, SB 23, Folder 281–282, CHRC of AoP.

59. Hart, "Multitude Observes Jubilee of Freedom at Mass in Stadium."

60. Hart, "Multitude Observes Jubilee of Freedom at Mass in Stadium."

61. Patricia Crosby, "A Stupendous Panorama," *Catholic Standard & Times*," October 9, 1926, SB 23, Folder 291, CHRC of AoP.

62. Crosby, "A Stupendous Panorama."

63. Crosby, "A Stupendous Panorama."

64. Letter from Joseph Dougherty to Evelyn and Mildred McCormick, October 4, 1926.

65. Sesquicentennial Catholic Celebration Position Memorandum, undated, SB 24, Folder 21–22, CHRC of AoP. For the distinction between "territorial" and "national" parishes, see Tricia Colleen Bruce, *Parish and Place: Making Room for Diversity in the American Catholic Church* (New York: Oxford University Press, 2017), 1–8.

66. Grimes, *Christ Divided*, 131.

67. Robin DiAngelo, "White People Assume Niceness Is the Answer to Racial Inequality. It's Not," *The Guardian*, January 16, 2019, https://www.theguardian.com/commentisfree/2019/jan/16/racial-inequality-niceness-white-people.

68. DiAngelo, *White Fragility*, 101–106.

69. DiAngelo, *White Fragility*, 141.

CHAPTER 6: DEFENDING

1. Jason Richardson et al., "Shifting Neighborhoods: Gentrification and Cultural Displacement in American Cities," National Community Reinvestment Coalition, March 19, 2019, https://ncrc.org/gentrification/.

2. Letter from Thomas Love, SJ to Raymond Cosgrove, SJ, August 8, 1936, Gesu Parish Improvement Association Collection, unprocessed, VASJP.

3. Letter from Thomas Love, SJ to Laurence Kelly, SJ, August 6, 1936, Gesu Parish Improvement Association Collection, unprocessed, VASJP.

4. Reprint, "Church in a Changing Neighborhood: Gesu Celebrates Centenary," *Catholic Standard & Times*, August 23, 1968, Gesu Parish/Anniversaries/1968, VASJP.

5. Homecoming pamphlet 1973, Gesu Parish/Jesuit Pastors, VASJP.

6. "Men and Things," *Philadelphia Evening Bulletin*, October 4, 1929, Gesu Parish/Anniversaries, VASJP.

7. "Men and Things," Gesu Parish/Anniversaries, VASJP.

8. "Men and Things," Gesu Parish/Anniversaries, VASJP.

9. *Gesu Golden Jubilee Book 1938*, Gesu Parish/Anniversaries, VASJP.

10. Letter from William Cosgrove, SJ to Thomas Love, SJ, August 10, 1936, Gesu Parish Improvement Association Collection, unprocessed, VASJP.

11. Gesu Parish Calendar, February 1937, 17, Parish Calendar Collection 36, CHRC of AoP.

12. Gesu Parish Calendar, April 1929, 4; and June 1929, 8, Parish Calendar Collection 36, CHRC of AoP.

13. Gesu Parish Calendar, May 1922, 40, Parish Calendar Collection 36, CHRC of AoP.

14. Gesu Parish Calendar, April 1925, 23, SJUHIS.0034, SJUA&SC.

15. Rothstein, *The Color of Law*.

16. Rothstein, *The Color of Law*, 21.

17. Rothstein, *The Color of Law*, 24.

18. Rothstein, *The Color of Law*, 62.

19. Rothstein, *The Color of Law*, 44.

20. Rothstein, *The Color of Law*, 39–57.

21. Rothstein, *The Color of Law*, 65.

22. Rothstein, *The Color of Law*, 65.

23. J. M. Brewer, "J. M. Brewer's Map of Philadelphia, 1934: South Section," Greater Philadelphia GeoHistory Network, Map Collection, Free Library of Philadelphia, 1934, https://www.philageohistory.org/rdic-images/view-image.cfm /JMB1934.Phila.002.SouthSection.

24. Rothstein, *The Color of Law*, 65.

25. Gesu Parish Calendar, July 1936, 15, Parish Calendar Collection 36, CHRC of AoP.

26. Gesu Parish Calendar, July 1936.

27. Letter from Dr. Francis Stokes to John L. Jenemen, undated, Gesu Parish Improvement Association Collection, unprocessed, VASJP.

28. Gesu Parish Calendar, October 1936, 17, Parish Calendar Collection 36, CHRC of AoP.

29. Gesu Parish Calendar, November 1936, 20–21, Parish Calendar Collection 36, CHRC of AoP

30. Grimes, *Christ Divided*, 90–94 and 124.

31. Undated GPIA flier, Gesu Parish Improvement Association Collection, unprocessed, VASJP.

32. Undated and unsigned petition, Gesu Parish Improvement Association Collection, unprocessed, VASJP.

33. Sample GPIA pledge card, Gesu Parish Improvement Association Collection, unprocessed, VASJP.

34. Gesu Parish Calendar, December 1936, 17, Parish Calendar Collection 36, CHRC of AoP.

35. Gesu Parish Calendar, September 1924, 22, Parish Calendar Collection 36, CHRC of AoP.

36. J. A. Emerick, SJ, "The Colored Mission of Our Lady of the Blessed Sacrament," *The Woodstock Letters* 42, no. 1: 69–81; vol. 41, no.2: 175–188; vol. 42, no. 3: 352–362, Woodstock College 1913, and vol. 43, no. 1: 10–23 and vol. 42, no. 2: 181–194, Woodstock College, 1914.

37. Our Lady of the Blessed Sacrament Visitations 1937-1940, H40 B2, Box 2, Sisters of the Blessed Sacrament Collection, CHRC of AoP.

38. Edward Schmidt, "A Vocation for Neighborliness: Anna M. McGarry's Quest for Community in Philadelphia," *U.S. Catholic Historian* 22, no. 2 (2004): 81–97; interview with Rev. John Bloh, October 19, 2018, Sicklersville, NJ.

39. Walter Fox, "Brotherhood & Anna McGarry," *National Catholic Reporter*, August 6, 1966, Anna M. McGarry Collection, VASJP.

40. Fox, "Brotherhood & Anna McGarry."

41. Fox, "Brotherhood & Anna McGarry."

42. David W. Southern, *John LaFarge and the Limits of Catholic Interracialism: 1911–1963* (Baton Rouge: Louisiana State University Press, 1996).

43. Anna McGarry, notes of oral history interview by Margaret Sigmund, January 1976, Anna McGarry Papers, Series 2, Box 1, MUA.

44. Leslie Houts Picca and Joe R. Feagin, *Two-Faced Racism: Whites in the Backstage and Frontstage* (New York: Routeledge, 2007). Picca and Feagin build on theories of performativity developed by Erving Goffman in *The Presentation of Self in Everyday Life* (New York: Anchor Books, 1959).

45. Houts Picca and Feagin, *Two-Faced Racism*, 43–85, 91–142.

46. Letter from Francis Stokes to Thomas Higgins, SJ, June 30, 1936, Gesu Parish Improvement Association Collection, unprocessed, VASJP.

47. Letter from Thomas Higgins, SJ to Thomas Logue, August 28, 1936, Gesu Parish Improvement Association Collection, unprocessed, VASJP.

48. Letter from Thomas Higgins, SJ to Matthew McCloskey, September 26, 1936, Gesu Parish Improvement Association Collection, unprocessed, VASJP.

49. Letter to Francis Stokes, from unidentified sender, August 1, 1936, Gesu Parish Improvement Association Collection, unprocessed, VASJP.

50. Letter from Thomas Higgins, SJ to the Board of Public Education of Philadelphia, May 8, 1937, Gesu Parish Improvement Association Collection, unprocessed, VASJP.

51. Letter from Cornelius O'Brien to Walter Biddle Saul, May 8, 1937, Gesu Parish Improvement Association Collection, unprocessed, VASJP.

52. Letter from Thomas Higgins, SJ to Cornelius O'Brien, May 13, 1937, Gesu Parish Improvement Association Collection, unprocessed, VASJP.

53. Letter from Thomas Higgins, SJ to A. L. Fitzpatrick, June 7, 1937, Gesu Parish Improvement Association Collection, unprocessed, VASJP.

54. Letter of Fr. Thomas Higgins, SJ to Harry McDevitt, June 7, 1937, Gesu Parish Improvement Association Collection, unprocessed, VASJP.

55. Gesu Parish Calendar, February 1937, 16, Parish Calendar Collection 36, CHRC of AoP.

56. Gesu Parish Calendar, February 1937.

57. Gesu Parish Calendar, February 1937.

58. Gesu Parish Calendar, February 1937.

59. Gesu Parish Calendar, February 1937, 16–17, Parish Calendar Collection 36, CHRC of AoP.

60. Gesu Parish Calendar, April 1937, 17, Parish Calendar Collection 36, CHRC of AoP.

61. Gesu Parish Calendar, June 1937, 18, Parish Calendar Collection 36, CHRC of AoP.

62. Gesu Parish Calendar, September 1937, 14, Parish Calendar Collection 36, CHRC of AoP.

63. Gesu Parish Calendar, December 1937, 14, Parish Calendar Collection 36, CHRC of AoP.

64. Gesu Parish Calendar, December 1937, 15, Parish Calendar Collection 36, CHRC of AoP.

65. Gesu Parish Calendar, July 1938, 16, Parish Calendar Collection 36, CHRC of AoP.

66. Gesu Parish Calendar, December 1937.

67. Letter from James Gorman to Thomas Love, SJ August 6, 1939, Gesu Parish Improvement Association Papers, unprocessed, VASJP.

68. E. Washington Rhodes, "Gesu Priest Advocates Segregation," *Philadelphia Tribune*, February 20, 1941, Gesu Parish Improvement Association Papers, unprocessed, VASJP.

69. Grimes, *Christ Divided*, 136.

70. Letter from Francis Stokes to Thomas Higgins, SJ, undated, Gesu Parish Improvement Association Papers, unprocessed, VASJP.

71. Letter from Thomas Love, SJ to Dennis Dougherty, October 18, 1940, File 80.6785, Dougherty Correspondence, CHRC of AoP.

72. Letter from Dennis Dougherty to Thomas Love, SJ, October 19, 1940, File 80.6788, Dougherty Correspondence, CHRC of AoP.

73. E. Washington Rhodes, "Gesu Priest Advocates Segregation," *Philadelphia Tribune*, February 20, 1941, Gesu Parish Improvement Association Papers, unprocessed, VASJP.

74. Arthur Huff Fauset and Lenerte Roberts, "Threat of Suit by Priest," February 27, 1941, *Philadelphia Tribune*, Gesu Parish Improvement Association Papers, unprocessed, VASJP.

75. Unidentified clipping, "115 to Give Money to Keep Race of out Girard Avenue," Gesu Parish Improvement Association Papers, unprocessed, VASJP.

76. Unidentified clipping, "Amazing Activity Brought to Light by Courier Probe," Feburary 13, 1941, Gesu Parish Improvement Association Papers, unprocessed, VASJP.

77. Letter from the Federated Colored Catholics of Philadelphia and St. Mary's Beneficial Society to Dennis Dougherty, May 1, 1940, File 80.5259, Dougherty Correspondence, CHRC of AoP.

78. Arthur Huff Fauset and Lenerte Roberts, "Church Groups Pushing Race Discrimination Not Frowned Upon," *Philadelphia Tribune*, May 8, 1941, Gesu Parish Improvement Association Collection, unprocessed, VASJP.

79. Arthur Huff Fauset, "I Write as I See: Cardinals Remain Silent," *Philadelphia Tribune*, June 12, 1941, Gesu Parish Improvement Association Collection, unprocessed, VASJP.

80. Gesu Parish Calendars, July 1938, 16, Parish Calendar Collection 36, CHRC of AoP; Anna McGarry notes from 1976 oral history, Anna McGarry Series 2, Box 1, MUA.

81. Letter from Anna McGarry to Thomas Love, SJ, February 12, 1941, Gesu Parish Improvement Association Papers, unprocessed, VASJP.

82. Letter from Anna McGarry to Thomas Love, SJ, February 12, 1941.
83. Letter from Anna McGarry to Thomas Love, SJ, February 12, 1941.
84. Anna McGarry, "Interracial Justice," *Philadelphia Tribune*, March 13, 1941, Anna McGarry Papers, Series 1, Box 2, Folder 1, MUA.
85. McGarry, "Interracial Justice."
86. Joseph Daughen, "Once-Thriving Gesu Church Notes 75th Year, Stands Out as Island in North Phila Blight," *Philadelphia Evening Bulletin*, December 8, 1963, Gesu Parish/Anniversaries/1968, VASJP.
87. *Gesu Parish Jubilee Book, 1968*, Gesu Parish/Anniversaries/1968, VASJP.
88. Reprint, "Church in a Changing Neighborhood: Gesu Celebrates Centenary," *Catholic Standard & Times*, August 23, 1968, Gesu Parish/Anniversaries/1968, VASJP.
89. Elijah Anderson, *The Cosmopolitan Canopy: Race and Civility in Everyday Life* (New York: W. W. Norton & Co., 2011), 2. For an overview of this phenomenon, see also Elijah Anderson, "The White Space," in *Sociology of Race and Ethnicity* 1 (2015): 10–21.
90. Anderson, *The Cosmopolitan Canopy*, 2.
91. Anderson, "White Space," *Sociology of Race and Ethnicity*, 14.
92. Anderson, "White Space," *Sociology of Race and Ethnicity*, 15.
93. Grimes, *Christ Divided*, 101.
94. Mindy Thompson Fullilove, *Urban Alchemy: Restoring Joy in America's Sorted-Out Cities* (New York: New Village Press, 2013), 12.
95. Anderson, *The Cosmopolitan Canopy*, 271, 276.
96. Anderson, *The Cosmopolitan Canopy*, 280.
97. Fullilove, *Urban Alchemy*, 39.

CHAPTER 7: HOMESTEADING
1. Ira Kaztnelson, *When Affirmative Action Was White: An Untold Story of Racial Inequality in Twentieth Century* America (New York: W. W. Norton & Company, 2006), 116.
2. William Piggot, "The Geography of Exclusion: Race and Suburbanization in Postwar Philadelphia" (master's thesis, Ohio State University, 2002): 8, http://rave.ohiolink.edu/etdc/view?acc_num=osu1166561231.
3. Kenneth Jackson, *Crabgrass Frontier: The Suburbanization of the United States* (New York: Oxford University Press, 1987), 232.
4. Dan Rottenberg, *The Outsider: Albert M. Greenfield and the Fall of the Protestant Establishment* (Philadelphia: Temple University Press, 2014), 60.
5. Morris, *American Catholic*, 186.
6. Rottenberg, *The Outsider*, 60.
7. Letter from Vincent Dever to Joseph Dougherty, April 26, 1924, MC84: Chancery Files, St. Katherine of Sienna (Torresdale), CHRC of AoP.
8. Letter from Vincent Dever to Joseph Dougherty, June 20, 1924, MC84: Chancery Files, St. Katherine of Sienna (Torresdale), CHRC of AoP.
9. Letter from Vincent Dever to Joseph Dougherty, June 20, 1924.
10. Letter from Vincent Dever to Joseph Dougherty, June 20, 1924.
11. Morris, *American Catholic*, 182.
12. Analysis of the *Archdiocese of Philadelphia Catholic Directory*, 2018 edition, CHRC of AoP, 102–105.
13. Rothstein, *The Color of Law*, 61.

14. Philadelphia City Planning Commission, "Comprehensive Plan for the City of Philadelphia: 1960," 70–71, https://www.phila.gov/media/20190603120413 /Comprehensive-Plan-1960.pdf.

15. Jackson, *Crabgrass Frontier*, 241.

16. Antonio McDaniel, "The 'Philadelphia Negro' Then and Now: Implications for Empirical Research," in *W. E. B. Du Bois, Race, and the City*, 163.

17. Rothstein, *The Color of Law*, 70.

18. Jackson, *Crabgrass Frontier*, 238–241.

19. "St. Francis Church and Minstrel Time," *Norristown Times Herald*, March 18, 1950, microfilm at MCHS.

20. Robert Nowatzki, "Paddy Jumps Jim Crow: Irish-Americans and Blackface Minstrelsy," *Eire-Ireland* 41, no. 3–4 (Winter/Fall 2006): 162–184, 165. See also Robert Nowatzki, *Representing African Americans in Transatlantic Abolitionism and Blackface Minstrelsy* (Baton Rouge: Louisiana State University Press, 2021).

21. Nowatzki, "Paddy Jumps Jim Crow," 163.

22. Roediger, *The Wages of Whiteness*, 115–118.

23. Nowatzki, "Paddy Jumps Jim Crow," 174.

24. Nowatzki, "Paddy Jumps Jim Crow," 179 and 166.

25. Roediger, *The Wages of Whiteness*, 115–118.

26. Nowatzki, "Paddy Jumps Jim Crow," 174.

27. Christian DuComb, *Haunted City: Three Centuries of Racial Impersonation in Philadelphia* (Ann Arbor: University of Michigan Press, 2017), 2.

28. Bonnie Cooke, "Horace A. Davenport, 98, first African American Judge in Montgomery County," *Philadelphia Inquirer*, April 3, 2017, https://www .inquirer.com/philly/obituaries/Horace-A-Davenport-98-first-African-American -judge-in-Montgomery-County.html; I also perused the Horace Davenport fileat the MCHS.

29. Ayanna Jones, "Horace A. Davenport, 98, Montco Judge," *Philadelphia Tribune*, April 7, 2017, https://www.phillytrib.com/obituaries/horace-a-davenport -montco-judge/article_f907a407-3a3f-58fe-b865-54a22a27ad78.html.

30. Katznelson, *When Affirmative Action Was White*, 115.

31. Jones, "Horace A. Davenport, 98, Montco Judge."

32. Rothstein, *The Color of Law*, 22.

33. Osborne, *The Segregated Covenant*, 160.

34. Pope Pius XII, *Sertum Laetitiae*, November 1, 1939, #9, http://www.vatican .va/content/pius-xii/en/encyclicals/documents/hf_p-xii_enc_01111939_sertum -laetitiae.html.

35. Morris, *American Catholic*, 182.

36. Morris, *American Catholic*, 182.

37. Matthew Cressler, *Authentically Black and Truly Catholic: The Rise of Black Catholicism in the Great Migration* (New York: NYU Press, 2017), 134.

38. Osborne, *The Segregated Covenant*, 165.

39. Osborne, *The Segregated Covenant*, 162–163.

40. Osborne, *The Segregated Covenant*, 162.

41. Darlene Eleanor York, "The Academic Achievement of African Americans in Catholic Schools: A Review of the Literature," in *Growing Up African American in Catholic Schools*, Jacqueline Jordan Irvine and Michele Foster eds. (New York: Teachers College Press, 1996), 11–46, at 18.

42. Grimes, *Christ Divided*, 143.

43. Grimes, *Christ Divided*, 143.

44. *Catholic Standard & Times*, April 14, 1950, CHRC of AoP, 4.

45. Massingale, *Racial Justice and the Catholic Church*, 50.

46. Federal Housing Administration (FHA), *Underwriting Manual: Underwriting and Valuation Procedure under Title II of the National Housing Act* (Washington, DC: US Government Printing Office, 1938), #9801.1, https://www.huduser.gov/portal/sites/default/files/pdf/Federal-Housing-Administration-Underwriting-Manual.pdf.

47. FHA, *Underwriting Manual*, #973.

48. FHA, *Underwriting Manual*, # 973.

49. Rothstein, *The Color of Law*, 66.

50. FHA, *Underwriting Manual*, #935.

51. Rothstein, *The Color of Law*, 87.

52. Rothstein, *The Color of Law*, 78–79.

53. Deed for 180 Liberty Ave, November 3, 1948, Montgomery County Recorder of Deeds, Deed Book 1955, 381–387.

54. Rothstein, *The Color of Law*, 182–183.

55. Analysis of the *Archdiocese of Philadelphia Catholic Directory, 2018* edition, 104–105; and Piggot, "The Geography of Exclusion," 9, citing a 1953 report from the Commission on Human Relations, City of Philadelphia.

56. Jackson, *Crabgrass Frontier*, 241.

57. Rothstein, *The Color of Law*, 179.

58. Grimes, *Christ Divided*, 133.

59. Rothstein, *The Color of Law*, 75.

60. Osborne, *The Segregated Covenant*, 121.

61. Massingale, *Racial Justice and the Catholic Church*, 100, referencing Eric K. Yamamoto, *Interracial Justice: Conflict and Resolution in Post-Civil Rights America* (New York: New York University Press, 1999).

62. Grimes, *Christ Divided*, 241.

63. John Paul Lederach, "Memoriale: Haiku and the Crowned Newness," April 8, 2020, https://onbeing.org/blog/an-unfolding-poem-for-the-moment-were-in/.

CHAPTER 8: DOUBTING

1. Glenn E. Singleton and Curtis Linton, *Courageous Conversations about Race: A Field Guide for Achieving Equity in Schools* (Thousand Oaks, CA: Corwin, 2006).

2. Craig Wilder, *Ebony and Ivy: Race, Slavery, and the Troubled Heart of American Universities* (New York: Bloomsbury Press, 2014).

3. Wilder, *Ebony and Ivy*, 11.

4. Wilder, *Ebony and Ivy*, 157.

5. Wilder, *Ebony and Ivy*, 158.

6. Wilder, *Ebony and Ivy*, 182.

7. Rachel Swarns, "272 Were Sold to Save Georgetown. What Does it Owe Their Descendants?" *New York Times*, April 16, 2016, https://www.nytimes.com/2016/04/17/us/georgetown-university-search-for-slave-descendants.html.

8. Thomas Murphy, SJ, *Jesuit Slaveholding in Maryland: 1717–1838* (New York: Routledge, 2001), iv.

9. Murphy, *Jesuit Slaveholding in Maryland*, 17.

10. Jesuit scholarship about Jesuit slave owning that I referred to in my 1994 thesis included Thomas Hughes, SJ, *The History of the Society of Jesus in North*

America: Colonial and Federal Documents, vol. 2 (London: Lonmans, Green & Co: 1907); Joseph Zwinge, SJ, "The Jesuit Farms in Maryland," in *The Woodstock Letters* 41 (Woodstock College Printing, 1912); Gerald Walsh, SJ, "The Spirit of the Maryland Ventures," in *The Woodstock Letters* 63 (Woodstock College Printing, 1934); and Emmet R. Curran, SJ, "Splendid Poverty: Jesuit Slaveowning in Maryland," in Randall M. Miller and John L. Wakelyn, eds., *Catholics in the Old South: Essays on Church and Culture* (Macon, Georgia: Mercer University Press, 1983), 125–46.

11. Joseph P. Mobberly, Joseph P. Mobberly Diary Part I, Box 1, Folder 1, SJ Papers, 139, Booth Family Center for Special Collections, Georgetown University.

12. Joseph P. Mobberly, Joseph P. Mobberly Diary Part II, Box 1, Folder 7, 33–36, SJ Papers, Booth Family Center for Special Collections, Georgetown University.

13. Mobberly, Joseph P. Mobberly Diary Part I, 80–81.

14. Mobberly, Joseph P. Mobberly Diary Part I, 83.

15. Maureen H. O'Connell, "St. Inigoes: A Jesuit Plantation," seminar in American History at Saint Joseph's University, December 16, 1994.

16. Wilder, *Ebony and Ivy*, 19.

17. Jennings, "Disfigurations of Christian Identity," 67–85.

18. Jennings, "Disfigurations of Christian Identity," 80–81.

19. Hill Fletcher, *The Sin of White Supremacy*, 9,

20. Hill Fletcher, *The Sin of White Supremacy*, 79.

21. James F. Keenan, SJ, "Coming Home: Ethics and the American University," *Theological Studies* 75, no. 1 (2014): 156–169, at 165.

22. Letter from Ethel Lee to Br. Edwin Anselm, FSC, December 3, 1937, 80.5257, Dougherty Correspondence, CHRC of AoP.

23. Cyprian Davis, "Black Catholics in the Civil Rights Movement in the Southern United States: A. P. Tureaud, Thomas Wyatt Turner, and Earl Johnson," *U.S. Catholic Historian* 24, no. 4 (2006): 69–81 at 77.

24. Karen L. Johnson, "Beyond Parish Boundaries: Black Catholics and the Quest for Racial Justice," *Religion and American Culture: A Journal of Interpretation* (Summer 2015): 264–300 at 281.

25. Letter from Thomas Wyatt Turner to Joseph Dougherty, October 21.

26. Letter from Ethel Lee to Br. Edwin Anselm, FSC, December 3, 1937, 80.5257, Dougherty Correspondence, CHRC of AoP.

27. Letter from Ethel Lee to Br. Edwin Anselm, FSC, December 3, 1937.

28. Letter from Ethel Lee to Joseph Dougherty, January 19, 1938, 80.5257, Dougherty Correspondence, CHRC of AoP.

29. Johnson, "Beyond Parish Boundaries," 272.

30. Community Council Meeting Minutes, February 16, 1938, LUA.

31. Osborne, *Segregated Covenant*, 173.

32. Dent, "The Share of Black Students at Philly Colleges Is Steadily Shrinking."

33. "How Diverse Is Catholic Higher Education?," Association of Catholic Colleges and Universities, https://www.accunet.org/Catholic-Higher-Ed-FAQs #Diverse. The ACCU reports data on four-year institutions. The Post-Secondary National Policy Institute reports that as of fall 2018 African American students made up 1.1 of the 16.6 million undergraduate students enrolled in colleges and universities across the country (or 13 percent) "but they were not equally represented at different institution types," which include two- and four-year programs

in private, public, and for-profit institutions. See "African American Students in Higher Education," June 12, 2020, https://pnpi.org/african-american-students/. For enrollment data as of fall 2018 on post-secondary education at large and by institution type, see the National Center for Educational Statistics Institute of Education Sciences, "The Condition of Education 2020," May 2020, 141, https://nces.ed.gov/pubs2020/2020144.pdf.

34. Anthony Carnevale and Jeff Strohl, *Separate and Unequal: How Higher Education Reinforces the Intergenerational Reproduction of White Privilege*, Georgetown University Center on Education and the Workforce, 2013, 11.

35. Dent, "The Share of Black Students at Philly Colleges Is Steadily Shrinking."

36. Gerald J. Beyer, *Just Universities: Catholic Social Teaching Confronts Corporatized Higher Education* (New York: Fordham University Press, 2021), 180.

37. Carnevale and Strohl, *Separate and Unequal*, 7.

38. Carnevale and Strohl, *Separate and Unequal*, 11.

39. Marcia Chatelain, "We Must Help First-Generation Students Master Academe's 'Hidden Curriculum,'" *Chronicle of Higher Education*, October 21, 2018, https://www.chronicle.com/article/We-Must-Help-First-Generation/244830.

40. Jacquelyn Elias, "Who Holds America's $1.5 Trillion Student-Loan Debt?" *Chronicle of Higher Education*, March 3, 2020, https://www.chronicle.com/interactives/who-holds-student-debt. For analysis of retention rates, see Emily Tate, "Graduation Rates and Race," *Inside Higher Ed*, April 26, 2017, https://www.insidehighered.com/news/2017/04/26/college-completion-rates-vary-race-and-ethnicity-report-finds.

41. Laura Sullivan et al., "Stalling Dreams: How Student Debt Is Disrupting Life Chances and Widening the Racial Wealth Gap," Brandeis University, Institute on Assets and Social Policy, September 2019, https://heller.brandeis.edu/iasp/pdfs/racial-wealth-equity/racial-wealth-gap/stallingdreams-how-student-debt-is-disrupting-lifechances.pdf.

42. Sarah Brown, "Nearly Half of Undergraduate Students are of Color. But Black Students Lag Behind," *Chronicle of Higher Education*, February 14, 2019, https://www.chronicle.com/article/Nearly-Half-of-Undergraduates/245692.

43. Johnson, "Beyond Parish Boundaries," 284.

44. See the Georgetown Memory Project for the most up-to-date number of direct descendants: https://www.georgetownmemoryproject.org/.

45. For biographical background on Cornelia Connelly, see Judith Lancaster, *Cornelia Connelly and Her Interpreters* (Oxford: Way Books, 2004) and Virginia Kaib Ratigan's compilation of biographies that predate Lancaster's in "In Search of Cornelia Connelly: Biographical Sources," *American Catholic Historical Society of Philadelphia* 107, no. 1 & 2 (1996): 25–43. For archival materials, see the Cornelia Connelly Digital Library Resource, https://corneliaconnellylibrary.org/hd-biographical.php?keywords=ccbio, particularly her correspondences and three volumes titled *Beatification and Canonization of the Servant of God Cornelia Connelly Foundress of the Society of the Holy Child Jesus* at the SHCJAPA. For more on the Grayson-Gough family from Jesuits archives, see Kelly L. Schmidt, "Ignatius Gough and His Family," Slavery, History, Memory, and Reconciliation Project, 2021, https://www.jesuits.org/our-work/shmr/family-histories/gough/.

46. For biographical information on Mercer, see Randy Penniger, "Inventory of the William Newton Mercer Papers," revised 2021, Louisiana and Lower

Mississippi Valley Collections, Louisiana State University Libraries, https://www
.lib.lsu.edu/sites/default/files/sc/findaid/0292m.pdf.

47. For history of Jesuit slave owning at St. Charles College in Grand Coteau,
see Kelly Schmidt, "Enslavement at St. Charles College, Grand Coteau," Slavery
History, Memory and Reconciliation Project, 2021, https://www.jesuits.org/our
-work/shmr/what-we-have-learned/st-charles-college-grand-coteau-louisiana/.

48. For history of slave owning in the Society of the Sacred Heart in Grand
Coteau, as well as the congregation's ongoing efforts at reckoning and reconciliation, see Society of the Sacred Heart, "Enslavement," https://rscj.org/history
-enslavement.

49. Society of the Sacred Heart, "Our History of Enslavement: Slavery, Accountability, Reconciliation Past and Present—Confronting our Racism," https://
rscj.org/history-enslavement.

50. Schmidt, "Ignatius Gough and His Family."

51. Schmidt, "Ignatius Gough and His Family." SHCJ archivists believe that
Phoebe may have lived her remaining days with the Jesuits at St. Charles Borromeo.

52. Letter from Mary Peacock and Adeline Duval, 1835, *Beatification and
Canonization of the Servant of God Cornelia Connelly Foundress of the Society of the Holy
Child Jesus*, Documentation Volume 2, 51–56, SHCJAPA. Abraham and Jenny are
also referenced in Radegunde Flaxman's biography *A Woman Styled Bold: The Life
of Cornelia Connelly, 1809–1879* (London: Darton, Longman and Todd, 1991), 34.
SHCJ archivists note that in Flaxman's account, the enslaved people are named
Abraham and "Jimmy," but they believe "Jenny" is more accurate.

53. See Flaxman, *A Woman Styled Bold* and the article "Brief History of the Society" on the SHCJ 175th Anniversary website: https://www.shcj.org/brief-history
-of-the-society/.

54. See Schmidt, "Ignatius Gough and His Family" and "Cornelia Connelly:
Founder, Society of the Holy Child Jesus 1809–1879," SHCJ, https://cornelia
connellylibrary.org/library-materials/texts/HCJ_CorneliaConnellyBook_FINAL
.pdf.

55. For more on white women's entanglements in slave owning, see Stephanie E. Jones-Rogers, *They Were Her Property: White Women as Slave Owners in the
American South* (New Haven, CT: Yale University Press, 2019).

56. "Report of Grand Coteau, Louisiana, Visit 1929," *Beatification and Canonization of the Servant of God Cornelia Connelly Foundress of the Society of the Holy Child
Jesus*, Documentation Volume 76, 2, SHCJAPA.

57. "College Commission Examines Cornelia Connelly's Ties to Slavery," *Rosemont Magazine*, Spring 2020, 9–10, https://issuu.com/rocomagazine/docs/spring
_2020_magazine_.

58. Marc Perry, "A New Path to Atonement," *Chronicle of Higher Education*,
January 20, 2019, https://www.chronicle.com/article/A-New-Path-to-Atonement
/245511.

EPILOGUE: UNDOING

1. John O'Donohue, "For the Traveler," Awakin, https://www.awakin.org/read
/view.php?tid=2191.

INDEX

abolitionists: in Chester County, 41–44, 47, 56, 58; Irish, 71–72

Abraham (enslaved man), 214–15

ACS. *See* American Colonization Society (ACS)

Act of Union (Great Britain), 1800, 64, 71

Advisory Committee on Zoning (Hoover), 145, 175

affirmative redress, 196–97

Africa, Ramona, 21, 23

Alexander, Michelle, 28

Allen, Theodore, 67–68

American Catholic Church: anti-Catholic propaganda, 70–71; and ecclesial supremacy, 56–57; emphasis on reconciliation vs. reconstruction, 91–93; mission churches, 50–53, 59; during the Obama administration, 8–9; Pastoral Letter of 1866, 91–93; pedagogical imperialism, 205; Philadelphia real estate holdings, 173; "respectability politics," 27; sacred role of parish halls, 182–83; social teachings, 149; and the Underground Railroad, 56; upholding of racial segregation, 188–89; and white Catholic support for Donald Trump, 28, 221; and white privilege, 149. *See also* Jesuits; US Catholic Bishops

American Catholic schools, colleges, and universities: and Christian supremacy, 206–7; gatekeeping powers, 213; Jesuit-inspired curriculum, 205–6; parochial schools, 12, 28, 71, 180, 189; in Philadelphia, 71, 200–201, 210; reinforcement of white supremacy, 199–200, 212; segregation of, 27, 71. 189. *See also* Jesuits *and specific educational institutions*

American Colonization Society (ACS), 56, 79

American Eugenics Society, 129

Americanization process: assimilation of white immigrants, 25–27; Catholic definition of, 102; and criteria for "belonging," 223–24; and the role of blackface minstrelsy, 179–80; and segregated property rights, 149–50

American Protestant Association, 70

amnesia, wall of, 25, 27–29, 35, 202–6, 224

Anderson, Carol, 87

Anderson, Elijah, 97, 165–68

Anselm, Edwin, 209–10

anti-Catholic prejudice, 29, 70–71, 75, 93, 149, 223

anti-racism, Catholic, 5, 12, 25, 28, 223, 227

atonement, 89, 91, 93. See also rounding ritual

backstage racism, 153–56, 163

Bagley, Lillian, 29, 183–86

Baldwin, James, 10–11, 17

baptism: of enslaved Catholics, 55, 68, 215–16; Katie Walker Grimes on, 119

Baptist-Jones, Clara, 127–28

Barbados, Irish immigrants from, 118–19, 128

Barbelin, SJ, Felix, 139–40

Barber, William III, 108